Secrets
of
America's
Best Bass Pros

By Tim Tucker

OTHER BOOKS BY TIM TUCKER

**Roland Martin's One-Hundred-and-One
Bass-Catching Secrets**

Advanced Shiner Fishing Techniques

**More Secrets of America's Best Bass Pros,
Volume Two of the Bass Pro Series**

**To Bob and Doris Tucker,
for lovingly fashioning the foundation
for a fantastic life**

Copyright 1990 by Tim Tucker

Second Printing 1991

Printed in the United States of America by
Atlantic Publishing Company
P.O. Box 67
Tabor City, N.C. 28463

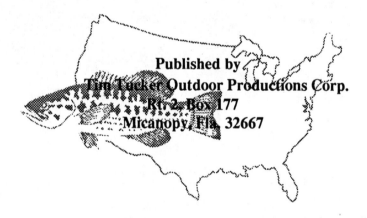

Published by
Tim Tucker Outdoor Productions Corp.
Rt. 2 Box 177
Micanopy, Fla. 32667

Library of Congress Card Number 90-090483
ISBN Number 0-937866-28-8

Photos and cover design by the author

About The Author

Tim Tucker is one of the country's most published outdoor writers and specializes in bass fishing. In addition to being a senior writer for *Bassmaster Magazine, Southern Outdoors* and *B.A.S.S. Times,* Tucker's work has appeared in *Field & Stream, Petersen's Fishing, Fishing Tackle Retailer, Southern Saltwater, Florida Sportsman, Florida Wildlife, Bass Fishing, Bassin'* and *Fishing Facts.*

Winner of more than 50 national, regional and state awards for his writing and photography, Tucker has three books on bass fishing to his credit. He also publishes *Tim Tucker's Florida Bass Update,* a unique monthly insider's newsletter on Florida fishing.

An outdoor columnist for the *Palm Beach Post* newspaper for the past decade, Tucker, 33, lives in Micanopy, Florida, with wife Darlene.

Table of Contents

SECTION ONE
Tools of the Trade

SECTION TWO
Techniques & Tips

SECTION THREE
Patterns & Conditions

Acknowledgements

Any book effort requires the meshing of many talents and the cooperation of many individuals. That is certainly the case with this book, which is, basically, a collection of the insights of America's top tournament anglers. Without their help -- their willingness to share their innermost secrets -- this book would not have been possible.

As a group, they have my utmost respect and sincerest appreciation.

Special thanks to Ann Lewis and Gerald Crawford of the Bass Anglers Sportsman Society for their help throughout the year and particularly with the compilation of this book.

From a more personal standpoint, there are several individuals in my life that need to be thanked publicly.

To Roland Martin, a living legend, great educator and the finest friend -- many thanks for your friendship and collaboration.

To Rick Clunn, my friend and an inspiration for all of those who know him -- my appreciation for the perspective that you have brought to my life.

To Dave Precht, *Bassmaster Magazine* editor and friend -- my heartfelt thanks for your role in my career and personal life.

To Doug Hannon, thanks for being such a good friend of both the bass and bass fishermen.

To Shaw Grigsby, fishing's rising young star and a fine man-- thanks for a friendship that knows no bounds.

To Guido Hibdon, a bass pro of literary proportions -- thanks for breathing new life into the sport of professional fishing and for your friendship.

To Mark Thomas, who understands the meaning of friendship.

To Mike Walker, my idea man, fellow entrepreneur and friend -- my appreciation for our relationship.

To Darlene, wife, companion, inspiration and saint -- because of her, life has real meaning.

To Dana Gehrman and Ed Whipple, dedicated teachers and leaders who had an incredible influence on my life, I am eternally grateful.

To my fellow outdoor writers, editors, guides, fishing industry friends, weekend anglers, bass club members and others who have crossed my path since my entrance into the outdoor field 10 years ago, I have enjoyed knowing you all. To borrow a move title, It's a Wonderful Life.

Tim Tucker
October 1, 1990
Micanopy, FL 32667

One Man's Plea

For the sake of the sport we love so much, please release a portion of your catch, particularly the trophy bass. Allow those magnificent genes to be passed to future generations and you will experience the same thrill in years to come.

Foreward

A writer's problem does not change. He himself changes and the world he lives in changes but his problem remains the same. It is always how to write truly and having found what is true, to protect it in such a way that it becomes a part of the experience of the person who reads it.

-- Ernest Hemingway

In the late 1960s, an insurance salesman from Montgomery, Alabama, decided the world needed a professional bass fishing circuit. After all, he reasoned, other recreational sports like bowling, tennis and golf had been elevated to the professional level. Why not bass fishing, where individual fishermen could match skills against other fishermen? Indeed, why not bass fishing?

He campaigned for his idea. He wrote letters to fishermen across the country. He made telephone calls to newspaper editors. He even spent time with noted outdoor writers, trying to gain enough initial support and encouragement to turn his idea into a reality.

The man, of course, was Ray Scott. Years later, even Scott would admit he was not fully cognizant of the enormous impact his simple idea would eventually have on the sport of bass fishing.

After all, bass fishing was merely a recreational pastime for the common man back in the late 60s. And Scott had visions of turning something as sacred as relaxing recreation into a three-ring circus, complete with bells and whistles. Many dismissed Scott as some sort of lunatic from the Deep South, a local boy from Dixie in dire need of a strait jacket.

But Scott pressed on. Eventually he formed the Bass Anglers Sportsman Society (B.A.S.S.) and the world finally had its professional bass fishing circuit. Through publications like *Bassmaster Magazine,* currently the largest fishing publication in the world, the American public has learned there is a lot more to the basic sport of fishing than mere luck.

Successful bass fishing also involves mental attitudes, proper equipment and physical skills — facts that have been consistently proven by the pros who compete on the national B.A.S.S. tournament circuit. These same professional fishermen have indirectly become America's fishing instructors, the trend-setters, the pioneering innovators and field-testers for new techniques and fishing equipment.

Through the attention Scott attracted to bass fishing, the sport soon became something more than a mere novelty and a recreational pastime. In the following years, the sport became a passion for millions of Americans.

It could be argued that no other single event in the history of outdoor recreation has had a greater impact on swelling the ranks of American fishermen. Ray Scott and those who shared his dream spawned a revolution. That transformation has been extraordinary, if not unparalleled, in the outdoor recreational arena.

Scott's dream and the impact it had on swelling the ranks of America's fishermen indirectly led to the formation of a multi-billion dollar support industry. To service the needs of millions of fishermen from California to Florida, manufacturers sprang up overnight, offering products ranging from boats to baits and everything in between. Scott single-handedly renewed America's passion for fishing. And the bass remains the king.

In the early 1980s, an A.C. Nielsen survey found that approximately 14 percent of the American population fished for bass. In other words, some 30 million people enjoyed chasing this widespread species each year across America. And the sport continues to grow and prosper.

Volumes have been written about bass fishing since Ray Scott elevated this sport to a higher level over two decades ago. Writers have attempted to explain virtually every facet of the sport. Some have been successful. Others have failed miserably.

As many have noted in the past, including writers like Hemingway, himself an avid fisherman, those who write about the world around them must be able to share the experience with the reader. In other words, a writer must be able to communicate the experience in a language and manner that the reader can understand and appreciate. To do that requires an intimate knowledge of the subject.

Few writers have been closer to the core of professional bass fishing than Tim Tucker. Considered by many to be one of the top outdoor writers in the country today, Tucker's award-winning work has appeared in virtually every major outdoor publication in America on subjects ranging from turkey hunting to bass fishing. But bass fishing remains Tucker's area of expertise.

As a senior writer for *Bassmaster Magazine,* and as a reporter who has covered the Bassmaster Tournament Trail for over a decade, Tucker is without question a qualified expert on the subject.

In his latest book, *Secrets of America's Best Bass Pros,* Tucker examines the entire spectrum of the sport, from the basics of bass fishing to the advanced techniques of some of the top bass fishing professionals in the world.

Whether you classify yourself as a weekend fishing enthusiast or a dyed-in-the-wool bass fishing fanatic, Secrets of America's Best Bass Pros is a guide to better bass fishing, a textbook offering the reader a better understanding of the intricacies of an oftentimes complex game. To his credit, Tucker has translated these complexities into simple language easily understood by anyone who has ever spent time on the water in pursuit of America's most popular gamefish.

If success governs the overall enjoyment of any endeavor, this book promises to make an already enjoyable activity even more exciting. As another noted writer once observed, "Success is a journey, not a destination."

Secrets of America's Best Bass Pros should be viewed as a rare opportunity to take a ride with some of America's foremost experts. And along the way, Tucker has given us the chance to learn how to become better bass anglers, ultimately increasing our passion for the sport.

Matt Vincent
Editor, B.A.S.S. TIMES
Staff Writer, Bassmaster Magazine
Oct. 1, 1990
Apache Junction, AZ

SECTION ONE

Tools of the Trade

Chapter 1

Tommy Martin's
Versatile Worm Tactics

On the surface, the plastic worm seems the simplest of all lures. A mere piece of plastic, it doesn't have the flash of a spinnerbait or the depth-defying dynamics of a crankbait.

It is a pretty simple lure to fish. For the most part, its action is built-in. Simply reel it in and the average worm shakes and shimmys back to the boat.

PROfile

And, at times, it isn't difficult to catch bass on a plastic worm. No artificial lure produces more fish nation-wide than these colorful pieces of plastic.

Yet, despite its simplicity, the most successful anglers are those who have developed worm fishing into an art. There IS more to worm fishing than its simplistic image and highly successful worm fishermen prove that day in and day out.

Tommy Martin, winner of the 1974 BASS Masters Classic and a two-time winner on the Bassmaster Tournament Trail, probably knows as much about this particular fine art as any man. Although he is among the most versatile of the traveling pros, Martin will tell you that the plastic

Former BASS Masters Classic champion Tommy Martin has qualified for 16 Classic appearances.

worm has more than paved the way to his 16 Classic appearances.

On the road to qualifying for competitive fishing's most prestigious event 16 times, Martin has refined worm fishing into a complete system that utilizes a wide variety of worm shapes and sizes, as well as different sizes of worm weights and hooks. It is a system that has rarely failed him in tournaments from Lake Mead to Lake Okeechobee.

"One of the biggest mistakes worm fishermen make all across the country is that they fish one particular style of worm almost all of the time," the personable Hemphill, Texas, pro and Toledo Bend guide says. "They pick one particular type of worm that they like — for whatever reason — and they fish it every day no matter where they go or what structure or cover they're fishing.

"Good worm fishermen will agree on one fact — no single worm style, shape, size or length will handle every job that you need a worm to handle. We find that is especially true as we travel all around the country fishing lakes that are often dramatically different from lakes we were fishing a week ago. We may be fishing a crystal-clear lake like Mead one week and be worming the thick milfoil at Chickamauga the next. And that requires different worms and techniques.

"No single worm style does everything a bass angler needs it to do. And when fishermen wise up to that fact and start experimenting with different types of worms, they will automatically increase their catch rate."

If pressed, Martin will admit that a 6-inch worm is the best all-around size for a variety of conditions. But by no means does he limit himself to any particular style or size of worm.

In the Tommy Martin system of successful worm fishing, the key is matching the worm size and shape to the cover or structure in each lake he's fishing. While it has taken him more than 20 years to accumulate such an extensive understanding of worm fishing, we have the luxury of simply putting what he has learned from experience into practice.

"There is no doubt that different styles and lengths of worms are better suited for different types of cover conditions," Martin says. "Once I discovered the absolute best type of worm to use in each situation, I became a much better worm fisherman."

In addition to various cover applications, Martin says certain worms are better suited (and more productive) for certain water clarity and temperature conditions. As a rule of thumb, in situations where the type of cover doesn't dictate the use of a particular type of worm, Martin prefers a flat-tail worm in water temperatures below 60 degrees. When the water warms above 80 degrees, he uses a curl-tail type worm, like the Ditto Gator Tail.

"The reason for those hot-weather and cold-weather choices are simple," Martin explains. "In real cold weather worms with tail styles that don't have much action produce the best. That has to do with the slower metabolism rate of the fish during the cold times when they just aren't very active.

"In the hottest months when the fish are naturally much more active, I like a worm like a Gator Tail that has a lot of action and gives off a lot of vibration. The warmer the water, the more action you want and the faster you can fish it."

Water clarity also plays an important role in Martin's worm selection. For example, in murky water conditions, the likable Texan believes a large worm is easier for bass to locate because it emits an abundance of vibration moving through the water. In clear water where the species relies much more on its sense of sight for feeding, such vibration isn't necessary and Martin uses a small (4-inch) worm. The smaller worm can be seen from considerable distances in clear water and some pros believe it stands up to closer scrutiny better than a large worm when examined by an interested bass.

4

Tommy Martin unhooks a nice West Point Lake largemouth that fell victim to a well-placed plastic worm.

But no condition dictates worm size and style as much as the cover or structure being fished.

"Cover, more than anything, should be considered when selecting a plastic worm," Martin explains. "Different types of cover require different styles of worms to work each type of cover effectively."

Here are some examples.

For fishing clear lakes that have little bottom cover like Nevada's Lake Mead, Martin believes no worm is as effective as a short (4-inch), small-diameter worm. There is a huge legion of western anglers who agree with Martin. In the West, the tiny worms are standard equipment for a large number of lakes and reservoirs.

"The small diameter worms are better for that situation because you have to fish light line with a light slip-sinker and a small (1-0) hook," Martin says. "You need light line just to get strikes in that clear water. We're talking about lakes with clear water, but not much cover, so you can get away with fishing light line. You need that small diameter worm so that small hook can penetrate it easily and stick into the fish.

"Regarding worm diameter, the opposite end of the spectrum is my home lake, Toledo Bend, which is just full of cover. We've got an abundance of hydrilla and other types of aquatic vegetation growing as deep as 20 feet. When I'm fishing real thick cover, whether it be grass or real thick brush, I am a whole lot more successful with a large diameter worm, as well as a larger worm."

For fishing heavier cover, Martin uses worms ranging from 6 to 10 inches in length. But all share a common characteristic — a thick diameter. A larger diameter is crucial when fishing thick cover because it creates more vibration and presents a larger silhouette in a crowded environment where visibility is limited.

"In heavy cover, you've got to attract the bass and when you're fishing real thick hydrilla or milfoil, you're not going to be able to draw him from very far away with a small worm that doesn't have a lot of sound to it," he adds. "A big 8- or 9-inch worm can sometimes pull a bass from 3 or 4 feet away."

(Martin emphasizes that large worms are not limited to thick vegetation applications. A large worm (8 to 9 inches) is often an effective tool for working deep drop-offs like river channels.)

The density of the vegetation will dictate worm style as well as size in Martin's system.

When flipping thick milfoil or other jungle-like vegetation, Martin switches to a straight-tail worm like the Mann's Jelly Worm. That type of worm will penetrate the grass much more easily than a large curl-tail worm like a Gator Tail. To proficient fishermen like Martin, that means being able to fish a little faster and cover more water than is possible with a worm-tail designed for more of a swimming-type action.

For fishing boat docks and similar structure, Martin uses 4- to 6-inch worms.

A boat dock in open water is perfect for the small 4-inch worm on light line, while a pier with brush piles beneath it or grass around it is better suited for the 6-inch version.

"Another thing you should take into consideration when selecting a worm is the size of fish you are fishing for," Martin interjects. "I firmly believe that you just naturally catch bigger fish on a bigger worm. That's something to keep in mind if you're fishing some of our Texas lakes where there is a 14-inch length (minimum) limit and the Missouri lakes that have a 15-inch limit or West Point (in western Georgia) that has a 16-inch limit.

"Take the size of the fish you're after into consideration even if there isn't such a restrictive length limit. For example, on a clear lake like Lanier, I know that most of the bass are going to be small, just by the nature of the lake. So, I drop down to a small 4-inch worm. On a place like Okeechobee or Kissimmee or other big-bass reservoirs where I stand a good chance of catching a quality fish, I have much more success with 8- to 10-inch worms. In that case, you may not get some of the little pound-and-half fish to strike, but I feel like the bigger worm has a better chance of catching a big fish."

Once a worm style and length is matched to the cover or structure, the task of preparing properly isn't over.

"The average fisherman doesn't pay enough attention to balancing his worm set-up with the proper size of hook and sinker," Martin says. "Most of them use a bigger hook than they need.

"In the past seven or eight years, I've had a lot more success hooking fish with a smaller hook than most fishermen usually use. I prefer a small diameter hook (which penetrates the worm more easily than larger hooks) and rarely use anything bigger than a 3/0 hook. I believe the average fisherman uses too big a hook. That creates a problem because a hook that's too large for the worm weighs it down and robs it of its action."

Attention should be paid to selecting a balanced worm weight as well. When fishing a large worm in thick cover, a 1-ounce sinker is often necessary to penetrate the vegetation. In contrast, when fishing a 4-inch, small-diameter worm, anything over a 1/8-ounce weight is usually excessive.

Another consideration when selecting the proper worm weight is the current season and the metabolism of the bass. For example, in cold water, the inactive bass are more likely to hit a slow-falling lure, which means using a smaller sinker than normal. In the summer months, bass are much more likely to chase a faster-falling worm, so you can get away with using a larger bullet weight.

Martin's Florida bedding-bass special seems unorthodox, but it produces. He combines a large 9-inch worm with a 1/16-ounce weight. The worm is large enough to intimidate the bedding bass into striking it, while the light sinker enables it to fall more slowly and stay in the strike zone (over the bed) longer.

Most importantly, Tommy Martin says don't be afraid to experiment with different worm sizes and shapes, as well as sinker sizes, on a regular basis.

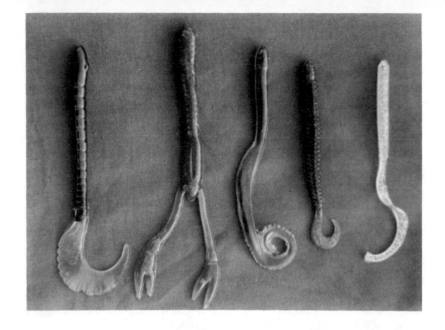

Tommy Martin relies on a variety of worm styles and lengths for different fishing situations.

"Generally, if I'm going to fish a worm, I'll rig rods up with two or three different size worms," he says. "I'll even rig up a rod with two or three different sizes of sinkers and different line sizes. I almost always have at least three different rods rigged in various ways for worm fishing. And I'll keep experimenting with them until I find the perfect set-up for that particular day. While I know in my mind what type of worm should work in a particular type of area before I ever step into my boat, I never know exactly what kind of mood the bass will be in and what they will like best."

Chapter 2

The Big-Bass Swimmin' Rig

For years, it was Doug Hannon's secret weapon.

And if you know anything about Florida's famed Bass Professor, then you know that Hannon's weapons are usually deadly. Few fishermen in America have caught as many bass over 10 pounds (more than 500) or understand the species better.

Back in 1973, Hannon discovered the best artificial lure he had ever come across for enticing big bass. It was crude, simple and extremely effective. It was a worm rig that resembles the action of an infant snake, one of the real delicacies of the largemouth bass. And it attracted so many big fish that he felt obligated to keep it a secret.

Fish like three bass that topped the 17-pound mark.

"It was a home-made rig that was similar to one that I came across that was used by an old guide who fished Lake Tohopekalgia for years and years," Hannon says. "That guide is dead now, but I took it and made a few modifications to it and discovered that it was extremely productive on big bass."

PROfile

Florida's Doug Hannon is America's top big-bass expert with more than 500 10-pound-plus bass to his credit.

That home-made rig was the forerunner to today's Swimmin' Worm Rig, part of the Hannon System of baits designed for Burke Lures of Traverse City, Mich., and one of the most innovative lures to enter the market in years.

"The first time I used that lure, I quit for using anything else for two years," says Hannon, known and respected in the fishing industry for his ethical stands on the sport and his knowledge of bass behavior. "It was so effective that I didn't fish any other lure for two years.

"I caught more bass than I had ever caught and I wasn't the fisherman I am now. One of the reasons that I got to the position that I am now is because of this thing.

"That lure and my dedication to it was one of my best-kept secrets for a long time. I had been shiner fishing for quite a while and I wanted to get back to fishing with lures. But I had never found anything that produced. Shiner fishing is very seasonal for big fish. In the summer, it slows down to nothing. The first summer I fished that lure, I caught 12 bass over 10 pounds. Obviously, there's a tremendous amount of nice bass involved in coming up with that many 10-pounders, too. On the lake that I live on, I used to be able to catch 40 to 60 bass a day on that lure any day."

The Swimmin' Worm Rig consists of a completely rigged worm made up of a camouflaged 20-pound test leader, four-ball black swivel and a special 3/0 hook Hannon designed that gives the lure its unique motion underwater.

When it's swimming in the water, Hannon's rig is extremely lifelike — the key to attracting big bass. "The secret is the totally natural swimming action when the lure is properly rigged," Hannon explains. "It triggers savage strikes from big bass because they perceive it as a living thing — not merely lifelike. A water snake swimming through the water may undulate and wiggle, but if you look closely, you will notice that the snake's head tracks straight and true. The Swimmin' Worm moves exactly the same way in the water when fished with a slow, steady retrieve."

The swimming action of the worm is dictated by the bend in the hook Hannon created. "There's a lot of ways to make a worm wiggle and swim by bending it," he says. "If you look at the way a snake swims in the water or an eel, their head stays in one position and the body swims. All of the lures classicly put some kind of interference bill in front of it to make the head wag back and forth. But that's not the way natural things swim. They use the tail section to swim and use the head to break water. So we had to get the bend in the hook in such a way that if the worm was rolling over and spinning, it wouldn't make the head go back and forth. When that happens, bass, particularly big bass, don't hit it nearly as well."

Hannon maintains that bass, particularly big bass, notice even the most subtle differences in the motion.

Although Hannon's rig will work with almost any type of plastic worm, Burke's Swimmin' Worms were designed specifically to enhance the motion the rig produces. The Swimmin' Worms are straight-bodied with a diamond-shaped flat tail.

"Worm preference with that rig was dictated by a natural, normal-shaped worm," Hannon says. "Something that didn't have any of these frilly, curly tails and stuff like that.

"Those tails work by creating a drag in the water, which forces the tail to flutter. That is not conducive to swimming in a nice even motion through the water, which these things do. So when you put a curly tail or something on there, it would drag the action down, because the worm doesn't get the nice, smooth

**Doug Hannon admires a trophy Florida bass that was fooled by the
lifelike action of the Swimmin' Worm Rig.**

water flow over it the way that the body of a natural creature would. I started out using a plain 6-inch worm and I used everything from Bagley's to Creme's to Mann's worms, which worked pretty well. But I found that this 6-inch worm works best.

"The other thing you want is something that works at the slowest possible retrieve. That's what attracts the biggest fish. The action had to be perfect and that thing had to be really tuned to make it work at a good, slow retrieve. Anybody can get them to work if you crank it fast enough. A small worm tended to work better at that slow retrieve.

"People think of a big lure as a big-fish lure and a small lure as a small-fish lure, but knowledgeable people know that a slow retrieve is better for big fish. We picked up more advantage from this small rig and being able to work it at a slow retrieve than we would have by going to a giant worm for big fish. This is really a big-fish bait."

During more than a decade of secretly enjoying his deadly rig, Hannon discovered that the rig has several different applications that would work in a wide variety of lakes, particularly in the South.

"It's the best drifting lure I've ever fished in my life for both wind drifting or using the electric trolling motor," he says. "It was a natural for the Florida lakes because it fishes between 2 and 5 feet down. And it will give you access to fish in about 8 feet of water with no weight at all.

"Unweighted, it's an excellent lure in any kind of situation where the water is 8 feet deep or less. Without a weight, it's perfect for fishing around objects and cover and weed beds and lily fields that are holding fish. Massachusetts would be a good example of a state that has a heck of a lot of those kinds of lakes. The backwater areas of many of the reservoirs all over the southeast and southwest have these weedy bays and jungles of hydrilla and standing timber in shallow water. This bait is ideal for those places.

"When the water gets over 8 feet, I recommend that you go to 1/8-ounce to 1/4-ounce sinker in front of it. Then you'll have a lead that runs 7 to 8 feet deep. If you stop it, it will go down to a level and then it will stay at that level. That makes it a lot more versatile to be able to add the weight to it."

Fishing clear water is one of the bass fisherman's biggest challenges, but the Swimmin' Worm rig is perfect because of its lifelike appearance AND motion. "It's one of the most fabulous baits for clear water for places like the springs in Florida," Hannon explains.

"In clear water, the fish really get a good look at your lure and it has to be convinced that it's a natural swimming creature. I got a call from a guy who fishes springs and he said this bait absolutely changed his life. And he was fishing it with a 30-pound leader in clear water.

"I went up there and tried it because it never occurred to me to fish that river with that bait. We caught just a boat load of bass. I had fished that river before and had been frustrated by it. The weird thing I noticed was that fish would come up to most lures that you threw in there — you could see hundreds of fish in that river in the period of a day — because lures are attractive. They see them from a distance, they come up to look at them and they get that cocked look like maybe they're going to hit it and you wonder if they are, but then they break away and leave.

"But with this bait, the fish would come charging in so fast that you'd never see them coming or following it. In this crystal-clear water, which was like looking through a pane of glass, you'd see the fish when he had a hold of it and he grabbed and shook it. But with this bait, the fish were coming in so fast, you had to look very closely to see anything. They'd charge in full-speed and just broad-side it, just hammer it. There was no hesitation. They were absolutely convinced it was alive. I think that's probably why it catches the big fish better than other lures."

The camouflaged leader also makes the lure more effective in clear water.

In shallow, weedy lakes (which are ideal for this lure), the Swimmin' Worm rig is surprisingly weedless, considering that the hook is exposed. But the bend in the hook and the unique action of the bait seem to shield it from getting hung up as it's worked through the grass.

With the natural lifelike look and movement built into the lure, color isn't as important as it would be with most worm rigs. But Burke and Hannon designed a series of iridescent colors that are extremely effective in clear water, Hannon says. "They contain crystals that catch certain colors of light," he explains. "It has a lot of flash, which attracts fish."

Hannon's favorite colors are purple with a red tail, pulsar blue and black with a chartreuse tail.

The concept behind the Swimmin' Worm rig enables it to stand atop the mountainous pile of baits on the market. Few lures are easier to use, yet produce as many fish as Hannon's long-time secret weapon.

"In essence, what we're doing is taking a plastic worm and turning it into something that's as easy to fish as a crankbait," Hannon adds. "You reel it up to the speed where you've got the action and then you add any weight to get the depth that you want.

"With a crankbait, you change bills (sizes) to change the depth. You always try to get them up to the speed where they vibrate. With this rig, you reel it to the speed that it swims. It should be easy for people to master. In everything I've ever read about plastic worm fishing, I found the feeling that people are totally frustrated with the fact that it is always discussed in terms of abstracts — the feel of the worm pulling on the brush and nursing it along the bottom and how indefinite everything is. You get the feeling you have to have your senses finely honed on all this.

"That's just not the case with this lure. It makes fishing a plastic worm easy, yet it's one of the most effective ways to fish a worm. You get all the attraction and the naturalness of a plastic worm, but you don't have to worry with it. The fact that you're reeling in the lure means that all of the slack is gone. When you're fishing conventional plastic worms, you're dealing with slack that you have to take up to set the hook. You don't have to do that with this rig. You just crank in the worm and pull and you've got it. That's it."

It sounds too easy to be true. But Hannon's reputation supports it and that's enough for most bass fishermen.

Chapter 3

Charlie Reed's Worming Primer

The line suddenly grew as taut as piano wire and began to hum with almost a music twang — much to the chagrin of Charlie Reed.

The tendons in the hammer-hard forearms of the tanned former BASS Masters Classic champion strained to regain some control over the bass that had just devoured his plastic worm some 25 feet below and had managed to penetrate some of the thickest timber that Broken Bow Lake has to offer. "Big fish," Reed managed to grunt. "Big fish."

PROfile

It is immediately obvious that the sizeable bass has put several limbs between itself and the boat, despite Reed's best effort. Maintaining pressure on the line and relying on the resourcefulness bred by more than 30 years of fishing, the Oklahoma angler works to manipulate the fish through the labyrinth of limbs and tree trunks of the decades-old timber. The see-sawing of line-on-wood has put creases of anguish on his 56-year-old face.

Suddenly, the tension breaks and the line goes slack. Reed's immediate thought is that the bass

Charlie Reed of Oklahoma is a past BASS Masters Classic champion.

has either pulled free or the line has parted. But almost before the thought is completed, a monstrous largemouth parts the water and does a tarpon-walk on the surface. Reed then discovers that the line is entangled with another branch located about 10 feet or so below the boat. And the intensity continues.

Finally, Reed is able to lead the bass away from the troublesome timber by easing the pressure slightly, moving the boat over the one side and finessing the fish through the limb in question. It is a masterful piece of rod work.

The bass weighs 10 1/2 pounds — a gigantic fish for this region. But Reed has another reason for the smirk on his face. "Ten-pound test line," he says proudly. He doesn't have to finish the thought.

That exhilarating battle with the bass of a lifetime illustrates just a portion of what separates Charlie Reed's system of worm fishing from the normal, standard ideas on fishing the colorful pieces of plastic. Through the years, Reed has refined his worm-fishing techinques into time-tested methods for catching largemouth, smallmouth and spotted bass in lakes and reservoirs throughout the country. In some respects, his worm ways are downright boring, but in others, they can be adventurous.

And catching a 10 1/2-pound bass on 10-pound test line in deep, standing timber borders on the adventurous.

"The most common mistake that fishermen all across the country make with worm fishing is using line that is too heavy," Reed explains. "They have a misconception that if they use anything under 17-pound line, they're going to get broken off. But I very seldom break off 8- and 10-pound line, because I'm patient and I've taught myself to know how much that line can take.

"And there is so much more benefit to using light line. Lighter line can be the difference between getting 15 or 20 strikes or just one or two strikes in a day's time. You get better sensitivity with lighter line and the worm has a lot more action with 10-pound line, compared to using 17- and 20-pound test line. And with 10-pound line, you've got enough stretch in the line to fight the fish once you've got him on. Stretch is important, although most fishermen don't realize it."

Reed's worm fishing begins with balanced tackle. He uses a 6 1/2-foot medium-action Berkley Series One graphite rod for most of his worm-fishing situations (except for flipping heavy cover) teamed with a Quantum Pro One baitcasting reel. The composition of the rod is crucial, according to Reed, who prefers a rod with the butt strength to move fish in cover and a fairly limber tip (which promotes accurate casting and a quick hook-set).

One of the most common worm-fishing mistakes among the average angler involves knowing when and how to set the hook, Reed believes. "Too many fishermen get involved in a 'feeling' game with the bass and that's a game that the bass is going to win with worm fishing," he says. "Too many people let the fish take the worm too long before they hit him. Instead, when you feel him touch the worm in any way, you should set the hook. Don't hesitate for any reason. When in doubt set the hook."

To illustrate the mechanics of hook-setting, Reed uses the face of a clock for a reference. While working the worm, he keeps his rod tip at about 10 o'clock. The instant he detects a strike, Reed immediately drops the rod to an 8 o'clock position, cranks the reel handle a couple of times to gather some of the slack line and then powers the rod upward to impale the hook. One hook-setting aspect that separates Reed from other worm fishermen is that he prefers to leave some

Charlie Reed rigs a plastic worm Texas style for fishing the shallow brush in Arkansas' Bull Shoals Reservoir.

slack in the line. "That slack gives your line a little snap that helps drive the hook home," he says.

Although the nerve-testing, patient method commonly referred to as "dead worming" has become the craze on the national tournament trail in recent years, Reed is not one of the converts. While he occasionally works the worm methodically when the conditions dictate it, Reed primarily relies on what he calls a medium retrieve in which he keeps the lure hopping and moving to maximize its action.

Another aspect in which Reed differs from the fishing crowd is in the area of worm colors. Although modern advancements in plastics technology has created shad-sided worms, the so-called bloodline insert models, translucent versions, metalflake sparkle and more color combinations than we could ever try, Reed is very basic about his color choices.

His favorite for most situations is a plum-colored worm. And that's easy to understand, since it is the worm that enabled him to catch enough bass during tough fishing conditions on Tennessee's Chickamauga and Nickajack lakes to win the 1986 Classic. His other basic color choices are red, blue and black.

From that point, Reed uses water clarity to dictate his worm color. He follows a simple rule of thumb in which he uses the lighter colors in clearer water and darker hues in off-colored waters.

His prowess with a plastic worm has enabled Larry Nixon to cash three $100,000-plus checks during his career.

Chapter 4

Larry Nixon's
Rules of Worm Fishing

In this day and time when the emphasis among the top tournament bass pros centers on versatility, it is often an insult to refer to someone as an expert with any single lure — a specialist.

But that isn't the case with Larry Nixon.

The Arkansas pro, who ranks as the all-time leading money winner (more than $700,000) in Bass Anglers Sportsman Society history, doesn't mind being referred to as a plastic worm specialist. In fact, he is flattered by it.

Although he has a high-caliber prowess with crankbaits, spinnerbaits and jigs, plastic worms are "my favorite bait," Nixon says. "I am partial to worm fishing."

That is understandable, considering his long line of successes that have come on a plastic worm:

• His biggest victory, the 1983 BASS Masters Classic title, came on the strength of a black 5-inch Ditto Baby Gator Tail worm with a blue tail. In what was at that point the most stingiest Classic in history, Nixon concentrated on making precise and quiet presentations with the worm on a 3/16-ounce sinker, which enabled him to catch 15 precious Ohio River bass that weighed 18 pounds 1 ounce.

PROfile

In addition to a BASS Masters Classic championship, two Angler of the Year titles, 10 victories and 14 Classic appearances, Larry Nixon is the all-time B.A.S.S. money-winner.

• Nixon cashed the first of his three $100,000 checks in 1987, when he was a member of the winning the B.A.S.S. Team Championship on New York's Lake of the Isles. Nixon developed the winning strategy for his four-man team, which centered around fishing underwater grass points with a small junebug-colored Baby Gator Tail with a 1/8-ounce sinker on 6-pound test line.

• Hundred-thousand-dollar check No. 2: Nixon fished an 8-inch junebug-colored Bass Pro Shops' Squirm Worm around offshore pads to win the 1988 B.A.S.S. MegaBucks Tournament.

• Hundred-thousand-dollar check No. 3: A 6-inch junebug-colored Bass Pro Shops' Tripple-Ripple worm produced a tournament record 31 pounds, 7 ounces (for the final two rounds) in MegaBucks V for Nixon on 17-pound test line and a 1/4-ounce sinker. During a qualifying round two days earlier, a green Tripple-Ripple worm with a chartreuse tail produced the largest bass of Nixon's career — a 10-pound, 10-ounce Lake Harris trophy.

With that track record in mind, you can understand why Nixon is a plastic worm fanatic. And it is also evidence that Nixon may be the country's best worm fisherman.

"I like plastic worms because they are such a precision bait," explains Nixon, a 14-time Classic qualifier and one of only three pros to win more than one B.A.S.S. Angler of the Year titles. "You throw it where you think the fish is at and you don't fool around very long. It is a pinpoint bait for me, as well as my big-fish bait."

Larry Nixon isn't the conventional worm fisherman, however. He has some definite ideas of how the baits are best used and some methods that separate him from the competition.

"With worm fishing, I concentrate on casting and pitching," he says. "I don't do a lot of flipping. I flip when I have to, but I feel like flipping bass are the hardest bass in the world to catch. So I don't want to flip for them unless I have to — like when the fish aren't biting and buried in heavy cover. When he's buried up in cover and doesn't want to bite, I wonder how many millions of times you flip in front of a fish before you actually get one of them to bite.

"I'd rather be out there hunting a fish that is active and aggressive."

Although the plethora of colors and styles available to anglers are mind-boggling, Nixon uses a rather simple criteria for selecting a plastic worm.

The most versatile worm, be believes, is a 6- or 8-inch ribbontailed worm like the Tripple-Ripple model by Bass Pro Shops. It is a worm that will penetrate a variety of cover types, according to Nixon. Worm color, he says, is dictated by the water clarity and temperature. In water colder than 65 degrees, Nixon uses a black or dark-colored worm. The warmer the water, the lighter the hue. Off-colored water demands darker colors, while clearer water allows lighter colors to be seen better.

Nixon differs from many anglers in that he pegs his bullet weight on the line slightly above the worm. "I feel that if you peg the lead down to your hook, you don't get nearly as good of a hookset as you do when the lead can move up and down the line freely," he says.

Few fishermen understand bass movement and behavior as well as Nixon, who recently returned to his hometown of Bee Branch, Ark., after guiding on

Texas' Toledo Bend Reservoir for more than a decade. It is his ability to follow the daily movements of bass that enables Nixon to take full advantage of the finesse, strike-provoking qualities of a plastic worm.

"Early in the morning or late in the afternoon, I believe that the bass will be holding on the outer edge of cover," Nixon explains. "During those times when the sun is low on the horizon, I will generally cast to the outside edge of whatever structure I am fishing and make my retrieve back to the boat. But when the sun gets up, I start pitching more to the interior of the cover.

"When the sun clears the horizon, I believe the bass move in close to the structure. To catch them, you have to drop the worm right in front of the bass' face. So I try to present the worm through the structure and bounce it right off of the bass' nose. If I am fishing down a log or fallen tree, I may swim the worm beside the log and let it fall into the hiding places where I think the bass may be.

"It's the same with a treetop or brushpile. I always start my retrieve well away from the cover when I don't know where the fish are. The bass may be holding 4 or 5 feet from a brushtop, halfway between the brushtop and the boat or right in the center of the cover. So the first thing I do is cast the worm 4 or 5 feet away from the cover and start my retrieve."

The speed of retrieve and patience involved in worm fishing is what separates the pros from the amateurs, Nixon believes.

"The type of retrieve used is critical for catching bass," he continues. "I believe that the bass prefer to take the worm on the fall, because 85 to 95 percent of my strikes on a worm occur when the worm is falling. For that reason, I jump the worm across the bottom.

"However, when I am trying to locate fish, I'll jump the worm up, let it fall back and then just use my rod tip to make the worm quiver on the bottom. I want the worm to shake on the bottom, while staying in one place. Then I will jump the lure off the bottom again, let if fall back and shake it once more. I will use this same jump-and-shake technique all the way back to the boat until I find out where on the structure the bass are positioned."

Nixon's meticulous methods were well illustrated during his 1990 Mega-Bucks victory. While the other competitors concentrated on the obvious shoreline cover, Nixon targeted deeper offshore grasslines and lily pads. Once he had established the approximate depth being utilized by the bass, Nixon was especially deliberate with his lure presentation. And it paid off to the tune of two 5-pound-plus bass on the final day.

"When I felt like I had my bait in a spot where a fish lived, I would leave the worm in there for 10 or 15 seconds," Nixon says. "You had to vertically jig them. Vertically jigging is something we do a lot in Texas in the fall, when the fish get real dormant. You get your bait over something (like a lily pad stem or limb) when it's in shallow water, because you can't do it right beside the boat in 5 or 6 feet of water without scaring the fish. It is better to cast the worm over a strand of grass and let it down on a real slack line to the bottom. Then you just lift it up about a foot and let it back down. Lift it up and let it fall back. You might have to do that six or seven times to get a bite when the fish are finicky."

Nixon's favorite structure/cover for worm fishing is vegetation — both shallow and deep. Vegetation holds bass throughout the year, a predictability that anglers should take full advantage of, he says. And pinpointing bass in a grass patch is not as difficult as it might seem.

"When looking at a weed bed, concentrate on any points as well as any change in the types of vegetation," Nixon adds. "More or less, you should concentrate on specific changes in the vegetation — like a point in a weed bed or a cut in the weeds — some type of irregularity in the weeds that could hold a fish.

"Then you should concentrate mainly on the windy side of those irregularities. You should always present your bait to a fish on the windy side. That's a good rule of thumb in all fishing. I believe a fish always sets up facing into the wind. Usually wind makes the fish bite, so therefore if you've got wind blowing into an ambush point, that's where you want to put your bait."

Nixon is asked to pinpoint the most common mistake that most fishermen make when using a plastic worm.

"A lot of people work the worm with the reel, instead of the rod," he replies. "That is entirely the wrong approach.

"To me, you cannot drag a plastic worm to get the proper effects. Maybe a small portion of the time and in very select bodies of water like the western reservoirs, you can catch fish by just dragging the bait. But that presentation rarely works in other parts of the country."

While manipulating the worm, Nixon keeps the rod tip fairly high, lifting it to move the bait, letting it settling back down to the bottom and then reeling in excess slack. For this fishing machine, it is an automatic movement.

That's the world of worm fishing, according to Larry Nixon. And when he speaks on this subject, every angler should give him his undivided attention.

Chapter 5

Doug Gilley's
Weedy Worm Ways

Doug Gilley was born and raised on the banks of the St. Johns River in Florida, one of the most renowned bass factories in America. His roots are solidly implanted in the southern portion of the magnificient river near Winter Springs.

It would be safe to say that Gilley — like most longtime Florida bass anglers — was practically born with a plastic worm in hand. You don't survive the weedy wars with Florida bass without becoming proficient at worm fishing and his years of experience qualify Gilley as a master at the art of fishing plastic worms. Few fishermen understand the more subtle aspects of this type of fishing.

PROfile

Doug Gilley is a past Super B.A.S.S. Tournament champion and expert worm fisherman.

And few catch as many bass consistently on this piece of plastic as Gilley.

It was a plastic worm that enabled him to capture his biggest moment in a lengthy career as a professional angler. Fishing his own St. Johns River waters, Gilley won one of competitive fishing's biggest titles when he won the Super B.A.S.S.-III Tournament in 1984 with almost 54 pounds of bass.

That was just another example of the power of the plastic worm.

"Day in and day out, no artificial lure produces like a plastic worm," claims Gilley, who fishes all types of lures well. "No other type of lure will get the number of strikes or catch as many big bass as a plastic worm. You won't get any argument on that.

"But there is more to fishing a plastic worm than just throwing it out there and reeling it in. There are various ways to work a worm and various types of worms for different situations. No one worm style will do every job any more. Worm fishing requires more thinking, concentration and skill than most people believe."

Gilley was asked to name the most common mistakes made by inexperienced (and unsuccessful) worm fishermen.

"I think a lot of people don't fish a worm long enough and stay steady with it," he replies. "If you fish an area real quick with a worm and then you come back over it with a crankbait or a spinnerbait, you don't usually have as much success as you would have had if you had stuck with a plastic worm longer.

"I think you've got to fish an area slowly with a worm to get them to hit it. If you fish a spinnerbait or a crankbait you might not get a strike in many situations where if you work a worm real slow, you can often trigger them into hitting it. The most common mistake with most worm fishermen is that they work an area too fast and switch to another lure."

Next on Doug Gilley's list of common mistakes is fishing the worm too fast. Gilley claims his success has been far greater over the years when he had worked the worm slowly and deliberately than when he retrieved it more quickly. And with his credentials, you can't argue with his claim.

A major reason for his success with a plastic worm over the years, Gilley says, is his use of a light worm weight. Many anglers make the mistake of using a slip sinker that is too heavy and often scares the bass. "My basic rule is you need to use as light a sinker as you can get away with," he explains. "But, of course, you can't fish a 1/8-ounce weight in 12 feet of water because you would spend all of your time waiting for the worm to get to the bottom. If you're fishing shallow water, you need to use a light weight for a couple of reasons. First, you won't spook the fish as much and, secondly, when the fish picks the worm up, he doesn't feel as much resistance with the lighter sinker. And you can feel them better."

Unlike many Florida fishermen, Gilley avoids heavy line whenever possible. In the Sunshine State, flipping heavy cover with 30-pound test line isn't unheard of.

While Gilley will flip with 17- to 20-pound test line when heavy-cover situations demand it, he prefers fishing 12- and 14-pound line for Florida's shallow waters. "I very seldom go below 10 when I'm worm fishing because I can't really set the hook as well with that light line," he says.

While Gilley matches different worm sizes and shapes to different cover situations, his favorite and most productive worm size is a 6-inch worm. "That just seems to be the most natural size to bass," he says. "A 7 1/2- or 8-inch worm feels a little bulky and I can't get the same action out of it that I get with a 6-inch worm. If I go to a smaller worm, I can't get the same action as with the 6-incher. And the 6- inch worm is the most versatile of all sizes. It's perfect for

Doug Gilley is a master at the delicate art of plastic-worm fishing.

a variety of types of worm fishing." Gilley prefers a worm with an abundance of tail action, like a ribbon-tail worm. But he doesn't limit himself to that shape. For example, when fishing clear water, Gilley scores consistently with the type of worm that has an extraordinarily long tail (that begins mid-way up the body of the worm). This type of worm has a tantalizing action that can be seen from great distances in clear water.

"For flipping, I prefer a straight tail worm," Gilley says. "It doesn't hang up nearly as bad as a ribbon-tail or curl-tail worm and most of the strikes you get when flipping are instinctive strikes where you drop it right on the fish and he nails it. The main reason, though, is that it's easier to flip with and penetrate the grass. That's why I use a straight tail for 90 percent of my flipping."

While flipping is a deadly technique for reaching heavy-cover bass, Gilley says the average bass angler would catch more fish if he better mixed both the flipping and casting methods of fishing a plastic worm. "Too many people will strictly flip or strictly cast during a day on the water," Gilley explains. "But they would be much more successful if they would learn when to flip and when to cast a plastic worm to cover. If you're flipping when you should be casting, you're going to spook fish. And if you're casting when the situation calls for flipping, you're not going to reach the fish. So, you have to get an understanding of what the situation calls for."

For that reason, Gilley keeps both a flipping stick and casting rod rigged and ready to go at all times.

His basic flipping outfit is a 8-foot graphite rod with plenty of backbone for setting the hook and pulling big fish out of thick cover. When flipping, the reel is unimportant, he says, as long as it is light-weight and has a good drag system. About 90 percent of his flipping is done with 20- pound test line. "I don't like to use any heavier line than 20 because it doesn't got through the guides or the grass as good and it has a tendency to coil more," Gilley adds. "I don't like to use anything lighter than that because you're fishing in heavy stuff and you can't get them out with 14- or 17-pound line."

If the cover is thick enough to demand it, Gilley will use a 1-ounce weight, which he pegs tight to the top of the worm with a small piece of toothpick. In lighter cover, he prefers not to peg his sinker, believing an un-pegged worm weight will produce a few more strikes.

Gilley's casting outfit is a 5 1/2-foot medium-action baitcasting rod with a smooth V-spool reel. For casting, he uses, primarily, 14-pound line with a 3/16- to 1/8-ounce sinker. For fishing a worm around boat docks and other similar structure, Gilley often switches to a spinning outfit. Spinning gear makes it easier to pitch a worm under a boat dock.

"The key is knowing when to flip and when to cast," Gilley says. "My advice to inexperienced worm fishermen would be don't get hung up on either casting or flipping. Even if you prefer flipping over casting or vice versa, use the prevalent conditions to dictate which way you present the worm. And don't be scared to change around a little bit.

"There are some obvious applications for each method. There's often a situation where flipping won't do the job. You have no choice but to back off and cast to the fish. A lot of people will keep on flipping in an area where they are spooking the fish and wonder why they can't get any strikes. You really need to mix it up a lot to be successful on a consistent basis. It's important to use the weather conditions to dictate whether you flip or cast. For example, if it's real bright, sunny and still, you should be flipping. If you've got a little ripple on the water, the fish will often be feeding on the outside of the cover, so you should be casting to them.

"If it's real cloudy, you can get away with casting a lot longer than you can flipping. A lot of times you'll start off in the morning casting and catch fish. But then the fish will shut off and you don't know what the problem is. But after the sun gets up, you can often ease up into the same area that you have been casting to — get tighter to the cover — and start flipping. And you will continue to catch fish."

A good illustration of the productivity of mixing flipping with casting is Gilley's victory in Super B.A.S.S.-III, in which he pocketed $100,000.

Fishing the Keeths Point area of the St. Johns River just north of Lake George, Gilley had found an abundance of bass holding in a stretch of eelgrass in shallow water, which he divided into two patterns: for both flipping and casting. On the edge of the grass, Gilley flipped a black Bandit worm with a blue tail. For fishing the thicker inside portion of the grassbed, Gilley would move even tighter to the cover and make a 15-foot cast with a blue-shad colored Bass Assassin worm.

"I had a different worm rigged up for each purpose," he recalls. "Because the grass on the outside edge of the vegetation was thinner, I used a Bandit worm, which has good action with a bigger head on it. The Bass Assassin worm has a smaller head and it would come through the thick portions of the grass better, so I used it for casting into the interior of the grass, which was thicker.

"When I was fishing the edge, I would flip the worm to the edge of the grass and let it fall as close to the grass as I possibly could. To catch the fish on the inside, I would stand up in the boat and look as far back into the grass as possible. I would then cast back into little openings in the thick grass and work those pockets. That combination of flipping and casting produced enough fish to win, but couldn't have caught nearly as many by strictly casting or flipping."

With the advent of the Color-C-Lecter and advanced multi-color molds by plastic worm manufacturers, today's bass angler seems hung up on selecting just the right hue. But don't put Doug Gilley in that crowd.

"You could throw a different worm color 50 times a day and not get around to all of the colors in a year's time," he says. "But I'm not one to try every color under the rainbow.

"I only use a handful of basic colors and I'm pretty successful."

To select worm color, Gilley uses a simple set of criteria. On bright, sunny day, he prefers a glitter-type worm color that will reflect the sunlight and attract fish from greater distances. When its cloudy and overcast, he uses a darker worm without any of the flash of glitter.

"There isn't a color that will not catch fish," he says. "You put a worm around enough fish and you'll catch them on any color. I have caught no less than a ton of fish on a plain clear worm. In clear water, it's an excellent fish-producer.

"Pure white is a worm that is overlooked more than any other worm color. I have good success fishing a small white worm on a small crappie hook on 6-pound line with spinning gear. It's deadly under a variety of conditions."

Regardless of the color, almost any angler on any skill level can improve significantly as a plastic worm fisherman by practicing the tips of a master like Doug Gilley. Any fisherman can take advantage of his years of experience by listening to his words and applying them to their specific fishing situations.

Chapter 6

The Time for Tubejigs

Guido Hibdon will never forget Alice.

Before his wife, Stella, gets upset, Alice was a roe-filled 10-pound female bass that he became well acquainted with in the St. Johns River during Super B.A.S.S.-IV.

"I could see all of the fish I was catching that day," the veteran bass pro from Gravois Mills, Missouri, remembers. "There were three fish in one place that would have weighed 10 pounds a piece.

"In fact, I broke one of them off twice in one day. The first time she hit and ran around the trolling motor and broke off. So I waited for about 30 minutes and went back and threw back in there. Somebody had put a little stick in there to mark the bed and she ran around it and broke off again. And she was still on the bed the next day. I would go by and wave at her. That was Alice."

Hibdon left Palatka, Fla., without catching Alice.

That's not the significance of the encounter. The importance of their regular meeting for several days was in how he had attracted her attention.

PROfile

Guido Hibdon's credentials include the 1988 BASS Masters Classic title, 1990 Angler of the Year and four B.A.S.S. victories.

Not to mention the attention of big bass throughout the country.

Guido Hibdon thinks small.

Hibdon, 1988 BASS Masters Classic champion, 1990 B.A.S.S. Angler of the Year and four-time winner on the Bass Anglers Sportsman Society circuit, was one of the first anglers to master the art of fishing tiny tubejigs for big bass. And he has proven that the miniature lures produce in lakes from Lake Mead out west to Georgia's Lake Lanier and the St. Johns River in Florida.

In Super B.A.S.S.-IV, his tubejig system produced 48 pounds, 11 ounces of bass, good enough for fourth place. Even more impressive was his victory in a national tournament on Lake Lanier in which he weighed in 50 pounds, 4 ounces of bass — in just two days of fishing.

"This is not something that a lot of guys have learned to do well," Hibdon says. "It's not the easiest way to fish or the easiest technique to master. But it's worth the effort to learn.

"It's an excellent bait for deep water and shallow water. But it takes patience because it is finesse fishing. It's something that I like to do because I know in a tournament I'm doing something that there aren't 90 other people doing. That's why I enjoy it."

Hibdon's idea of a small, but deadly weapon is a 1/32- ounce tubejig, although he occasionally uses a 1/4-ounce model. Although he originally learned finesse fishing with the Fat Gitzit, made by Bobby Garland's Bass'n Man Lures in Arizona, Hibdon developed the highly successful G-2 for Lucky Strike Manufacturing, Inc., which has become his main weapon. Both have an ultralight plastic hollow-bodied jig that seems to breathe as it falls or is pulled through the water.

Hibdon usually fishes the little lure on 4- or 6-pound test line, but occasionally ties on 8-pound line when fishing for big bass, like on the St. Johns River. For the most part, fishing tubejigs on ultralight line requires the touch of a surgeon.

"You certainly get more strikes with light line," the personable Hibdon explains. "That's because the fish can't see it as well.

"I've always figured you have to get the strikes before you have to worry about catching the fish. If I use 8-, 10- and 12-pound line, I believe I cut my strikes just about in half. If I can get the strikes with these little jigs, I'll worry about catching the fish later. Maybe that's all in my head, but that's the way I've fished for years."

Hibdon's rod choice for tubejig fishing is from the Guido Hibdon line of signature finesse rods he designed for Daiwa. The graphite rods are light enough to promote sensitivity, yet strong enough for setting the hook at considerable depths — a combination not found with many light spinning rods.

"You can set the hook hard with 4- and 6-pound test line and if you've got your drag set halfway right, you can jerk as hard as you want without breaking the light line," Hibdon says. "These rods have that much give to it. I don't know of very many rods on the market that you can do this with. It has a fast tip that goes halfway down the rod, which is important. Most of the time you can jerk just as hard as you can with this rod without breaking the line."

On the surface, it would seem that hooking a decent-sized bass with the tiny hook of these tubejigs would be a challenge. But Hibdon insists it's not terribly difficult.

"It's not hard to hook fish with this little jig, even though the hook is small," he explains. "The fish usually eat it.

"It's a No. 4 hook, which is like a perch or crappie hook. But if you can get any part of that little bitty hook in him, he's yours because these hooks are needle-sharp. They're needle-point sharp. It will penetrate that bone, so you can land big fish."

Fishing tubejigs on light line not only requires patience, but concentration as well.

"With a jig this small, it's very important to watch your line constantly," Hibdon says. "You really can't feel anything.

"You'll never feel one of them hit. You're able to tell the very instant the line stops. Because a lot of times it will stop and move. It will stop and go right on. And when it moves, you should never set it on the spot. It will stop and then move. Most people set the hook as soon as it stops. But that's when he's grabbing it the first time. When the lure moves again, he has already turned and sucked it in his mouth. You can set the hook and catch him then. You have to have the patience to wait until he moves with the bait to set the hook."

Once the hook set is made, Hibdon cautions that even more patience and finesse is required for battling big bass on this light line.

"You've got be to patient when fighting the fish," he says. "You can't horse him to the top. You hold him more than you do anything. The key is to hold him and let him play himself out. It doesn't take that long. As long as you hold tension on him, he'll work his way up."

Although he has experimented with tubejigs in all types of water clarity, Hibdon says clear water is where the tiny lures are most effective.

"Anytime you have clear water, it calls for light-line finesse fishing," he explains. "The clearer the water, the better this works.

"Most people use 8- and 10-pound line and that's extremely light line to them. But that isn't light line to me. In clear water, light line is 2- or 4-pound line. You can land some awfully big fish on 4-pound test. I mean super big fish.

"And you have to fish it very slow. There's more movement of the boat than there is movement of the jig. If you're fishing a 1/32-ounce bait and you lift it a foot with the rod, it might fall 10 feet in deep water. So you do very, very little lifting. It's strictly a matter of moving the boat around as you fish it. The boat's movement gives it subtle movement and you really don't have to put much action on the jig at all, other than the basic retrieve."

Fishing these tiny jigs requires an attitude adjustment of sorts.

"You have to realize that you'll be making shorter casts than normal," Hibdon says. "You can't throw that jig very far.

"You're fishing right around the boat. A 20-foot cast would be a long cast. Very seldom is it longer and if it is, you're just kidding yourself because you

Guido Hibdon was the first to apply the finesse techniques of the West to eastern bass waters.

can't control what the jig is doing. You can't let that much line out and fish effectively. You have to keep it where you have constant contact with the bait. In other words, you feed so much to it and slow it. That keeps the slack out of your line."

In clear water, "color makes all the difference in the world as far as light line jig fishing is concerned," Hibdon adds. "I use smoke colors 90 percent of the time. In Florida, a smoke with copper and red flake has been real effective. On Lake Mead, I use smoke with blue and silver metal flake. These color combinations reflect a lot of light."

Although Guido Hibdon has won a considerable amount of money on the magical little lures, he admits that tubejig fishing is just plain fun as well.

"I can fish different baits and I can fish heavier line, but I prefer to be doing something different from what everybody and his brother are doing," he says. "That's the reason I fish these little jigs on light line. There's a lot of sport to it.

"I won a tournament on Lake Lanier with over 50 pounds of fish and every fish I caught was on light line. It was nothing special I was doing except that I was doing something that nobody else was. That's what separated me from the rest of the fishermen. I had 50 pounds and second place had 18 pounds. It was just a matter of they couldn't do what I was doing. There were a lot of guys who knew exactly what I was doing, but they didn't have the skill with this kind of finesse fishing to duplicate it."

But you can bet that America's top bass fishermen have learned the basics of tubejig fishing since Guido Hibdon took them to school in recent months.

The jig-and-pig, when worked properly, closesly imitates the shape and action of a live crawfish, a bass delicacy.

Chapter 7

The Crawfish Connection

Few Floridians had ever thought much about the relationship between crawfish and bass until Kentuckian Corbin Dyer came to Lake Okeechobee in 1985.

While live crawfish and artificial imitations have been standard bass baits throughout the South for years, the Sunshine State anglers had completely ignored that particular predator-prey relationship. Solid evidence of that was the absence of the jig and pork chunk combination as a main weapon for catching Florida largemouths.

The vast majority of America's tournament pros believe that the jig-and-pig better represents the crawfish than any other type of artificial bait, including the soft-plastic look-alike lures. Corbin Dyer is a big believer of that, as well as the bass' preference of crawfish as a food source.

He proved both to Floridians and fellow tournament fishermen during the 1985 B.A.S.S. tournament on Lake Okeechobee.

PROfile

Dr. Loren Hill is America's best-known bass biologist, as well as a tackle innovator and avid angler.

During the second day of the tournament, Dyer revealed what he had learned about the jig-and-pig in Florida with a seven-fish stringer that weighed 31 pounds — one of the largest stringers in B.A.S.S. history. Four of his bass topped the 7-pound mark. He was forced to admit the secret he had discovered two weeks before when his jig-and-pork combo produced an 11-pound trophy in Lake Tohopekaliga.

"I had read where Florida has several species of crawfish in its natural lakes," Dyer explained. "I didn't realize that or the fact that crawfish is a major food source for Florida bass."

Florida bass are no different from any other state. Its native bass love crawfish.

There are more than 250 species of the 10-legged crustacean in North America. And they are more abundant in the South than the North. Georgia alone has 60 different species, while Louisiana claims 29. Texas must have its share when you consider that the former state record smallmouth was caught on a live crawfish and the current record was taken on a crawfish-colored crankbait.

The bottom-dwelling crawfish, often called crawdads, are found in fresh-water systems of all types, including natural rivers, lake and streams as well as man-made reservoirs.

And in places where bass have a choice, crawfish are a real delicacy, their No. 1 food choice.

"There's a real story to crawfish that a lot of people really don't realize," says bass-fishing legend Bill Dance, who is constructing a 2-acre crawfish pond near his home in Memphis, Tenn., with the help of biologists from Louisiana State University and Memphis State University. "I didn't know it until I started to investigate it.

"It's the most prevalent forage that lives in rivers, ponds, streams and lakes across the United States. The biologists say it represents 75 percent of an adult bass' diet where it is prevalent. That's because the little creature is high in protein and easy to catch. Fish eating a crawfish diet grow fast and fat."

Renowned fisheries biologist Loren Hill, chairman of the Department of Zoology at the University of Oklahoma, confirms Dance's contention about the bass' preference toward crawfish.

Hill reports that several experiments were conducted in which largemouth, smallmouth and spotted bass were offered frogs, salamanders, crawfish, shiners and sunfish. The obvious top choice with the smallmouth and spotted bass was crawfish, while it ranked near the top of the largemouth's preference list as well.

"You have to remember that bass are more or less an optimum forage predator," Hill explains. "They normally take advantage of what is abundant.

"In many lakes, the populations of crawfish are limited to certain locations, depending on the substrate of the bottom or the rocks. In certain areas where the crawfish are abundant, the largemouth will be feeding almost exclusively on crawfish. Where crawfish aren't very abundant, largemouth bass, being opportunistic feeders, will seek the forage that is most abundant.

"So it is difficult to rank crawfish, but if given an opportunity with all

Some flipping lures and crankbaits feature a realistic look that consistently fool bass.

forages available in equal concentrations and numbers, crawfish are very high on the preference list."

Crawfish, biologists tell us, are bottom dwellers that feed mostly at night. They are especially active during the spring and summer months, but crawfish-imitation baits like the jig-and-pig will produce even in the coldest months (although the bait has to be fished slowly).

When confronted by a bass, a crawfish typically flips its tail violently, making a clicking sound and creating a cloud of bottom silt that sometimes allows it to escape by slipping behind a rock or other object. Biologists say the threatened crawfish will react one of three ways: it will sometimes try to face the predator down, with its pinchers out; it will slowly back away; or it will flee in short, rapid spurts.

It is for that reason that both biologists and bass anglers try to vary the retrieve of a crawfish-imitation lure, especially with a crankbait.

"The secret to using a crawfish-type or crawfish-colored crankbait is to be very erratic in your retrieve," says Loren Hill, the inventor of the pH meter, Color-C-Lector and several lures, who is also a fine bass angler. "If you have a constant retrieve, that is not a crawfish pattern.

"Crawfish are very erratic movers and swimmers. They dart around crazily. I try to get a bait that I can jerk real hard, stop it and allow it float back up. I'll jerk the rod in all directions. And it really makes a major difference. I was fishing on Lake Texoma with some friends recently and using a crawfish-colored crankbait. I was jerking my rod around in every direction and catching fish so well that they wanted a crawfish lure on their rods. They fished it with a normal retrieve and I out-fished both of them 16 to one."

The fishing industry obviously recognizes the irresistible predator-prey relationship between bass and crawfish. A vast array of soft plastic lures imitate crawfish (one of the most popular among the tournament pros is Hale's Craw Worm made by Stanley Jigs), which are usually fished as jig or spinnerbait trailers. During the spring spawning season, these plastic crawfish are often fished similar to a worm.

The hard-bait makers haven't ignored the bass' love of crawfish either. Advancements in the photo printing system on lures have created some natural looking finishes on crankbaits ranging from lipless vibrating lures to deep divers.

The company that has exploited the bass-crawfish relationship the fullest is Rebel Lures, which makes seven models of crawfish crankbaits (ranging from a 2 3/8-inch Deep Sinking Wee-Crawfish to the ultralight Deep Teeny Wee-Crawfish, which reaches remarkable depths for a 1/10-ounce lure). More importantly, Rebel offers its crawfish imitations in 10 colors, which is important, the pros say, because crawfish in different waters often have different coloring. And some claim that crawfish change shades of color from season to season.

My personal favorite crawfish-type crankbait is the Rebel Teeny Wee-Crawfish, an ultralight floater-diver that has produced all types of gamefish in streams, rivers, ponds and lakes throughout the South. On 2- and 4-pound test line, it is an enjoyable lure to fish.

Two very realistic crawfish copies are Flow Rite, Inc.'s Dance's Craw, a soft-bodied crankbait, and Strike King's Flip-N-Craw, which is designed to be fished similar to a jig. Both have a lifelike appearance that could fool both fish and fishermen.

But the lure that best resembles a crawfish to the bass — and therefore produces most consistently — is the jig and pork chunk.

"There is no other lure that more closely resembles a crawfish in the water than the jig-and-pig," claims all-time tournament king Roland Martin. "I have filmed a jig-and-pig working on the bottom the way you ought to work it. And I also have film of crawfish scooting along the bottom. I'm telling you that thing looks like a crawfish. It really does.

"You can't throw any kind of crankbait or worm that looks more like a crawfish. There are all kinds of crankbaits that physically look like a crawfish, but from a distance underwater, they don't look much like a crawfish coming through the water. It looks like a darn wiggling lure coming through the water. Crawfish don't wiggle like that. Crawfish work like a jig works. When that jig-and-pig comes hopping along, that looks like a crawfish, not a crankbait. There's a lot of difference."

It is that close resemblance to this bass delicacy that makes the jig-and-pig the best big-bass lure on a year-round basis, the pros agree.

Martin credits a simple black jig with a brown No. 11 Uncle Josh pork chunk with playing a significant role in most of his national tournament victories. But like other anglers, Martin often selects a color that best resembles the crawfish in that particular lake at that particular time of the year.

The jig-and-pig combination is largely weedless, so it can be fished in a variety of cover and structure situations where big bass live. And it is a good bait for covering large areas in search of fish.

For many years, Martin followed the lines of conventional thinking that discounted the jig-and-pig as a productive summer lure. Most fishermen didn't want the bother of trying to keep the pork from drying out, so they switched to a plastic trailer for jig fishing. Besides, a jig-and-pig wasn't effective during the hottest months of the year, they claimed.

During an entire summer several years ago, Martin experimented to discover which was a better summertime big- bass lure — a plastic worm or jig-and-pig. He fished the two lures equally on lakes and rivers throughout the southeastern United States, keeping a record of his catches. What he found was that the worm produced more fish, but the jig-and-pork lured the largest bass. The fish Martin caught on the jig-and-pig had an impressive 4-pound average.

"I've always believed that it produced big fish in the summer because crawfish are universal in this country and especially active during the summertime," he says.

Whatever the reason, crawfish imitations like the jig-and-pig are effective bass-fishing tools because they take advantage of the natural predator-prey relationship that exists. And the special craving that bass seem to have for this little crustacean.

A big Strike King spinnerbait produced this trophy smallmouth for Charlie Ingram on a summer evening on Pickwick Reservoir.

Chapter 8

Lessons From the Master

Although you have be most versatile to stay among the elite ranks of national tournament winners, Tennessee's Charlie Ingram could rightfully be considered the "king of the spinnerbait."

Consider that two of his three Bass Anglers Sportsman Society tournament victories came on the strength of his ability to fish a spinnerbait. Consider that he has won a tournament on various levels in every month of the year (except winter) with the bladed bait and you begin to understand his affinity for this type of fishing.

PROfile

His spinnerbait victories have come in all corners of the country as well. Two B.A.S.S. wins illustrate the allure of the bait. In October of 1985, Ingram won the B.A.S.S. stop on Missouri's Truman Reservoir by slow-rolling a spinnerbait along creek channel ledges in 50-degree water. In late May, he won by catching pre-spawn bass on a spinnerbait fished around warm-water stumps and grass just off of the Mississippi River in LaCrosse, Wisc.

Spinnerbait expert Charlie Ingram of Tennessee is a three-time B.A.S.S. winner and five-time Classic qualifier.

The diversity of those two tournament victories illustrates the undiscriminating appeal of the spinnerbait to bass in every state except Alaska.

Ingram has been sold on spinnerbaits since he was a young man.

"A lot of people live by the spinnerbaits alone," Ingram says. "Jimmy Houston is a prime example of that.

"But the fact is that spinnerbaits will work 90 percent of the time in almost every imaginable condition or situation. If a person wants to learn how to fish for bass, it's the one lure he should master, because it can be fished so many different ways at so many different depths and so many times of the year. It's the most versatile bass bait of all."

One facet of the spinnerbait's allure that greatly appeals to Ingram and should be of great interest to many weekend anglers is that bass usually don't become immune to this type of lure in heavily-pressured waters. Bass don't become conditioned to a spinnerbait, Ingram says, because they don't have an opportunity to closely examine it before striking it. And a large percentage of the strikes come from a reactionary instinct rather than the urge to feed.

Successful spinnerbait fishing begins with well-balanced, specific-purpose tackle designed to accomplish its unique needs.

The rod deserves the most consideration. Ingram's spinnerbait rod choice may be a little surprising. Most bass fishermen use one of two rod types: a 5 1/2-foot rod for making short pitch-casts to targets and a 6 1/2- to 7-foot version for making long casts across vegetation fields or stumps flats. Ingram uses the same rod for both common situations. He cuts a 6-foot-6 Quantum Quartz Lite rod down to 6 feet to create a general-purpose rod.

"One of the keys to becoming a good spinnerbait fisherman is casting accuracy," Ingram says, explaining his rod choice. "The more you cast with the same rod, the more accurate you will become with it. That's why I use the same type of rod for all of my spinnerbait fishing."

The composition of the rod is critical. The rod must have a limber tip that won't hamper the action of the spinnerbait, yet must possess enough backbone to set the hook and move big bass out of heavy cover.

The reel choice isn't as crucial as the rod for spinnerbait fishing. But Ingram recommends using a reel with at least a 5-to-1 gear ratio, so that you have enough speed to get the bait up quickly and enough power to move fish from within cover.

After years of being a dedicated heavy-line fisherman, Ingram has completely changed the line he uses for spinnerbait fishing. The reason for the change is the introduction of DuPont's Magnum 14-40 line. It is a unique, oval-shaped line that its makers claims casts like 14-pound test and has the strength of 40-pound line. "I use it for all of my spinnerbait fishing now, because it casts much better than the 25-pound line I had been using and is a lot stronger," Ingram claims.

Although there are a variety of spinnerbait styles on the market, along with a mind-boggling array of blade and skirt sizes, shapes and colors, Ingram has developed a system of spinnerbait fishing that is seasonal in nature. But before exploring his seasonal approach, it is important to understand some other facets of his spinnerbait system.

Ingram uses only the safety-pin style of spinnerbait, preferring those with the "R" wire design (without a loop in the middle of the wire). That design creates less problem with the line tangling on the wire during the flight of the cast.

Veteran pro Ricky Green found that a large willow-leaf spinnerbait was the perfect answer to Lake Chickamauga's off-colored water.

Two types of plastic trailers suffice in every conceivable fishing situation and weather condition in the Ingram system. In warm-water conditions, Ingram uses a Burke Twin-Tail trailer, which has a tantalizing action when the bait is retrieved rapidly. For cold-water conditions, Ingram works the spinnerbait slower and uses a trailer that offers plenty of vibration coupled with enough action to entice the less active bass into striking. His choice for these times is a 4-inch Harville curl-tail worm-like trailer.

Unlike most pros, Ingram does not use a trailer hook, saying it would hamper his efficiency in heavy-cover situations. Instead, he believes he has an innovative answer to catching short-striking bass.

"I've found that if the fish are missing your bait, you need to change your blade color," Ingram explains. "If you're using a gold blade on the back and the fish are missing the bait, change to a nickel or copper. Or vice versa. I don't know why it works. It just works. If you change that blade color, they'll usually start taking that bait."

When selecting a spinnerbait, perhaps the most important consideration is the vibration factor — the amount of fish-attracting vibration it emits while being pulled through the water. To get more vibration out of a spinnerbait, Ingram flattens the factory blade out a little, reducing its cupping arc.

But more vibration isn't always better. "Early in the year, you don't want as much vibration as you do late in the year," Ingram says. "When the shad are smaller, you should use a blade with a little vibration, which is when I prefer a willow-leaf blade. Later in the year, the shad are bigger, so you want more vibration. So I use a big Colorado or Indiana blade. I know from fishing for smallmouths at night how crucial the right vibration is."

Ingram recommends making one change to almost every spinnerbait on the market — exchanging the Colorado blade on the front of most baits for a smaller version. Most manufacturers use a front blade that is too large and reduces the action of the rear blade. The purpose of the front blade is to provide a little different flash, without hampering the movement of the rear blade.

To reduce the confusion created by an endless variety of skirt and blade colors, Ingram uses a simple criteria — water clarity. In gin-clear water, he uses a copper blade and white skirt. In clear water, a nickel blade and chartreuse skirt works best. For off-colored water, Ingram prefers a gold blade and chartreuse skirt. In muddy water, the best color combinations are a gold blade and a chartreuse-and-orange skirt.

One small trick that has paid off handsomely for Ingram in muddy-water situations involves the color red. Ingram uses a red curl-tail trailer and even paints the backside of his spinnerbait blades red.

The ideal conditions for spinnerbait fishing, Ingram says, is an overcast day with wind. "Or any day with wind," he adds. "A calm day is a worm or jig day. But a windy day moves the fish a little shallower and makes them more aggressive and they're a little easier to catch. There is no such thing as too much wind for spinnerbait fishing."

There is a limit to the depth he will fish a spinnerbait, though. For Ingram, the bottom line is 15 feet.

Two aspects of his spinnerbait skills separate Ingram from many other fishermen, he believes. First of all, he is not afraid to fish the bait in some bad places, jungle-like cover that the average angler might avoid.

Secondly, Ingram has the ability to consistently make picture-perfect casts that enter the water without much sound or disturbance. To accomplish that, Ingram uses short pitches, sending the spinnerbait along the water at a low trajectory so that it hits the water with less force and less commotion.

Since Charlie Ingram has developed his spinnerbait system through years of trial and error on natural lakes and man-made reservoirs throughout the country, the average angler can take advantage of his knowledge by following his seasonal approach to spinnerbait fishing:

SPRING

Throughout the many faces of spring, Ingram uses the same spinnerbait — a 3/8-ounce white-skirted bait with a small gold Colorado on front and a No. 4 1/2 nickel willow-leaf blade on the rear.

But he changes the speed of his retrieve as the water warms up. In early spring, Ingram uses the slow-rolling technique, but his retrieve gradually speeds up as the water gets warmer throughout the season.

"In real early spring, I concentrate on what I call vertical cover like steep banks and bluffs, which are the first places where the fish will move up after the winter," Ingram says. "I parallel them with my spinnerbait.

"But during the spawn and post-spawn periods, I concentrate on bumping the bait against logs, stumps, brush and grass in shallower water."

SUMMER

Ingram's summer spinnerbait selection is a 3/8-ounce bait with a No. 2 Colorado nickel blade on the front and a 4 1/2 gold willow-leaf on the rear. The skirt color is white-and-chartreuse.

"I look for fish in the summer in vegetation or up the river where there's flowing water," Ingram explains. "I especially like grass. The fish are going to be relating to the edge of the vegetation, so it is important to parallel that edge."

FALL

"I go to a bigger blade in the fall because the shad are bigger and I look for some off-colored water," Charlie Ingram says. "I primarily concentrate on wood like stumps, lay-down logs and treetops."

Ingram uses a 3/8- or 1/2-ounce spinnerbait with a No. 3 nickel Colorado on the front and No. 6 gold Indiana on the rear. The skirt color depends on the water clarity. "I like the heavy thump that the big Indiana blade gives off," he adds. "That extra vibration better imitates the vibration of the bigger shad during that time of year."

LATE FALL/EARLY WINTER

The colder temperatures of late fall and early winter force Ingram to make a drastic change in his spinnerbait selection. He uses a 1/2- to 1-ounce spinnerbait body (depending on the depth being fished) and a single blade. His usual choice is a No. 8 Indiana blade (usually gold in color), which has a slow fall and can be fished methodically.

"Always with spinnerbait fishing, you should bump the cover with the bait," Ingram explains. "But in the late fall and early winter, you should fish it slowly. Bring it across the cover and try to let it drop 6 to 8 inches on the edges and in the holes of the cover. If you hit a stump, log, tree or brushpile, immediately drop your rod tip and stop the bait. The vertical fall of that bait will often produce a vicious strike."

Ingram puts his spinnerbait rods away when the water temperature drops below 50 degrees. There are better tools for catching bass in cold water, he says, citing the jig-and-pig combination and a plastic worm.

Spinnerbaits are among the most versatile and appealing artificial lures known to fish and fisherman. By selecting the right bait and applying it to each seasonal situation, spinnerbait fishing can also be the most productive form of bass fishing known to man.

Chapter 9

Emergence of the Willow-Leaf Spinnerbait

It's one of the strangest-looking lures ever to hit the water. It doesn't resemble anything a bass would ever pay any attention to. It's actually a little gaudy.

But it's a winner with impeccable credentials. It's such an effective big bass lure that the priviledged few who have mastered the bait have done their best to keep it a secret on the Bass Anglers Sportsman Society circuit.

PROfile

Just ask Roland Martin. Or Hank Parker. Or Kim Carver.

All have ridden the secret lure to great success.

Martin, winningest professional fisherman of all time, was in the midst of a three-year winless slump during which he rarely challenged for a tournament lead. But after he was introduced to this lure, Martin went on a hot streak, winning twice and finishing fourth three times in five consecutive tournaments.

The mystery lure played no small part in the revival of a magnificent career.

Top pro Hank Parker's credits include two BASS Masters Classic titles, B.A.S.S. Angler of the Year and five victories.

The first day Hank Parker threw this bait, he caught 15 fish in a single practice day for the St. Johns Bassmaster Invitational in Florida several years ago. He then went on to lead the tournament for two days using this lure before finishing third.

And Kim Carver, a relatively-unknown Georgia angler, used the radical bait to win his first B.A.S.S. title, stealing the St. Johns tournament from Parker.

The secret bait is a secret no more.

It's referred to most often as the Okeechobee spinnerbait, because the roots of its origins are deep within the massive south Florida lake. But whatever you call it, it is unparallelled when it comes to catching big bass — unless you want to consider wild shiners.

"I guess my secret's out," said Martin, winner of a record nine B.A.S.S. Angler of the Year titles. "I've done exceptionally well with it, so I didn't think it would stay a secret too long.

"It enabled me to win two tournaments and to come close to winning three others. The significance of it is that it's really a big bass lure."

The big spinnerbait was a major factor in Martin's win in the Georgia Invitational in 1983, a victory that enabled him to erase his longest slump as a professional fisherman. The next tournament, on Okeechobee, Martin's home waters, he weighed in a 27-pound stringer — the largest of the tournament — on opening day, using the big spinnerbait and ultimately finished fourth. Martin then took the lure to La Crosse, Wisc., where he finished fourth again.

Martin opened the 1984-85 B.A.S.S. season by winning the Green County Hudson River BASSmaster Invitational on the lure, which provided him with big bass in a tournament dominated by small fish. Martin's five-fish limits for three days added up to 50 pounds, 2 ounces, and he also took big bass honors. He added a fourth-place finish at Truman Lake in Missouri, where the lure provided him with an impressive final-day stringer — five fish that weighed 15 pounds, 6 ounces.

Martin alone has proven that this big-bass bait will produce anywhere.

By now, your appetite should be whetted.

The Okeechobee spinnerbait is a regular spinnerbait (3/8- to 5/8-ounce leadhead) rigged with a huge willow leaf blade. Although there are several versions and color combinations, the key to its effectiveness is the willow leaf blade, a No. 6 or 8 Hildebrandt, according to those who have fished it.

Martin remembers the first time he fished the unusual-looking lure seriously.

"My friend George Smith of Naples (Fla.) put me on this bait," Martin says. "He gave me this special blade and I put it on a couple of spinnerbaits and right away I started catching humongous fish on the thing.

"Then, I was practicing before the cutoff for the Okeechobee tournament with Orlando Wilson and I had probably the best day I've ever had on lures. That day, I had a couple over 9 pounds, a couple around 7 pounds, a couple of 6s, a couple of 5s. I had a string of seven that would have gone well over 40 pounds. It would have been an awesome stringer and if it had been during the tournament, it would have been the record stringer for seven fish. I'm positive of that.

"Orlando was skeptical of that spinnerbait. When we started out that morning, he said `Heck, I don't think that's any big deal.' He was throwing a regular small spinnerbait and he catches two or three small fish right off the bat. But all of a sudden, I catch one about 6 pounds. Then we go to the next spot and

I catch another one about 6 or 7 pounds.

Finally, he says 'Gosh Roland, that's certainly a big fish. Do you have another one of those lures?' "

The Okeechobee spinnerbait has made a believer out of everyone who's witnessed its effectiveness.

"I had been throwing a spinnerbait with a No. 6 blade for a long time, but I had never tried a No. 8," says Parker, a former Angler of the Year and two-time Bass Masters Classic champion. "I'm sold on it."

"This is a super big bass bait," said Carver, who charged from 32nd on the final day with 18 pounds, 9 ounces, to win the St. Johns tournament by a single ounce. "It's proven itself in several tournaments this year."

But why is this bait so effective? What does it do to attract such big bass where more conventional lures fail?

The experts explain their theories:

Martin: "It's a great big lure that gives off a tremendous flash. It's a big mouth full. It's just like using a shiner. I do a tremendous amount of shiner fishing and one thing that you'll always find is that if you fish nothing but small shiners, you'll catch nothing but small fish. But if you use nothing but monstrous shiners, you'll catch fewer fish, but more big fish. It's the same with this big spinnerbait.

"It's a reflex-action lure. I don't think it does anything radically different than a regular spinnerbait. A regular spinnerbait flashes and it's a reflex thing. A small spinnerbait normally coming by a real big bass, it might not bother them or intimidate them. But this big spinnerbait does. I really think this giant spinnerbait makes so much more noise and so much more flash that it intimidates the big fish to the point where they just blast it out of reflex."

Parker: "It's a neat bait. The reason it works so well and the reason the good fish hit this big spinnerbait when they won't hit a regular spinnerbait is because it puts off so much more vibration.

"It's a good bait to throw in the grass because the fish are often roaming out in the grass and that thing puts out so much vibration that it attracts them. And it's slow. You can keep it in a hole or pocket longer. To get a lot of vibration out of most spinnerbaits, you've got to get it moving pretty good. But that old No. 8 Hildebrandt willow leaf puts out so much vibration and it's so slow, they can come through the grass and home in on it."

Carver: "That big No. 8 willow leaf is about 4 inches long and it puts off a very big flash. I think the fish come up and hit the flash. And it's slow. It gives the fish a better opportunity to look at it — more time and with a lot of flash. You can work it slow and stop it or drop it into holes. It's a good drop bait."

While Martin has proven that the lure has big-bass appeal throughout the country, the Okeechobee spinnerbait's effectiveness is not limited to just grass lakes. Because it's largely weedless, no type of cover is immune from its attraction.

"I throw it in typical spinnerbait cover," Martin says. "But I like to fish spinnerbaits in some of the thickest, nastiest stuff you've ever seen. This bait will work anywhere — in stick-ups, underneath boat docks, around pilings, the edge of grass beds. But I don't throw it in open water."

"It'll work anywhere there's big old bass," Parker says, smiling. "It's such a good-running bait, it will run through just about anything."

The big-bass lure has proven its worthiness during a variety of retrieves. "Basically, I like a medium retrieve," Martin explains. "The only time I would work it slow would be in real cold weather. In real hot weather, I might run it real fast. I've caught a number of fish waking it under the surface in shallow water.

"It all depends on the water depth. If you're fishing, say, spawning bass in 2 feet of water, you might want to wake that thing. If the water's muddy, you might not want to fish it slow. You might want to fish it fast, like in real shallow stump flats. But in real deep weedlines like an 8- or 10-foot hydrilla line, you might want to sink it 8 or 10 feet and work it."

Rigging the lure is subject to personal preference.

Carver won the St. Johns tournament using a No. 8 copper willow leaf blade, teamed with a No. 4 Colorado blade on a 3/8-ounce leadhead. He was using a white skirt with a white twin-tail grub trailer, his favorite combination.

Parker uses a gold No. 8 willow leaf blade on a 5/8-ounce head, but switches skirt colors depending on water clarity. His favorites are white, chartreuse and lime. "I usually put on the brightest skirt for dingier water," he says.

"There are about 10 different ways you can rig it," says Martin, but his most successful version has been a 3/8-ounce head with a long spinnerbait wire teamed with a No. 7 or 8 willow leaf, either gold or silver. "I've had good success on both silver and gold and I'll switch them around a lot."

Martin usually puts the big blade on a spinnerbait manufactured by Blue Fox called the Roland Martin Muddy Water Special, a 3/8-ounce tandem-blade model. "I take the rear blade off of it and leave the little No. 1 brass blade on the shaft. It's so small it doesn't rob much water and it allows that big blade to turn real easy. It comes with a chartreuse skirt, which is a good color."

Whatever version you come up with, Martin, Parker and Carver all agree on this — be prepared for a big battle. Arm yourself with heavy tackle, because the fish won't be small.

Carver was using 30-pound test line when he won the Florida tournament. Parker usually uses 20 and above. Martin throws the bait tied to 17-pound line on rare occasions, but usually relies on 20- to 25-pound test. All use strong rods, usually flipping sticks.

"When you throw this lure, be prepared for war," Martin warns.

He's serious.

Chapter 10

Advanced Cranking

Over the past decade, the diving crankbait has won over a legion of followers that stretch from California to Connecticut and Maine to Florida.

As the nation's lure manufacturers refined the first crude wooden diving plugs of yesteryear, crankbaits began to earn a place in the tacklebox of every bass angler, from the weekend fisherman to tournament pro.

The rise in popularity is understandable. Besides the fact that crankbaits produce fish on a consistent basis from every corner of the country, these lures are not discriminating. Novice anglers adore crankbaits because they require none of the skills a plastic worm demands. Simply retrieving a crankbait ignites its built-in fish-attracting action. Even the smallest child can catch bass on a crankbait.

PROfile

Paul Elias is a former Classic champion who is credited with popularizing the kneel-and-reel cranking method.

While there is beauty in its simplicity, crankbait fishing has become a real art to dedicated diving-lure fishermen, who have taken the time and effort to learn its intricacies. These knowledgeable anglers have taken crankbaits from its "dummy bait" reputation to an advanced form of angling.

In the hands of a talented fisherman who understands the principles of advanced crankbaiting, these wooden or plastic diving baits are the most versatile of all fishing tools. With the proper education and enough practice, it's possible to catch bass in places you could never reach; places you had avoided; or places where you never fished before.

Advanced crankbait fishing begins before ever leaving home with the choice of equipment.

The rod, an often-overlooked instrument among early crankbait anglers, is the absolute key to getting the most out of a diving lure. Standard equipment among good crankbait anglers is a long (7 1/2-foot), stout rod (some pros use flipping rods). The long rod accomplishes two tasks: It allows you to get more depth out of a crankbait by creating a longer cast (you can also put the rod tip in the water for added depth). Secondly, it enables the fisherman to better set the hook after a long cast, which is especially important when fishing clear-water structure with light line.

Until 1985, few anglers ever gave much thought to the composition of the rod they used for crankbaiting. Most were caught up in the boron/graphite craze of the past eight years, charmed by the sensitivity and feather-light weight of those rods.

Then Texan Rick Clunn broke all B.A.S.S. records by crankbaiting 75 pounds of bass in three days to run away with the BASS Masters Classic (the most prestigious event in competitive fishing) on an old fiberglass rod he had found buried in the back of the Daiwa catalog.

Although Clunn recently designed a special crankbait rod for Daiwa that features a graphite body with a fiberglass tip, his Classic massacre took the lid off a secret he had maintained for years. Graphite rods can cause even the most seasoned fishermen to lose fish when using fast-moving lures like crankbaits.

"Through years of fishing both graphite and fiberglass rods, I am convinced that the action and sensitivity of graphite rods work against hooking fish well on fast-moving baits," Clunn explains. "And the better a fisherman you are, the more it will hurt you.

"What happens with graphite is that those rods are so super-sensitive that we're reacting a split-second faster than we had been able to react before. And the fish is just not getting the lure into his mouth far enough and long enough before the rod and the fisherman feels him and reacts. We're talking about split-seconds, but that's the amount of time that's going to determine whether the bass is hooked deep or it's hooked on the outside and is able to spit the lure out."

Clunn discovered the value of using fiberglass rods for crankbaits during extensive testing as a guide. And he proved his theory so well in his Classic victory that most of the bass pros seem to share his belief.

The reel is also an important consideration for advanced crankbaiting.

In the past decade, reel manufacturers have made tremendous strides in increasing the take-up speed of their products. Ten years ago, the fastest gear-ratio found on a baitcasting reel was 3.7 to 1. Today, 5 to 1 ratio reels are commonplace and one manufacturer, Daiwa, markets a model with a 7 to 1 ratio.

Don't get the idea that faster means better when it comes to crankbait fishing, though. Veteran diving-lure anglers emphasize that more speed does not necessarily translate into more depth, which seems to be the aim of most crankbait enthusiasts.

"The development of high-speed reels has changed the game and a lot of fishermen haven't adjusted to it," says Joe Hughes, a superb crankbait fisherman employed by Plastics Research and Development Corp., parent company to the Heddon, Cotton Cordell and Rebel line of lures. "First of all, you can actually reel too fast and rob a lure of some of its depth. You can easily over-crank it.

"The biggest problem, though, is that fishermen everywhere have bought these new high-speed reels to replace their older, slower ones. Then they tie on a crankbait, head out to the lake and proceed to retrieve that bait at the same speed they were accustomed to with the older, slower reel. They don't make a mental adjustment to the fact that they are using a reel that is moving that lure about twice as fast as the old reel did and slow down.

"Two things happen when you over-crank a lure. First, you change the action of the lure and, secondly, it won't run at the same depth. You may have a bait that will run to 12 feet with a moderate retrieve, but if you speed it up, it may only run 10 feet. The common thought among many weekend fishermen that you get more depth the faster you crank, is one of the biggest fallacies in bass fishing."

In 1987, five lure manufacturers introduced crankbaits that shared a common claim—all have broken the 20-foot barrier. Before this development, crankbait fishermen had to be content with flirting with the 15-foot mark (on an average cast).

If the claims of these companies prove true, it opens up a new arena for crankbait enthusiasts. But since some independent tests have found inconsistencies between some of the super-deep lures and the claims that accompany them, we will concentrate only on getting more depth from other lures.

Lee Sisson is a crankbait expert and a genius at getting maximum depth from these deep-diving baits. But then, he should be. As lure designer for the Jim Bagley Bait Co. for more than a decade and now maker of his own Lee Sisson Lures' Ticker Series of wooden baits, Sisson created crankbaits that found their way into the tackle boxes of most American bass fishermen.

"The first thing to get out of your mind is that the harder you crank, the deeper a lure goes," Sisson says, echoing Hughes' statement. "Once you overcome the buoyancy factor of the lure itself, it will run at its deepest from that point. To accomplish that, it usually just takes a moderate, comfortable retrieve."

The most critical aspects involved in getting optimum depth from a crankbait are length of cast and line size, Sisson says.

Flipping sticks and long crankbait rods, which allow two-handed casting, are a necessity. "A long cast is crucial because deep crankbait fishing is a game of angles," Sisson explains. "The longer the cast, the longer your crankbait can work at its maximum depth range.

"For example, say you make a 50-foot cast and your goal is getting the bait to reach 20 feet. If you were somehow able to drop that crankbait straight down, it would take almost half of the line you have cast out to reach 20 feet. So you can eliminate that 20 feet of your line. Now you've only got 30 feet for that bait to work its way down to the structure and back up (as it nears the boat) in a single retrieve. So you can see with a 50-foot cast, your crankbait is not going to be at its maximum depth very long."

One way to instantly gain more depth is to drop to lighter line. Sisson insists that the smaller diameter of the line means less friction coming through the water. So the difference in diameter between 10-pound test and 20-pound line can mean a couple of additional feet of depth.

Lighter line usually translates into additional strikes when fishing all types of artificial lures.

"Another way you can lose depth with a crankbait is if the bait is not running dead center," Sisson adds. "If it's running even a foot off to the side, that can cost you a couple of feet of depth. It's critical that the lure run straight."

A crankbait that is not tracking true requires tuning. To tune a crankbait, use a pair of needlenose pliers to slightly bend the eye of the crankbait in the direction in which you want it to run. For example, if the crankbait is running too much to the left, (while holding a crankbait with the lip facing you) turn the eye (where the split ring is attached) slightly to the right. "If you see it move, you've probably gone too far," Sisson advises. "You just have to develop a feel for it."

Another trick developed in recent years to increase crankbait depth by a foot or so is commonly called "kneeling and reeling." Mississippi's Paul Elias popularized this crankbait technique en route to winning the 1982 BASS Masters Classic on the Alabama River.

The technique is simple. Using a long rod, the angler kneels in the boat and keeps as much of his rod tip as possible underwater. Not only does this lower rod profile allow the lure to run deeper, but it eliminates the surface tension that the monofilament line must penetrate (which means less friction and more depth).

While most crankbait fishermen seem obsessed with breaking the depth barrier, an angler that limits the use of crankbaits to deep water is cheating himself.

"The guy who heads for deep water and only fishes a crankbait deep and fast shouldn't consider himself much of a crankbait fisherman," says Cliff Shelby, an executive with Ranger Boats and an excellent angler. "A crankbait is a tool like any lure and to get the maximum amount out of that tool, you've got to apply it to many different situations.

"For example, most people don't realize it, but a crankbait can be worked very, very methodically and catch fish on or near the surface. I often use the larger, more buoyant baits as top-water baits. In shallow-water situations, a real effective technique is to jerk the bait down a couple of feet and then release it and allow it to float back to the surface. With the deep-diving baits that have a big lip and are real buoyant, that bait won't hardly leave that spot. It will actually back up as it floats up. So now you have a lure that you throw into a little hole in the lily pads and work effectively. That jerk and floating motion seems to drive bass wild. And you can keep this lure in the strike zone a lot longer than other types of baits."

Fishing deep-diving crankbaits in shallow water is nothing new to knowledgeable crankbait anglers. Texan Tommy Milam, who guides on Lake Monticello, used a similar technique with deep-diving lures like the Bagley DB-III and the Rebel Deep Maxi-R to catch more than 120 bass that topped the 7-pound mark in a two-year period. Fishing in 4 to 6 feet of water, Milam would crank the lure down to the lake bottom and reel it slow enough to keep it bumping along the bottom.

A common technique practiced nation-wide is known as "bumping the stump." Crankbait experts agree that these diving baits are most effective when kept in contact with some type of structure—a submerged log, standing timber, underwater ledge or even sparse types of vegetation. The action a crankbait makes when it careens off of a log or bounces over a tree limb or pulls off of submergent vegetation seems to consistently trigger strikes.

While the tournament pros and veteran fishermen understand well this technique, the weekend angler is often reluctant to cast his crankbait around some of the densest cover available — the types of places that hold bass.

"Some people will never fish a tree top, because it means using a lure that cost $3 to $5 and has a pair of sharp treble hooks on it," says Shelby, who was instrumental in the design and testing of crankbaits while working for the Jim Bagley Bait Co. "They're simply afraid to lose that bait.

"But knowledgeable fishermen will catch a lot of fish off of that tree because they know that they can fish it with a crankbait. There's a very simple art to fishing a crankbait in structure like a fallen tree or a tree top. Most deep-diving lures are fairly buoyant, so you use that to your advantage. It's just a matter of cranking the lure down until you feel it bump a limb. Once it hit the limb, if you will stop the retrieve, the lure will float above that limb. Then you crank it until you lure hits another limb and repeat the procedure. The key is not to be in a big hurry. You can walk a crankbait through some incredibly thick structure."

When fishing treacherous structure like a submerged tree top, Roland Martin has a tip that the average angler will appreciate. In situations where there is a danger of numerous hang-ups, Martin replaces the heavier hooks on his crankbaits with lighter wire hooks.

"The wire will straighten out a lot easier than the factory hooks once you hang-up in a tree," Martin explains. "That means I'll have fewer lost lures, less time spent tying on new crankbaits and more time spent fishing."

For just general crankbait fishing, four-time Classic champion Rick Clunn always removes the factory hooks and replaces them with stronger and sharper models. "Almost every hook put on crankbaits today by the manufacturers are not very good," he says. "They are not sharp enough or strong enough for my liking."

Although active bass usually hook themselves, constantly re-sharpening crankbait hooks is essential, particularly with the smaller diving lures. Ultralight crankbaits like Bagley Honey B, Sisson's Diving Tiny Ticker and Rebel's Wee Crawdad have developed a following of their own. But because these lures require light line and sport smaller hooks, sharpness is at a premium.

Long cast as a "dummy lure," crankbaits can be the most versatile tool available for bass fishermen. And only those who have learned the art of advanced crankbaiting reap the full benefit of these deep-diving baits.

Maltuning A Crankbait

Although a crankbait that does not run straight can cost you precious depth, there are some situations when the more knowledgeable crankbait anglers purposely tune the lure to run off-center.

"To get the most out of a crankbait as a tool, you've got to learn when to maltune a bait," says Lee Sisson, a lure designer and crankbait expert. "By maltuning a crankbait, you can get it to perform certain jobs that a straight-running crankbait can't."

By slightly turning the eye of the crankbait, you can make it run radically right or left while being retrieved. This can be a deadly weapon for reaching bass in certain situations.

"This is an excellent technique for fishing boat docks and other types of standing structure," Sisson explains. "Let's say you're fishing a boat dock and you're trying to reach the fish that are underneath in the shade.

"You don't want to try to make a difficult cast under the dock and take a chance at spooking the fish in the process. So your next best option is to ensure that your crankbait runs as closely to the pilings as possible. You can do that by maltuning the crankbait.

"Position your boat out in front of the dock. If you are fishing the right side of the dock, maltune the bait to run off to the left. Then make a cast parallel down the side of the dock to the bank. Now, as you retrieve the lure, it will run off to the left and run around to the back of each piling underneath the dock. It enables you to thoroughly work that dock and keep your bait in the strike zone longer."

And when fishing stick-ups (standing timber), you can actually swim the crankbait around the structure. While fishing structure surrounded by moving water, a maltuned diver could be worked against the current and stay closer to the structure.

Chapter 11

Fishing Lipless Crankbaits

If you were to quiz 100 avid bass fisherman and ask them to select the most versatile artificial lure known to man, you would likely get a variety of answers.

But one answer you would get repeatedly may be a little surprising.

Lipless vibrating crankbaits.

What are lipless vibrating crankbaits, you ask? That category includes a variety of brands of baits that share these common characteristics: flat, shad-shaped, sinking lures that have no plastic or metal lip to serve as a diving plane, but are filled with rattles that crank out a distinctive vibrating noise as the lure is pulled through the water.

You'll recognize the brand names: Bill Lewis' Rat-L-Trap, Cordell Spot, Bagley's Chatter Shad, Storm's Texas Shad, Heddon's Sonic, Rebel's Racket Shad, Mann's Finn Mann and the Bayou Boogie and Rippin' Rattler by Whopper Stopper. All represent a type of lure with enough versatility deserves a place in every fisherman's tackle box.

PROfile

Texan Rick Clunn is a four-time Classic champion and the first angler to win $1 million in tournament earnings.

"These are extremely versatile lures," says Joe Hughes, public relations director for Heddon, Rebel and Cordell lures, as well as one of the country's finest crankbait fishermen. "You can fish them more ways than you can any other type of bait.

"The nice thing about these types of lures for the consumer is that you almost never have to worry about these lures performing other than the way they were designed to perform. It's almost always going to run right, where with crankbaits with lips, you often have to tune it by hand to get it to run correctly.

All you have to do with these types of baits is cast it out and wind it back and you will catch some fish.

"However, you will greatly enhance the fish-catching ability of these kinds of lures by learning to utilize different techniques."

Although Hughes and others have proven that lipless crankbaits will produce under a variety of conditions and around different types of structure and cover, it would seem that they were invented with aquatic vegetation in mind. Few lures can saturate a weed bed or grass line as effectively as a Rat-L-Trap or Spot.

"The Rat-L-Trap-type bait is a year-round bait anywhere you have weeds," says Rick Clunn. "I utilize it more for weed beds than anything else."

Clunn understands well the value of lipless crankbaits around submerged vegetation. In April of 1987, he won a national tournament on Alabama's Lake Guntersville using a gold 1/2-ounce Rat-L-Trap around isolated, submerged milfoil patches.

In Clunn's winning situation, the milfoil beds were located in the middle of a large open-water flat. His most productive area offered a challenge to fish properly. It had the thickest vegetation and deepest water on its perimeter, but became thinner and shallower toward the middle of the weed bed, which featured an open spot where the bass had spawned earlier.

To effectively fish the weed bed, Clunn chose a lure that would allow him to work all depths of the grass — a lipless, vibrating crankbait.

"I used a Rat-L-Trap because that lure does several things for you," Clunn explains. "I could control it very well over the top of the weeds with the position of my rod tip. With all of these weeds, every one I fished had a little different depth, so that was important.

"Crankbaits, to me, are the best baits for fishing for what I call non-positional fish—fish you can't position or pinpoint. Non-positional means that I can't predict where the fish is going to come from. Is he going to come from the left or right side of the stump or underneath that log? You're blind fishing. I could position the fish generally on these weed beds, but I couldn't specifically position where they would be. I had to search for them."

Clunn found almost 43 pounds of bass with his Rat-L-Trap.

Another reason he was able to effectively cover the weed beds, Clunn insists, was the reel he was using. Clunn was utilizing a prototype of Daiwa's new 7 to 1 ratio baitcasting reel, the fastest retrieve reel on the market. When first asked to test the new reel, Clunn was skeptical, but soon found it to be an excellent tool for fishing lipless crankbaits around submerged vegetation.

"I didn't like it much at first because it made a Rat- L-Trap, which is a pretty easy bait to reel, feel like a deep-diving crankbait," he says. "But what I noticed was the extreme variables of speed that you don't have with other, slower reels.

"If you're using a regular ratio reel and you slow down a little bit, the Rat-L-Trap drops. But with this reel, it's almost like a variable control power on a

Despite not being weedless in nature, a lipless crankbait is one of Rick Clunn's most productive tools for probing vegetation.

trolling motor. You could drop the bait on the weed line so much easier without killing the bait. The bait would maintain its vibration even though you were slowing it down to different speeds. I really felt like I had the kind of control of the bait over the weeds that I had never had before."

In Clunn's case on Lake Guntersville, a worm or spinnerbait would have produced in these submerged milfoil patches and certainly would have been easier to fish in the grass. But those lures would not have attracted as many strikes, Clunn says, because of the control he had with the Rat-L-Trap and its ability to cover water.

"Those fish were post-spawn fish, which are typically heavy-shad feeders," Clunn adds. "And the Rat-L-Trap is the perfect imitation.

"Plus, it pulls bass out of the weeds. There's no doubt that the Rat-L-Trap moves bass to the bait. With a slow bait like a worm, you've got to put it right on the fish. But the Rat-L-Trap will draw fish that are buried in the weeds. It will get their attention.

"It's the best of both worlds when you can get a bait that works the weeds efficiently and, plus, attracts fish to the bait, so that you don't have to put the bait right on the fish."

Grass fishing with a lipless crankbait requires patience, though. During his tournament week on Lake Guntersville, Clunn says he rarely made a cast in which he didn't have to remove grass from the lure once the retrieve was completed. To get a strike, the Rat-L-Trap had to touch the top of the submerged vegetation and a considerable number of strikes came as a reaction to the lure being pulled free from the milfoil.

"With this type of fishing around weeds, you've got to understand that you'll have to put up with a certain amount of frustration," Clunn emphasizes. "The average guy won't tolerate it, though. He'll either fish outside of the weeds or move to a place where there are no weeds. You have to control yourself when fishing weeds and be willing to put up with fighting them all day long."

Despite its many virtues, lipless crankbaits like the Rat-L-Trap seem to have a common problem — hooking ability. Even the most talented anglers will lose some fish on these types of lures. Some say it is because the weight of the lure (usually 1/2-ounce) can actually work as leverage once a bass is hooked and help force the hooks loose.

Clunn combats the problem several ways. First, he replaces the factory hooks with heavier versions. He then bends the barbs out so that they flare out significantly. To avoid taking the lure away from a fish by reacting too quickly to the strike, Clunn uses a fiberglass rod instead of a super-sensitive graphite model.

His most successful technique for fighting the bass and keeping it from throwing the lure is to bury the end of the rod in the water and power-crank the reel. "The only jump you can't avoid is the initial jump right after he hits and charges to the surface," Clunn says. "But with this method, I've had good success keeping them from jumping. If you keep them out of the air, you'll lose a few, but the jump is the most dangerous part of the fight."

In an effort to combat the bass' ability to throw these lipless crankbaits, many of the top pros had been quietly using an adaptation that many swear by. After drilling a hole through the top the lure, they inserted the line through the body of the bait and attached the belly hook directly to it. That created a free-swinging hook that allowed the heavy lure body to pull away from the frantic fish.

This eliminated any leverage the lure weight provided for the bass. The pros also removed the tail hook to ensure that the fish hit the free-moving belly hook.

Recognizing a good idea, several lure manufacturers followed suit and the 1988 introductions included free- swinging versions of the Rat-L-Trap (called the Pro-Trap), Mann's Finn Mann and Cordell's Spot. In fact, PRADCO, Inc., parent company of Heddon, Cordell and Rebel, introduced similar hook systems in the Zara Spook and Pop-R.

While lipless crankbaits are extremely effective tools for probing aquatic vegetation, these lures are much more effective than that. If you fish these baits exclusively around vegetation, you aren't taking much advantage of the power of these lures.

"There aren't very many situations where these lipless crankbaits won't produce," says Joe Hughes. "To get the most out of them, you have to try different retrieves and techniques.

"The most univeral way of fishing a Spot-type lure around some type of submerged structure or cover is to cast it out and let it run 4 or 5 feet below the surface, while making it run erratically. The most productive way to fish it is by making it bump into whatever cover you're fishing, whether it is a point or sandbar on a river system or the edge of a weed line or over submerged grass."

Although most people don't consider these lipless vibrating crankbaits to be suited for deep-water structure fishing, Hughes and others have proven otherwise. These lures, generally, will sink at a rate of a foot per second, so they will reach underwater humps, ridges or breaklines that even the deepest-diving plastic-lipped crankbaits can't touch.

If you are fishing a hump in 25 feet of water, the sinking ability of these lures allows you to (after making a long cast) effectively work the lake bottom. A productive way to work a bottom irregularity with these lures it to allow the bait to hit the bottom and then perform a series of short hops, followed by free-falls. The strike will usually come on the fall in that situation.

These lures can be fished vertically along bridge pilings and standing timber with great results.

"Back when Sam Rayburn and Toledo Bend in Texas were new lakes and really hot, one of the techniques that produced the best for Cotton Cordell (renowned lure maker and creator of the Spot) was dropping the Spot straight down to the base of a big tree in the flooded timber areas," Hughes says.

A selection of lipless crankbaits: top row (left to right) -- Bagley Chatter Shad, Ed Moore Lures Sugar Shad; middle -- Cordell Jointed Spot; bottom -- Storm Texas Shad, Bill Lewis Lures Pro Trap.

"He would keep it tight against the trees, rip it off of the bottom and let it fall back down. If he didn't get a strike, he would crank the lure to a different depth and do the same thing. He caught a tremendous amount of fish that way. And since Cotton told me about that technique, I have used it very effectively. It has proven particularly valuable on the tough days when the fish were holding right next to the structure. It doesn't take long to fish a tree this way and with the sound that the Spot generates under water, you can really attract strikes.

"This is an excellent technique for fishing cold-front conditions. When the fishing is tough and the fish are tight to the cover, this is an excellent way to put fish on the stringer."

Lipless crankbaits are the perfect tool for a variety of structure and cover situations that fisherman face throughout the year. While they don't have the glamorous appeal of their deep-diving counterparts, these vibrating baits are among the most versatile lures known to man.

Chapter 12

Jerkbaits:
The Professional Tool

After 17 years as a touring professional, four world championships, numerous national tournament victories and the B.A.S.S. Angler of the Year award, it takes something spectactular to get Rick Clunn truly excited about his fishing exploits.

PROfile

Four-time Classic qualifier Zell Rowland of Texas used a jerkbait to win the 1987 Tennessee B.A.S.S. Invitational.

During a remarkable week on New York's St. Lawrence Seaway one recent June, Clunn enjoyed such a moment. Listen as he describes it:

"It was the most unbelievable fishing. You would be out in 15 feet of water jerking that minnow-bait and, all of a sudden, there would be about 10 smallmouths weighing 2 1/2 to 5 pounds swimming up under it. I would then stop it and let it sit. And the minute they would start to turn away from the bait, I would just pop it. Every single time one of those big smallmouths would come back and just explode on the bait.

"I had one big boulder in that clear water where you just couldn't bring the bait by without seeing those big brown objects that looked like they were coming from the heart of that rock. It was exciting — the most exciting fishing I had ever done. I hadn't been so eager to go out the next day in a long time. I just couldn't wait to get back out there the next day. It was just incredible."

If that doesn't make your pulse race, you had better check the level of your embalming fluid.

It was at that tournament that the jerkbait, a shallow- diving, angled-lipped minnow-style lure also referred to as a ripbait, began to garner some serious attention from those on hand to witness the outrageous fishing it produced in the clear water of the St. Lawrence. While that river harbors the kind of fishing that makes almost every type of artificial lure productive, it was the jerkbait — in the hands of several knowledgeable pros — that produced the quality bass.

It raised some eyebrows, much to the chagrin of certain pros.

"The jerkbait is a very confidential bait among the professional fishermen that are in the know, you might say," Clunn says today. "It's a lot like the Pop-R was. Certain fishermen have really kept the jerkbait to themselves.

"In this day and time, the way you keep a bait to yourself is the way you work them. That was true with the Pop-R. You can't keep the bait itself a secret, but you can usually maintain that secrecy if there is something different about the way that you fish it."

And for a small, select fraternity of pros, the secret of the ripbait lies in the way they fish it — with power.

Jerkbaits like the Bomber Long A, Rebel Spoonbill, Rattlin' Rogue, Rapala, Deep-Diving Bang-O-Lure and Rebel Minnow have suddenly assumed a more important role in the tackle boxes that travel the national tournament circuit, an updated importance of the past two years. The pros have discovered that with the right technique, these minnow baits will produce impressive results under a variety of weather conditions and cover/structure situations.

But these types of lures are most effective in the hands of the fisherman who isn't afraid of working up a sweat and creating a blister or two. The design of these baits create a substantial drag in the water, which makes them harder to pull. And the only way to drive the bait down and make it perform correctly is to muscle it. Pros like Clunn, Zell Rowland, Gary Klein and Jimmy Crisp drive the lure down and through the water with powerful sweeps (or jerks — the origin of the term jerkbait) of the rod, which can create bulging biceps. Coordinating single turns of the reel handle with each sweep, they always leave enough slack in the line to allow the bait to walk from side- to-side — which many believe is the key to the bait.

The idea is to make the lure dart frantically through the water and then pause to allow it to suspend momentarily. That combination of power-and-pause is important because a bass can either ambush the bait while it is motionless or strike out of reflex-action as it steams by him.

"Done right, it will wear you out and if you don't have blisters at the end of the day, you're not fishing it right," Clunn says. "That is the secret with the jerkbaits — how hard you work them. Very few people will commit to working that hard.

"And if you upgrade to the big No. 18 Magnum Rapala that Jimmy Crisp throws, you'll discover what hard work is. That bait is definitely a secret. It's a deadly, deadly bait when you step up to that size. But there is not one in 100 guys who can work that bait right all day. I know I can't."

It doesn't require the demeanor of Hulk Hogan to catch bass on these lures, however. Simply retrieved steadily just below the surface, jerkbaits will catch fish. But the true power of the bait lies in the power of the angler. That is just one example of what separates the top pros from the rest of us.

The design of the bait, with its long, slender body shape, gives it a natural appeal to bass. Its shape resembles that of a shad, minnow or shiner — all prime food sources for largemouth and smallmouth bass. And biologists tell us that bass are more likely to consume prey with that shape than others with the build of a bluegill, for example. The elongated shape of a minnow will more easily slide through the fish's throat.

The jerkbait, Clunn believes, is about the most versatile hard bait available to fishermen. The fish-attracting qualities of these lures are numerous.

"The thing that makes it special is that it catches numbers, but it also catches quality fish," he explains. "I think that is because of the size and shape of the bait and its unique action. It's an elongated bait that you can get down pretty deep — deeper than most people realize. It has the Zara Spook `walking the dog' type of action that's actually done under the water, which, for some reason, is very enticing to largemouth bass. And you can also hover the bait. Stop it and almost most suspend it, which is, again, attractive to larger fish."

It is one of the few lures that will both allow the angler to quickly cover water in search of bass, yet finesse individual fish holding on an isolated piece of cover into striking. A rare combination of power and finesse.

For most anglers, the seasons for fishing jerkbaits are spring and summer, although Clunn will use it other times of the year in special situations like a wind-blown bank or bluff where it is one of the few lures that can be fished effectively.

But fellow Texan Zell Rowland also fishes it through the fall and into the beginning of winter. "I've caught fish on a jerkbait when it was snowing outside," adds Rowland, who credits the Bomber Long A with helping him win the 1986 B.A.S.S. Super-Invitational on Tennessee's Lake Chickamauga. "I just worked it real slow and made it stop a lot."

A major appeal of these lures to the tournament pros is the wide range of cover and structure types that can be fished with jerkbaits. Almost no fish-holding habitat is immune to them.

Clunn believes these baits are at their best when fished over submerged vegetation, but he has been known to drive the big ripbaits through brush as well. With the exposed treble hooks, it takes experience and considerable skill to be able to manipulate it through brush, but it can be done.

But Rowland and Arkansas' Cliff Shelby, a talented bass angler and Ranger Boats executive, say the baits are most alluring when used to parallel rocky shoreline like that found in reservoirs like Bull Shoals, Shelby's home lake.

And Bull Shoals has the one ingredient most crucial with this type of fishing — clear water. The clearer the water, the more productive a ripbait can be because its ability to attract fish from considerable distances is greatly enhanced.

Once a bass is located, these jerkbaits can be transformed into enticing finesse lures, thanks to their near neutral-buoyant quality. Experienced anglers drive the bait down to the desired depth and then pause it next to the cover, where the bait can maintain its position for several seconds if enough pressure is applied to the line. Twitching the bait while it suspends is often enough to trigger a strike from an inactive bass.

To enhance its suspending ability, Rowland adds weight to a Rebel Minnow by drilling a hole just above the front hook, inserting a 1/2-ounce piece of lead and re-sealing the hole.

"But you don't need to do that with the Spoonbill," adds Shelby, who is a firm-believer in the persuasive powers of that Rebel ripbait. "In the clear water here at Bull Shoals, you can really get a good idea of how a lure performs and I've found that the Spoonbill is an amazing bait for finessing a bass into striking.

"Not only does it suspend well, but you can actually make it back up 2 or 3 inches. I'm not talking about the tail rising up. With a little practice, you can make the entire bait back straight up. And that initiates some vicious strikes out of a fish watching it."

At other times, the strike on the Spoonbill will be anything but vicious, though. So Shelby advises paying close attention to your line.

Because of the Spoonbill's suspending quality, it is surprisingly effective in the late winter/early spring when the water is still cold (40 degrees or so) and the bass are inactive.

Knowing the bait's ability to draw bass from a distance, Shelby emphasizes the importance of working the lure all of the way back to the boat.

The depth that these baits will run ranges from 3 to 9 feet, depending on both the diameter of the monofilament used and the brand of lure, Clunn says. The pros seem to agree that the Rebel Spoonbill, which features a large lip, is the deepest diver among the jerkbaits.

When selecting a ripbait, Zell Rowland has a single criteria — weight. The heavier the lures, the farther it can be cast and the deeper it will dive.

Although line size will help dictate the depth at which you can drive these types of lures, Rowland refuses to use less than 12-pound test. Smaller line will not withstand the pressure he puts on it, Rowland says, referring to his technique of power-fishing. Like many Bull Shoals fishermen, Shelby uses 4- to 8-pound test for finessing the clear-water fish.

The choice of rod with this type of fishing is crucial. Both Shelby and Rowland prefer long (6 1/2- and 7-foot) medium-action rods with a slightly limber tip. The composition of the rod should have enough backbone to drive

B.A.S.S. Times editor Matt Vincent unhooks a nice Kentucky Lake bass caught on a jerkbait.

these big baits through the water, yet have enough tip to enhance the action of the bait.

The type of reel isn't nearly as critical. Almost any type of reel would suffice, but a high-speed model makes this type of fishing a little easier.

Rowland isn't one to go overboard on colors. For jerkbait fishing, he relies on two color patterns — shad imitations and chrome with either a blue, black, green or gold back. "The way we power these jerkbaits, a chrome finish really flashes under water," Rowland says. "And in this clear water, that flash will attract bass from as much as 25 or 30 feet away."

The attractions of these diving minnow baits are many. And in the hands of a fisherman willing to put forth the effort involved in fishing them correctly, these big jerkbaits simply overpower bass.

The secret is out.

After flipping a jig-and-pig into a tangle of fallen trees, Roland Martin
battles with a big Lake Okeechobee bass.

Chapter 13

The Allure of Jigs

During a five-month period in 1980-81, one of the most phenomenal feats in all of sports took place.

It was during that time that Roland Martin further solidified his position as the country's best bass angler by winning an unprecedented three consecutive Bass Anglers Sportsman Society tournaments, an accomplishment that ranks with Joe DiMaggio's 56-game hitting streak and the Miami Dolphins' perfect 17-0 season in 1971.

PROfile

To outdistance the nation's top pros in three consecutive contests was unimaginable — until it occurred. Martin started the streak by catching 48 pounds of Lake Okeechobee bass. He followed that with a whopping 84 pounds of Toledo Bend largemouths and 43 pounds from Lake Eufaula.

If a man was ever on a roll, it was Martin, the model of efficiency during that stretch. But if you ask him to cite a common denominator between the three victories, he would single out his skill as a jig fisherman.

Roland Martin's accomplishments are legendary: nine B.A.S.S. Angler of the Year titles, 16 victories and 18 Classic appearances -- all records.

"Jigs are my favorite bait for most lakes in this country and I'll tell you why," Martin says. "I've probably had more success with that lure as anything I've ever fished. It played a significant role in my three straight wins. And the last four tournaments I've won came on a combination of baits and the jig-and-pig played a big role."

That's quite a statement of confidence in a specific lure, particularly considering that Martin has collected more than $300,000 in B.A.S.S. winnings, 16 tournaments and nine Angler of the Year awards in the process.

A down-sized jig-and-pork chunk is an excellent bait for catching both trophy smallmouth and spotted bass (above).

From his experience with the rubber-skirted, lead-headed lures in lakes and rivers all over America, Martin has come to consider the jig — particularly the jig-and-pig combination — to be the best big-bass bait of all in a wide variety of conditions. With a degree in fisheries biology to support his thinking, Martin believes the ability of the jig to produce large bass can be attributed to the fact that it resembles one of the bass' favorite food sources—crawfish. And a major reason why jigs are effective in radically different waters in all parts of the country stems from the fact that crawfish are a prevalent food source throughout America.

"It is such a great big-bass lure because it simulates a crawfish better than any lure known to man," he explains. "There's no question that the basic size and shape of a jig and the way it moves and hops emulates a crawfish more than anything else. The addition of a pork chunk makes it look even more like a crawfish.

"Crawfish are a big source of protein for bass everywhere. Some southern lakes, particularly the rocky lakes, like Truman Reservoir and Lake of the Ozarks, and others like Toledo Bend have a lot of crawfish and, therefore, they are better jig lakes than others. For example, Florida has some lakes that aren't as good for jigs as they are for plastic worms because the basic make-up of the lakes are different from the rocky southern reservoirs and they have fewer crawfish. But Okeechobee sure fooled me."

Despite living on massive Lake Okeechobee in southern Florida for the past six years, Martin rarely tied on a jig. That all changed when Kentuckian Corbin Dyer used a jig-and-pig to catch 31 pounds (one of the largest seven-fish stringers in B.A.S.S. history) on the final round of the 1985 BASSmaster Florida Invitational to come from nowhere to finish third. That opened the minds of many Floridians and others to the productivity of the lure in these shallow, weed-laden lakes.

Martin admits he should have realized the power of a jig on Okeechobee bass long before Dyer's heroics. Years earlier, Californian Dave Gliebe introduced Floridians to the art of flipping by winning a national tournament on Okeechobee with an amazing 96 pounds — on a jig-and-worm combination. The second-place finisher had more than 60 pounds, a guy named Roland Martin.

"The value of fishing a jig on Okeechobee doesn't escape me anymore," he says, smiling. "I've come to the conclusion that if you want to catch a big fish, use a big jig — anywhere."

In the last few years jig-makers have gone wild with colors, manufacturing every hue and color-combination under the rainbow (or Color-C-Lector). As a result, the average jig angler is faced with deciding between as many skirt colors as a spinnerbait fisherman. But Martin has simple system for selecting jig color.

"The simplest way to choose color is to match the hatch," he explains. "I use color combinations involving only four colors — brown, black, red and blue. All are colors that are found on crawfish during different times of the year in different parts of the country. There are probably more than 100 different species of crawfish and I think almost every lake has a slightly different coloration to its crawfish. So take the time to examine the crawfish and try to match your jig color to it."

The most productive color combination for Martin over the years has been brown and black. He teams either a black jig with a brown pork chunk or vice versa.

Jig fishermen have adapted a variety of trailers for their use, including pork eels, plastic worms of various types, grubs and frogleg-like plastic extensions. For 90 percent of his jig fishing, though, Roland Martin relies solely on a jig teamed with a No. 11 Uncle Josh pork chunk, the combination that best resembles a crawfish, he says.

"But don't rule out a jig-and-worm combination," Martin adds. "I still use a jig-and-worm or a jig with a Mr. Twister Twin Tail as a trailer sometimes when flipping isn't my main pattern that day.

Let me explain that. If you're fishing a hot day or you're running down the lake, the pork chunk can dry out very easily if flipping isn't your primary pattern. What I mean by that is you may stop first at a crankbait point. Then you might run to a surface-plug spot. Finally, 5 miles down the lake, you might see a tree that's fallen over in the water, which you decide to flip. By that time, you're pork chunk has dried into nothing but a hard mass. So if you're just casually flipping, it might be best to have something like a worm or Twin Tail tied on as a trailer. Then, when you pull up to that tree, you're ready to go."

Jig fishing is most effective in water temperatures less than 60 degrees, Martin says, and, over the years, most of his big bass hit a jig in water between 45 and 55 degrees. Generally speaking, that makes a jig most effective in the winter and early spring for catching sheer numbers of bass, while a plastic worm is a better choice for late spring, summer and fall. But don't abandon the jig in the hot portions of the year if you're after big bass, he says.

"For many years, I thought jigs where just not a good summer bait, so I would automatically use worms once the water got over 60 degrees," Martin explains. "But I conducted a pretty extensive experiment in '79 or '80 that convinced me that jigs are a good big-bass lure in the summer, too.

"I knew that Dave Gliebe and (fellow Californian and flipping pioneer) Dee Thomas had really done well flipping jigs most of the year, so rather than switch to worms when the weather got warm, I decided to stick with a jig-and-pork rind combination to see what would happen. That summer, I fished jigs in water with 90- and 95-degree temperatures all through Oklahoma and Texas and the tournament stops on the east coast. I fished it in every kind of condition.

"I carefully documented everything and I found that I caught a lot fewer fish than I had on a worm. I had probably caught three or four times more bass on a plastic worm. But the fish I caught that summer on a jig-and-pig maintained a 4-pound average. A 4-pound average is fantastic. That proved to me that the jig is an excellent big-bass bait throughout the year."

Although Martin's favorite size is a 3/8-ounce jig, he advises anglers to match the lure size with the type of cover (and, to a lesser degree, water depth) they are fishing. The 3/8- ounce jig is ideal for shallow-water situations like fishing a tree top or stump field because it falls at a tantalizingly slow speed. But thick cover like bulrushes, milfoil, hyacinths and hydrilla usually form an impenetrable barrier for jigs of that size. So Martin will usually switch to a 5/8- or 1-ounce jig — whatever size it takes to puncture such cover.

And Martin concentrates his jig attacks in some of the toughest cover imaginable, while avoiding open-water situations.

"I never throw a jig in something that it can't bump through," he says. "When I'm fishing a jig, basically, I'm throwing it over things and through things.

"Unless I can feel it pull up over a limb or pull up on a rock — actually be in contact with the cover — I don't feel like I'm fishing the jig in the manner that would be most productive. I've found a jig is most effective when you bump it into the cover or slowly pull it over a tree limb and, at the last moment, shake it over the top and let it flutter down the other side. As soon as I see it sink, I really concentrate hard because that's when bass will often hit it. So it's important to be a line-watcher when fishing jigs."

It was during his amazing winning streak in 1980-81 that Martin developed a three-pronged attack for jig fishing that involves three distinctly different methods of getting the lure to the fish.

His most common method was the conventional California-born flipping technique that allows you to quietly and accurately present the lure to bass in heavy cover. The technique involves stripping off line from reel with one hand and using a pendulum motion to propel the jig just above the surface of the water before dropping it into the desired location.

But it was during his tournament victory on famed Toledo Bend in 1980 that Martin developed his "flip-cast," a method of flipping long-distance that has paid major dividends for him since its invention.

"It was a spring tournament and I was fishing water so clear that I could actually see the fish spook every time I got close enough to flip a big stump or tree," Martin recalls. "I tried to flip these places the conventional way from a farther distance away, but the best I could get was a flip of 25 or 26 feet. Even at that distance, I was scaring the fish.

"I couldn't cast to it because there was no way that regular a casting rod could handle these big fish in this heavy, heavy cover. So I had to use my flipping stick and that's when I developed my flip cast. The flip cast is a very

TROPHY TAMER: The jig-and-pig is unparalleled by any other lure when it comes to attracting bragging-sized bass.

simple cast. You simply let out enough line to match the length of your 7 1/2-foot rod. You then grasp the jig in your left hand (assuming you are right-handed). Now, as I make an under-handed motion by swinging the rod upward sharply, I take the jig and both aim and propel it with my left hand like I was bowling. By using your left hand, you can get another 10 or 15 feet more than conventional flipping. That gives you a cast of 35 to 40 feet that is very accurate and still has a quiet lure presentation."

But even with the ability to flip-cast 40 feet, Martin found there were times when a fish would break the surface off in the distance and he had no way to present his jig to it. Or he was unable to fish a solitary piece of timber away from the line of stick-ups he was flipping without taking the time to motor over to it. It was then that he realized the potential value of being able to cast jigs on heavy tackle like flipping sticks.

It takes practice to develop a feel for using the big rods to make long casts, Martin says, but the versatility this particular skill provides is well worth the effort to learn it. "Not only can you make a long cast and cover more water," he says, "but you will also have the good hook-setting ability that a stout flipping stick gives you."

Roland Martin has taken the time and trouble to expand his system of jig fishing into a real art. And it has paid off handsomely over the years. After all, it helped him garner a piece of fishing immortality in 1980-81 and stay atop of the sport he helped glamorize.

Chapter 14

Steve Daniel's Jig Prowess

When Steve Daniel first moved to Lake Okeechobee several years ago, he brought with him the weapons he used to catch bass in his home state of Tennessee and throughout the country.

Included in an arsenal good enough to garner a coveted spot in the 1985 BASS Masters Classic were a variety of jigs, which he promptly began to experiment with on Okeechobee, where he would soon begin a guide service. Experiment is the proper term, because Florida's legion of bass fishermen rarely fished a jig in their shallow, weed-laden lakes and most didn't believe a jig-and-pig would even be retrievable below the Georgia line.

PROfile

Lake Okeechobee guide Steve Daniel is a three-time qualifier for the BASS Masters Classic.

On one of the first days that Daniel began trying a plastic jig and pork chunk combination, Lake Okeechobee yielded a pair of bass that topped the 9-pound mark.

"I knew I had something. I knew then that a jig-and-pig would be productive in Florida," Daniel says today. "But I really wasn't surprised, because I knew you can fish a jig anywhere in the country and catch fish around any kind of structure or cover. It's just a good big-bass bait."

Steve Daniel, a three-time BASS Mastres Classic qualifier and Lake Okeechobee guide, is a very versatile angler with many talents. He can fish every lure effectively, whether it be a deep-diving crankbait or a Do-Nothing Worm. He has proven his ability on waters as different in nature as Lake Mead in the west and Tennessee's Chickamauga and Nickajack.

But he credits a major portion of his success to his ability to fish a variety of types of jigs and the systematic approach he has developed to cover almost every conceivable condition.

"I am really crazy about jig fishing," says Daniel, who now makes his home in Clewiston, Fla., where he guides out of Roland Martin's Clewiston Marina. "When you have confidence in jig fishing like I have, there is a good anticipation every time you fish it, because you know it's such a great big-fish bait. That anticipation keeps you on your toes and ready.

"And the jig itself is such a versatile bait, regardless of what you put on it (as a trailer). You can fish it so many different ways. I might throw it on a drop-off or brushpile or a log and work it real slow across the bottom. And you can jig it vertically over a piece of deep structure. It's a good lure for finding fish, because I can cover a lot of water with a jig. I swim it slow, which is a good way to find fish. I fish a worm and a jig pretty much the same way, but I'll fish a jig more whenever I can.

"I fish a jig around any type of shoreline cover, real thick cover or any kind of cover. I will especially fish it anywhere where there might be crawfish, which is what a jig really imitates. It's also a good river bait for fishing drop-offs and tail-waters where there's plenty of current. A lot of people don't like to fish current situations with a jig because it's not easy to do. But you can find areas below dams where there are lots of crawfish in that current and catch a variety of fish — largemouth, smallmouth and spotted bass. I think it's the most effective lure you can use below a dam."

Included in Daniel's jig fishing gameplan are five combinations: jigs with no trailer, jig-and-pig, jig-and- spring lizard, jig-and-plastic crawfish and small hair jigs with a tiny pork chunk. Each have separate applications in Daniel's system, although he doesn't limit his jig choices exclusively to certain conditions.

The jig-and-pig combo is probably his favorite.

"It's a real good bait here in Florida, but that was a well-kept secret among the ones that were fishing it down here until Corbin Dyer came along," Daniel says, referring to Dyer's 31-pound-plus (third-largest seven-fish limit in B.A.S.S. history) stringer in the 1985 BASSmasters Florida Invitational on Lake Okeechobee. "It's a good hot weather bait.

"The reason it's such a good hot-weather bait is that it's a big-fish bait and big bass are lazy, especially in the hot times of the year. Crawfish are easy prey for bass because they don't move real fast and even when it's real hot and the fish aren't real active, bass will hit a crawfish when they would pass up other food sources."

Daniel's most productive jig-and-pig combination is a brown jig with a black No. 11 Uncle Josh pork chunk. "But I try to match my jig-and-pig colors with the seasonal colors of crawfish," he adds. "For example, in the springtime, they'll have a greenish tint to them, so I use a lot of greens on my jigs — black-and-green and black-and-chartreuse."

A significant portion of Daniel's success throughout the year comes on a combination of brown jig and black plastic spring lizard, a home-made twin-tailed trailer that resembles Burke's Split Tail Eel. "I've caught some real big fish on Chickamauga on that combination," he says. "It's really effective in the summer and fall when the water's warm."

For Daniel, a prime clear-water combination is a brown jig teamed with a brown-and-black Ditto Fire Claw trailer. "It's a real good bait in clear water where the fish can get a good look at your bait before deciding whether to hit it," he explains. "This combinations resembles a crawfish more than any."

A productive, but overlooked smallmouth lure is a brown hair jig coupled with a tiny black Uncle Josh No. 101 pork chunk, which is about 1 1/2 inches in length. "This is a super smallmouth bait in rivers," Daniel says. "It's one of my favorites for fishing below a dam."

Daniel uses a hair jig made of arctic fox and suggests rigging the small piece of pork with the fat side down. "It looks so much better in the water that way," he adds.

A jig without a trailer has a place in his system, but Daniel has limited applications for it.

"I seldom use a plain jig, but it's a good bait for fishing real deep and vertically jigging it like a spoon," he says, "Out west they call it shaking. You just drift through an area of deep water and just barely shake it vertically. I don't use a piece of pork on the end of it because that makes it slower to fall and slower to fish."

For this type of fishing, Daniel sticks to basic blacks and browns, although he will occasionally mix in a brown-and- orange jig that resembles a crawfish.

Generally, Daniel fishes a heavy jig, usually a 5/8th- ounce version. He says he needs the heavy jig to work the bottom, which is his approach about 75 percent of the time. The heavy jig enables him to keep in good contact with the lure (which makes it easier to detect a strike) and he says "the fish don't seem to care how heavy it is."

Daniel admits he fishes jigs on heavier line than most anglers use.

"I use as heavy a line as I can get away with," he says. "Even if I'm fishing reeds in real clear water, I'll use 25-pound test line. The only time line size seems to matter is in open water, where it definitely makes a difference. But as long as you're around a lot of brush or reeds or any kind of cover, you can get away with heavy line.

"Remember, this is a big-fish bait, so you need to make sure you can get these big bass in the boat once you get a strike. And that's not an easy thing to do around thick cover."

Presentation of the jig is especially critical in clear water, Daniel says.

"Lure presentation is the part that a lot of fishermen fail at, particularly in real clear water," he adds. "In dingy water, you can fish right on top of the fish and flip to them. I don't think even the trolling motor makes much difference in dingy water because I've had fish hit my jig as I was taking it out of the water with the trolling motor running.

Steve Daniel uses a variety of jig and trailer types to counter different fishing situations.

"But in clear water, you need to back off and learn to pitch your jig into the water without making a big splash. That's especially important if there's a lot of fishing pressure on the area and the fish are real spooky. Presentation means everything in that case. You need to be as subtle with it as you can be."

Finally, Steve Daniel reminds us that jigs are enjoyable — and easy — lures to fish.

"If you went out and bought a 1/2-ounce jig and a bottle of No. 11 pork chunk, you could fish it anytime during the year and have good success with it under a variety of water conditions and types of structures," he says. "Any fisherman of any skill level can catch fish on it. I don't think you could beat it with any other bait."

pork chunk combination. But he doesn't hesitate to down-size the jig and switch to a small No.101 Spinning Frog trailer for smallmouth bass.

And the pork strips make excellent trailers for spinnerbaits, spoons and buzzbaits because they combine tantalizing action with durability.

But the pros most often utilize the No. 1 or 11 pork chunk as a trailer behind a lead-headed jig — the most common pork companion. The jig-and-pig combination is considered by most pros to be the best big-bass lure known to man.

A major reason why the pork chunk is such a cherished professional tool s its ability to be altered to better perform in changing situations. This is most often in relation to water temperature, which regulates the metabolism (and activity level) of the fish.

Johnnie Borden adds the element of sound by inserting rattle chambers into his pork chunk.

"The key to fishing a jig-and-pig is the speed of the fall," veteran Missouri pro Johnnie Borden claims. "When the water is cold and the fish are sluggish, you need the bait to fall slowly through the water. When the fish are aggressive, you need a fast fall. And the beauty of using pork is that you can change the speed of the fall in seconds with a pocket knife. If you shave off some of the fat, it will increase the speed of the fall — yet it still has that bulky appearance that is so important. It will also give the trailer more action."

Borden also inserts a small plastic rattle chamber (more commonly used with plastic worms) into the fat portion of the pork for an added attraction. Using the hook point of the jig, Borden first creates a small opening in the side of the thick section of the pork for the rattle.

There is a common problem with attaching pork chunks to a jig that often translates into missed opportunities. The pork will often move up on the shaft of the jig hook, rotate slightly and become impaled on the hook point. To eliminate this problem, Shaw Grigsby places a 1-inch section of a plastic worm on the shaft of the hook between the jig head and pork trailer.

"You can do virtually anything with pork that you can do with soft plastics," Doug Hannon says. "The main thing is that it's more naturally supple — bulk for bulk — than plastic. In the water, it's very close to the same specific gravity as water is. When you add a lure to it, it gives you good tail and leg action.

"If it wasn't for some of the detriments of pork like getting them off of the hook, having to store pork in a compound and having them dry out, it would put soft plastics out of business. But it is certainly worth the trouble."

Pork Rind Alternatives

While natural pork is an excellent tool for catching bass, it has some inherent problems.

The common problem comes from the fact that it has a tendency to dry out on warm days when it is exposed to the air and sunlight. Some anglers avoid the problem by simply switching to a plastic crawfish or worm as a trailer. But some alternatives have emerged in recent years.

Although pork hide is the basis for Berkley's new Strike Rind, it doesn't seem to dry out as easily as a conventional pork chunk. This can be attributed to the lack of a thick, fatty section and a tanning process that gives it a softer, chamois-like texture. And when it dries out, the Strike Rind (Berkley and Co., Inc., One Berkley Drive, Dept. BT, Spirit Lake, IA, 51360) seems to quickly recover when it comes into contact with water. It comes immersed in Berkley Strike fish attractant.

Two other alternatives contain no pork, however. The Dri Rind (Dri Rind Co., P.O. Drawer 1676, Many, La., 71449) and Better Leather Trailers by Jim Cates (Circle C Lures, P.O. Box 235, Brownsville, TN, 38012) are made of a soft, leather-like material that is supple and has plenty of action. The new Soft Fall Dri Rind has a wool underbelly that closely resembles the fat portion of a pork frog, but has a slower descent through the water because of its light weight.

"The neat thing about the Dri Rind is that you don't have to worry about it drying out, which is a big problem," Florida pro Shaw Grigsby says. "If it dries out, it comes back to life after about 30 seconds in the water and gets real flexible and pliable. And a lot of fishermen trim the pork chunk to get more action, which is where Dri Rind comes in. It is thin and a lighter bait, which allows it to fall faster, which can be the key to catching fish at times."

Although it has the same tendency to dry out as conventional pork trailers, Californian Lloyd Osgood has developed a rind that is a departure from tradition. His Hog Hair Pork Rind Bait (22407 Whipple Tree, Dept. BT, Palo Cedro, CA, 96073) has the hair intact, which Osgood believes provides a more natural feeling to the fish and promotes longer contact.

Chapter 16

The Jigging Spoon Scores

The jigging or structure spoon is one of the most underrated bass lures in the country, especially during the summer and winter months.

In this age of cranking-fever and plastic bait-mania, the jigging spoon remains one of the most dependable lures on the market today for putting fish in the boat.

PROfile

People have gotten away from spoons in some areas and are trying a lot of the new lures that they read and hear about. But they're just as dependable as ever for catching fish down deep.

"Jigging spoons will catch the big largemouths which are down deep, but the reason I don't think they catch more big bass is that a lot of the 7- to 10-pounders are in shallower cover rather than down 20 to 30 feet deep" says Roland Martin. "At Santee-Cooper Reservoir during the seven years I fished regularly there, I caught 24 bass over 10 pounds, but only two of them ever came off of deep structure.

Alabama's Jack Chancellor is a deep-structure specialist who won the 1985 Classic.

"However, jigging spoons are super for catching bass from 2 to 5 pounds and that's the size I'm sure after when I'm in a tournament. That is also the size that most fishermen would be satisfied with during the average outing."

Expert jigging spoon fisherman Jack Chancellor agrees that the metal slab can be unmatched in terms of the numbers it produces. A former BASS Masters Classic champion, Chancellor says that it is a weapon has gotten him out of more jams in crucial times than any other lure. It helped him win that Classic title back in 1985 and helped him make a charge at two other Classic championships.

The jigging spoon, Chancellor says, is "the fastest way I know of to catch fish."

Chancellor, who manufacturers his own Jack's Jigging Spoon, insists that although it is a easy lure to use, there aren't many of even the top pros who have learned how to fish it effectively.

That may be why so many many misconceptions exist about the simple bait. The most common misconception is that most fishermen consider it to be limited to fall and winter, according to Chancellor. The bass are more likely to be concentrated during those seasons, but Chancellor has proven time after time that the jigging spoon can be productive almost year-round. The one season he puts the jigging spoon away is during the spawning cycle.

"Most people don't realize it, but the jigging spoon is an excellent lure when you get into schooling fish," Chancellor says. "It's excellent for throwing at fish that are schooling on top of the water. My favorite method is to throw it past the point where the fish are breaking water and as soon as it hits the water, start retrieving it real fast to make it skip across the top of the water. Then once you get to where the fish are, just stop reeling and let it start to sink. That's when you'll get most of your strikes."

Most fishermen consider the jigging spoon to be a "limit bait," a tool for catching good numbers of small bass. But Chancellor has caught bass weighing up to 9 3/4 pounds.

Jigging spoons are at their best in the hottest and coldest times of the year. In the summer, a good jigging spot could be a submerged hump, a point or the edge of a creek channel, according to Martin. But in the winter, creek channels generally pay off better. Bass generally prefer high spots in the summer and creek channels in the winter.

"I prefer jigging heavy spoons rather than casting lures because the jigging is more direct," Martin adds. "The only time I cast is when I'm looking for fish, but I miss a lot of fish casting because I don't have direct control of the lure."

The pro agree that the best way to catch jigging bass is to get vertical and drop the lure right down on the fish and jig it on the structure. Martin doesn't fish the spoon shallower than 15 feet because deep-structure fish are usually 15 feet or deeper. Most of the deep-structure lakes where you can catch bass consistently with jigging spoons are clear-water lakes and particularly in the summer those bass on structure are at a minimum of 15 feet deep and often 20 to 30 feet deep.

Some of the most popular jigging spoons on the market today are the Jack's Jigging Spoon, Tor-P-Do by Blue Fox, Hopkins, Salty Dog by Bagley and the Mann-O-Lure, heavy spoons with strong treble hooks that enable you to jig one of them all day without losing it.

Roland Martin alters a jigging spoon by adding a split ring, which gives the bait more action, while eliminating any chance of line wear.

"For the majority of my spoon fishing, I use a No. 2 Blue Fox Tor-P-Do, which I modify as I would any type of jigging spoon," Martin says. "I automatically remove the factory hook and replace it with a No. 2 light-weight hook. The reason for this is that the factory hooks are gaudy in appearance, but, more importantly, I can recover a spoon hung on brush by simply pulling hard enough to straighten out one of the hook points.

"I also add a split ring on the front of the spoon where the line is tied to give the spoon a little more action and often the stamped-out hole on the spoon can be sharp and actually cut the line."

Martin won a B.A.S.S. tournament on a jigging spoon, concentrating on deep-structure bass in South Carolina's Lake Moultrie in the summer of 1975.

"The bass were active and I found that when I lifted the spoon much higher, they hit much harder," Martin explains. "I was using a large popping rod, which enabled me to easily lift the spoon 4 to 8 feet off the bottom. With a 6-foot rod, you can lift a spoon 15 feet off the bottom when you put the rod tip almost to the water and then bring it back over your head. We learned this while jigging these spoons for striped bass at Santee and we found the rockfish like a much higher lift and much more violent jigging motion.

Winter jigging is quite different, though, according to the pros.

In the summer, the jigging is done in a very quick sequence and the spoon may move 4 or 5 feet each time you jig it. In the winter, you have to slow the jig down and limit its range of movement to catch the sluggish fish.

It is important to understand that when the water temperature plummets, the fish become lethargic, which forces you to change your lure presentation to catch these sluggish bass. That means moving the lure no more than a foot at a time.

Winter fish often hit the lure as it falls and, many times, strike the lure softly. For that reason, winter jigging requires a rod with sensitivity. And winter jigging usually necessitates lighter line, since these fish don't put up much of a battle. Martin uses 14- to 17-pound test, but 8- or even 6-pound line can be used successfully.

"I prefer using small spoons for winter jigging (1/2- to 3/4-ounce) and even smaller when the water really gets cold and fishing slows down," Martin interjects. "Under those conditions, I turn to a 3/8-ounce spoon to entice the sluggish fish into striking."

Blake Honeycutt of Hickory, N.C., who took the saltwater Hopkins Spoon and used it to great success on the B.A.S.S. circuit, is one of the real jigging spoon masters. Honeycutt was one of the first pros to master structure fishing, which he learned, largely, from fishing with the legendary Buck Perry.

Honeycutt's prowess with a Hopkins Spoon around structure enabled him to set the B.A.S.S. record for a three-day tournament with 138 pounds, 6 ounces (15-fish limit) en route to winning a tournament on Lake Eufala in Alabama.

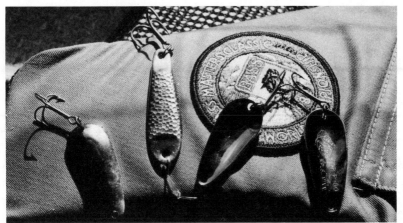

Jigging spoons are most productive during the coldest and hottest times of the year.

One Honeycutt technique that is often effective, is holding the spoon about a foot or so off of the bottom without moving it. Bass will often blast a spoon used in this manner. Honeycutt believes the water current causes the spoon to move slightly when it's suspended off the bottom.

"I agree," Martin adds. "I also believe that vertically dropping a spoon causes a slight line twist to develop and when the spoon is held motionless, the line straightens out, causing the lure to turn slightly, attracting the fish."

Jack Chancellor refers to the jigging spoon as a specialty bait, better suited for fishing bottom-contour structure like drop-offs, humps, roadbeds and sharp breaklines. The lure is much less effective when fished around such structure as stumps, standing timber, tree tops and so on, he says.

Chancellor avoids fishing jigging spoons in rivers with a considerable amount of current, believing there are better tools for catching bass in moving water. But there are times when it is difficult to get a lure down to deep-water fish in that situation. Chancellor has a little trick that has paid big dividends while fishing deep in current situations.

"On a river like the Arkansas River where there's a lot of current, I've had to add a little more weight to my spoon," he explains. "Instead of switching to a bigger spoon, which might eliminate the smaller fish, I take a Slinker (a unique type of bullet-shaped worm weight), which Doug Hannon designed for Burke Lures, and I put my treble hook on it and connect it to the spoon. That makes it heavier, but it doesn't hamper the action of the spoon or the hooking ability of the lure."

Veteran fishermen like Blake Honeycutt, Jack Chancellor and Roland Martin have proven that the jigging spoon is a highly versatile lure that deserves a place in everybody's tackle box. Don't underestimate the jigging spoon.

The weedless Johnson spoon has survived the test of time.

Chapter 17

Spoon Tricks and Tactics

One of Roland Martin's favorite stories involves his introduction to spoon fishing.

In the late 1960s, while guiding on South Carolina's famed Santee-Cooper Reservoir, Martin had discovered just how potent a black Johnson spoon with a short black plastic worm trailer could be During a single month, Martin had caught 42 bass that topped the 8-pound mark. During that time, he had a day that produced a 10-fish, 87-pound stringer. On another day, his 10-fish weighed 79 pounds.

You could understand Martin's excitement about his discovery and the fact that he couldn't wait to show off for one of his best customers. "I rigged a spoon and worm trailer up for him and the first cast he threw out by this grass bed and caught a 7- or 8-pound bass that just inhaled the bait," Martin recalls. "I'm all excited and I'm still talking about how great this brand-new technique is. It was all I had talked about all morning. But he wasn't saying a word.

Finally, he said — in a real patient manner — 'Son, I'm 76 years old and the Johnson spoon was my father's favorite bait.' "

PROfile

Past BASS Masters Classic qualifier Jim Nolan has proven the allure of the weedless spoon throughout the country.

That story illustrates the stamina of one of America's oldest and dearest lures, as well as the time-tested productivity of spoon fishing.

Another story brings the illustration into a more modern focus.

The setting is drought-stricken Lake Okeechobee in 1982, where only a few large fishable bays exist in what is normally a 763-square-mile body of shallow, weedy water. The leading man in this mini-drama is Ron Shearer, a 28-year-old unknown Kentuckyian yearning for a career as a professional fisherman.

On the second day of the tournament, with tournament boats all around him, Shearer fished a shallow peppergrass bed with a 1/2-ounce Johnson Silver Minnow (teamed with a white skirt) and put together a Bass Anglers Sportsman Society seven-fish record stringer of 36 pounds, 8 ounces. He went on to win the tournament, qualify for the prestigious BASS Masters Classic and secure the career he could only dream about before.

That's just two cases of the 'spoon swoon.'

Although they are today made in various shapes and sizes, spoons are among the oldest lures known to man. The first metal spoon was patented in 1834, but archaeologists tell us that primitive man used pieces of polished shell and bone the same way as far back as 3,000 B.C.

Today, the common, unsophisticated metal spoon (with the exception of jigging spoons, which will not be discussed here), is among the most weedless lures available. Almost no vegetation is immune to the spoon, which will catch fish from Florida to Maine and California to Connecticut.

"There's just not many lures that are as productive as a Johnson-type spoon for fishing in grass," claims Jimmy Nolan of Bull Shoals, Ark., a knowledgeable angler who qualified for the 1985 Classic. "In fishing all over the country, I haven't faced a situation where a spoon couldn't be fished effectively in a grassy lake.

"The wobble it has and the flash it gives off will produce in grass that's just laying under the surface as well as grass so thick that it's matted over. In grass as thick as milfoil, the flash of the spoon may not penetrate it, but that wobble will still make a vibration that the fish will zero in on. I've seen them blow up through the grass and take milfoil, moss, spoon and all in their mouths."

And fishing a Johnson-type spoon isn't difficult to learn. The spoon's flat, oval shape allows it to wobble, rather than spin, as it is pulled through water and vegetation. As a result, an ordinary straight, slow retrieve will attract strikes, meaning that even beginning anglers can catch fish on it.

As unsophisticated as that sounds, knowledgeable spoon fishermen have developed some definite tricks and tactics using a variety of types of spoons that solve a wide-range of bassin' needs and conditions.

For example, Roland Martin's most productive spoon pattern that has produced in tournaments throughout the country is what he calls "grazing the grass." Grazing the grass is a relatively simple technique that is used by thousands of fishermen. It involves working the spoon slowly (but fast enough to keep it from sinking) across the top of thick vegetation and almost out of the water. Sounds easy enough, right?

It is, but there are a couple of tips that will mean more strikes, and just as importantly, more catches. "The most important aspect of fishing grass with a Johnson spoon and other type of spoons is the position of your rod during the retrieve," Martin explains. "Always point your rod at the spoon. If you hold your rod high, you won't have a way to set the hook effectively. Keeping the rod tip low and pointed straight at the spoon also gives the spoon better action.

"Another important thing to remember when spoon fishing and trying to get fish to come up and hit your spoon on the surface is the way you position yourself to fish a grassbed. In order to keep the fish from being spooked by your shadow, learn to cast into the sun as much as possible to keep your shadow from causing any problems."

Probably the biggest problem the average angler has with spoon fishing is setting the hook. Veteran spoon fishermen say the novice angler — caught up in the exhilaration of visibly viewing the surface strike — simply takes the spoon away from the attacking bass before it has a chance to completely engulf it.

Russ Bringger of Pompano Beach, Fla., a winner on the BASSmaster Tournament Trail, is a spoon specialist, who has an effective technique for setting the hook in spoon-fed bass.

"So many guys reaction instantly to the fish first blowing up on the spoon and they yank the spoon away before the fish has a chance to eat it," Bringger says. "The most productive way, I've found, is to make five or six cranks of the reel handle and keep the bait coming toward you before attempting to set the hook. This gives the fish ample time to eat the spoon. I always keep my rod tip a few inches off of the water, so that when he hits it and I actually feel him on the lure — not just see him take it — I can bring the rod straight up to set the hook. It takes a little patience and composure during a time when you're excited."

While the built-in action of most spoons is enough to entice strikes, Bringger became interested in a spoon that could both be buzzed across vegetation, as well as be used as a drop- bait in small holes in the grass. He came up with an adaptation of a Johnson spoon that he calls a "spinner-spoon" about eight years ago.

Bringger took the blade and neck off of a Snagless Sally and attached it with a stainless-steel O-ring to the front of a 1/2-ounce Johnson spoon. To get even more action, he added a Mr. Twister Double-Tail plastic trailer. And promptly went out and started catching fish on his new lure. The lure has produced consistently well through the years, including a 10-pound, 10-ounce large-mouth in a tournament.

"This is really a big-fish bait," Bringger says. "It gives you the best of both a spoon and a spinnerbait with that Snagless Sally blade spinning around on the front. I knew that spoons certainly catch fish and spinnerbaits catch their share of fish, but there are times when you want to use a spinnerbait in thick cover, but you just can't effectively. But this spinner-spoon will go through almost any grass and the vibration from that blade turning, even in heavy cover, triggers bass to come from considerable distances to hit it.

"And it's an easy bait to fish. It comes across whatever type of cover you're fishing real easy. You can work it slower than most spoons because the blade will help keep the lure up. In fact, it will keep the lure on the surface so well that you have to consciously let it fall once in a while, which is one of the lure's most productive qualities. When you hit an open pocket in the grass, if you stop retrieving it, that lure will sink slowly with the blade whrilling around as it drops. I can't tell you how many times I've let it flutter down and had bass just bust it."

Bringger didn't realize it at the time of his invention, but Arkansas' Bobby Murray won the 1978 BASS Masters Classic on a similar adaptation.

Murray used a Timber King black spoon (which is shaped a little differently than a Johnson spoon) with a chartreuse skirt and a gold Snagless Sally blade to work the lily pad fields of Mississippi's Ross Barnett Reservoir. Murray caught all of his 37 pounds, 9 ounces on the lure on the supercharged spoon.

Although the basic action of the metal spoon allows it to be worked relatively slowly across the surface of the water, there are times when a Johnson spoon cannot be maneuvered quite slow enough. And it certainly won't float. But under some conditions, a spoon that would both float and could be worked slowly across the top of the water would out-score the more conventional metal spoon.

Doug Hannon and Sam Griffin have developed answers to those problems.

Hannon, the famed Bass Professor, designed the Skitterfish under the Doug Hannon system for Burke Lures, a lure that is billed as a "weedless surface-plug spoon." The Skitterfish is a 2 3/4-inch soft-plastic lure that features a V-shaped design that is buoyant in the water. Despite a pair of exposed hook points that ride atop of the lure's tail, the Skitterfish is amazing weedless.

"It's important to remember that spoons are basically for active fish," Hannon says. "Even though it's a wonderful lure, your use of spoons is limited to active fish because you have to crank a traditional spoon so fast to keep it on top.

"The Skitterfish has the same ability as a traditional spoon to be skittered across the top quickly, but you can also stop it in small holes and twitch it and work it. So you can cover several basic patterns on the same retrieve. You can fish for the bass that might hit it moving fast across the water and when you see some good water where you want to work the bait slowly, like holes in the grass, you can stop it and twitch it a couple of times. It's a lot more versatile than the traditional metal spoon."

Unlike most spoons, the Skitterfish's ability to be worked like a twitch-bait makes it adaptable to cover and structure other than grass, like standing timber. Hannon says another advantage is its lifelike paint design and body shape. The deep V-shaped body "represents a baitfish profile to the bass as it's floating on the surface," he says.

Sam Griffin, a topwater expert and owner of Griffin Lures in Moore Haven, Fla., was seeking similar qualities in a spoon when he developed the Sugarwood Spoon, which has an army of followers around Lake Okeechobee.

The Sugarwood Spoon, is a 2 1/4-inch piece of lightweight wood with a single hook, wire weedguard and short skirt. Unlike other spoons on the market, the Sugarwood Spoon has no built in action, which is exactly why Griffin created it.

"You can work the same type of structures you would normally work a Johnson spoon with my Sugarwood Spoon, but my spoon is just so much more versatile," says Griffin, a talented fisherman, who has three top-10 B.A.S.S. finishes to his credit. "By using your rod tip, you can get similar action to a Johnson spoon from my spoon and you can get it through even thicker cover, because of the buoyancy of it. It will go through a lily pad a lot better than a Johnson spoon.

"There are several ways to fish a Sugarwood Spoon. I make it 'walk the dog' (similar to the action of a Zara Spook) at a semi-fast rate of speed to find fish. You can fish it fast across the surface and they'll hit it that way. If the fish aren't as aggressive, you can present the Sugarwood quieter than a Johnson-type spoon and work it slowly by just letting it sit and twitching it. One of the best applications I've found for the Sugarwood Spoon and a big advantage it has over metal spoon is during situations when the fish are striking short. If a bass strikes and misses a Johnson spoon on the surface, it will sink if you stop it and the bass will usually swim away. With my spoon, if he hits just short of it, you can stop it and it floats. I've had good success twitching it a couple of times in that situation and the bass will come back up after it."

Obviously, today's spoon fishermen have decided that no one model will handle all situations. But with a little ingenuity and some experience, you can make the proven fish-catching ability of the common spoon work to your advantage under almost any circumstances.

Larry Lazoen ties on a weedless spoon, a bait that has produced big bass for him from Florida to New York.

Chapter 18

Spoon-Shaking for Bass

The black spoon skips across a seemingly impenetrable mat of peppergrass, slapping the surface with every turn of Larry Lazoen's reel. Without pausing, he makes another long cast across the top of vegetation so thick that small birds and animals could walk on it.

The rhythmic slapping sound begins again, but it is suddenly interrupted by the sweet music that only a bass enthusiast can enjoy. In between beats, the 1/2-ounce Johnson spoon simply disappears, enveloped by an explosion of grass and water.

Despite the unnerving nature of the vicious strike, Lazoen calmly plays the bass, strong-arming it toward the surface. After a few seconds, the bass tires and Lazoen trolls over to it. A little gardening is in order. After picking his way to the fish, Lazoen locks his thumb firmly under the bass' lower jaw and pulls it into the boat.

PROfile

Florida's Larry Lazoen is a three-time BASS Masters Classic qualifier.

Inside the mouth of this 5-pound-plus largemouth we find a well-buried Johnson spoon. This fish was so determined to ambush the bait that he had inhaled it, peppergrass and all.

Unfazed, Lazoen unhooks the fish and drops it gently overboard. He's seen it all before.

"That's what happens with this technique," he says, firing another cast across the jungle-like vegetation. "It just seems to agitate them like nothing else."

The technique is called spoon shaking and it was devised by a man who is one of the top guides on Lake Okeechobee as well as one of the country's premier tournament bass pros. Lazoen, who lives in Port Charlotte, Fla., and also guides in saltwater, is one of only four anglers to qualify for the BASS Masters Classic through both the pro tournament route and the club Federation system.

Spoon shaking is a variation of weedless spoon fishing that has paid some handsome dividends in Lazoen's career. In addition to several Florida tournament victories, the technique has played a role in securing two of his three Classic appearances.

In his first Classic appearance, the 1984 event on the Arkansas River, Lazoen finished fifth — then the best performance ever by a Federation representative. But he never would have gotten the opportunity to compete in fishing's most important event without the help of his spoon shaking technique.

Spoon shaking produced fish throughout the long and grueling road that Federation anglers must endure to qualify for the Classic. Its greatest moment was the Southern Division tournament in which it produced 51 pounds of bass and lifted Lazoen into the Classic as the top qualifier in the division.

Spoon fishing in vegetation is basically a simple affair. Untold thousands of largemouths have been caught by fishermen simply tossing out and winding in a Johnson-type weedless spoon, but through years of experience on Lake Okeechobee, Lazoen devised a spoon technique that has paid off in weedy lakes and rivers from Florida to New York.

With the basic retrieve of a Johnson spoon, the lure runs just below the surface, bouncing off of a submerged or thin surface vegetation. But that technique often isn't very productive (or a very enjoyable way to fish) in extreme heavy-cover situations such as matted hydrilla and peppergrass or large fields of thick lily pads.

In those situations, even a weedless spoon has difficulty coming through the vegetation. But with Lazoen's spoon shaking technique, it doesn't have to penetrate the grass, yet it is consistently productive. The spoon simply skirts across the top of the vegetation, creating a commotion as it comes.

It is a faster and noisier way to work a Johnson-type spoon.

"When I'm fishing grass that isn't very thick, I'll run a spoon under the surface like everybody else," Lazoen says. "But this is a technique that works in heavy cover where there's very little else you can throw in it."

For this type of spoon fishing, Lazoen uses a long (6- foot-10) rod, heavy line (20- to 25-pound test) and a 1/2- ounce spoon with a plastic grub trailer.

The long rod is important. After making a lengthy cast, Lazoen begins retrieving the spoon, keeping his rod tip high to ensure that the nose of the lure stays up as he pulls it across the grass. He uses a quick retrieve, similar to that of a buzzbait, with one major difference.

As he reels the spoon, Lazoen constantly shakes his wrist, which makes the lure slap the top of the weeds and water at regular intervals that must be either

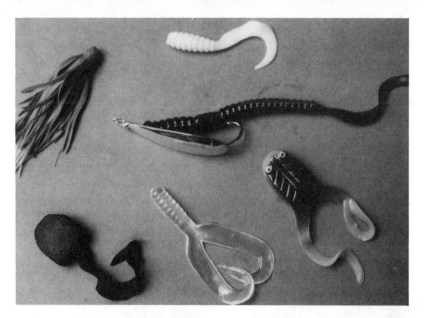

Various types of trailers make a weedless spoon more attractive.

enticing or aggravating because the bass respond to spoon shaking with amazing aggression.

"I think the speed of the spoon causes a reaction type of strike rather than a hunger type of strike," Lazoen explains. "They hear it coming for so long because it's beating the water as it moves toward them. Once it arrives, they nail it, even if they have to blow through the grass to get it."

Lazoen theorizes that the rhythmic noise of the spoon also makes it easier for the bass to home in on.

The most productive size for this technique is a 1/2- ounce spoon, Lazoen says, because it casts farther and has more hooking power than the 1/4-ounce size, yet it comes through the vegetation easier than the larger (3/4-ounce) size.

Surprisingly, Lazoen's color choice is a black spoon — day in and day out. A black spoon will produce on both clear and overcast days, he says, contrary to the belief of some. His trailer choice is a yellow flat-tailed grub like the Mann's Swimming Grub, although he says a rubber skirt of similar color will also produce.

The black spoon-yellow trailer combination will produce in both clear and off-colored water, he says.

It's a slight variation of an old standard way to catch fish. But spoon shaking has a place and a purpose in weedy lakes throughout the country.

**Rich Tauber with a Lake Guntersville trophy that could not resist a
Heddon Zara Spook worked in the "walk the dog" manner.**

Chapter 19

Favorite Topwater Situations

When we die, those fortunate enough to travel skyward will undoubtedly find that all of the bass fishing in heaven is topwater fishing.

There will be no flipping fish. No arm-wearying deep- cranking fish. No finicky finesse fish.

Just great topwater action.

PROfile

No other single type of bass fishing is as universally revered as surface action, where aggressive fish attack most of the human senses with a torpedo-like charge that we are privileged to witness — unlike any other lure. The topwater dance of a charging bass startles the senses and leaves a lasting impression that sub-surface baits just can't duplicate.

While bass enthusiasts throughout the country would list that topwater fishing is their favorite way to catch fish, surface plug fishing — like so many good experiences in life — seem to come in limited and often unpredictable quantities. Perhaps it is for that reason that we savor each topwater strike with more fervor than we do the tug on a worm or the sudden stop of a crankbait.

Jimmy Houston is one of only three men to win two or more B.A.S.S. Angler of the Year titles.

And we aren't likely to forget those precious situations in which the conditions were primed for topwater success. We remember them with an eye toward the future when the same pattern may present itself again.

Fall & Flooded Timber

For Charlie Campbell, one of the country's most renowned topwater fishermen, that means fishing reservoirs like Missouri's Table Rock or Bull Shoals in Arkansas in the fall — September through early November.

"My favorite top-water situation is when the water temperature gets down to about 60 degrees and the fish — particularly the big fish — get real active," says Campbell, a tournament veteran and former BASS Masters Classic qualifier. "During this time, I've seen days when I could go out to places close to home where I knew big bass usually stayed and catch eight or nine lunkers over 5 pounds, which is good for any type of fishing.

"That's particularly good topwater fishing, which is the most exciting form of bass fishing there is — especially in a big-bass situation like this."

For Campbell's favorite topwater situation, he concentrates on standing timber. Once the water temperature warms up in the early afternoon, Campbell says the fish move up near the surface of the water and hold in the shade of the dead trees. It is the shallow positioning of these bass that make them especially receptive to a topwater plug. "There are times when you can bring them up from depths of 10 feet or more, but it's a lot easier to catch them when they're holding just below the surface of the water," he says. "This can be the absolute ideal time for catching big bass on a topwater bait."

Campbell, runner-up in the 1986 B.A.S.S. Super-Invitational, is a big fan of the Heddon Zara Spook, a fat, cigar-shaped stickbait. He has spent so many hours both fishing and experimenting with adaptations to the lure that Heddon used his expertise to transform the original Spook into the modern version that is both more effective and easier to use.

In both his favorite conditions and all topwater situations, Campbell advises anglers to throw the Spook well past the target (whether it be a grassline, stick-up or submerged brush) and keep it as close as possible to it during the retrieve. Primarily, Campbell uses the "walking the dog" retrieve, a method he helped make famous. By both simultaneously reeling and rhythmically twitching the rod tip, the Zara Spook will dart back and forth in a straight line. Campbell is so proficient with this technique that he can "walk the dog" practically around a tree — maximizing the allure of the bait.

Another important point to remember, he says, is to use the wind to your advantage. Campbell prefers to cast the Spook into the wind and work it with the current back to the boat.

Winter & Weedbeds

Although surface plugs aren't considered prime winter lures because cold-water bass are usually inactive, David Fenton's favorite topwater situation revolves around the first Texas freeze of the year.

"A lot of people think that because they are cold, the fish won't be active enough to hit a topwater plug," says Fenton, a guide on Lake Conroe and two-time Classic qualifier. "But that's not always true.

"There's definitely a cold-water application for topwater fishing. I can remember catching fish on a chugger when the guides were freezing up on the rod."

Fenton's favorite cold-water topwater technique uses hydrilla as its centerpiece. The first Texas freeze usually occurs when the hydrilla has just topped out and it is this exotic vegetation that attracts the more active bass. "I believe the hydrilla absorbs more heat and that heat dissipates slower than other types of cover," Fenton says. "I've seen cases where there is a 3- to 5-degree difference in the water temperature around the hydrilla."

Fenton's favorite topwater plug is the Rebel Pop-R, a 2 1/2-inch chugger that became the secret bait of several Texas pros who won numerous national tournaments with it in recent years. During these chilly times, Fenton works the Pop-R slowly, concentrating on the edges of isolated weedbeds and small openings in the grass.

"In my opinion, the first freeze of the year provides some of the best big-bass topwater fishing to be found in the state of Texas," he says.

Spring & Spawners

Spring has always been considered prime-time for topwater action.

Roland Martin, the all-time B.A.S.S. tournament winner, has fished surface lures all over the country throughout the year, but has little trouble selecting his favorite topwater situation.

"Spring and spawning bass, no doubt about it," Martin says. "Fishing for spawning bass, to me, is the most exciting fishing of the year, particularly for topwater fishing. There's just such a great anticipation with this type of fishing because you know that nearly all of the really big bass in the lake will be spawning and their protective instinct will make them extremely aggressive."

Martin's ideal topwater situation involves fishing for bedding bass in open-water areas of a lake. For that situation, he uses a light spinning outfit, 8-pound line and a small Rapala, a swimming minnow-type plug.

Concentrating on shallow-water bedding areas, Martin patiently fishes the surface plugs over beds that he can see, slowly twitching the lure to entice or anger the protective female bass into striking.

"This is some of the most explosive topwater fishing in the world and it can be duplicated from Connecticut to California during the spawn," explains Martin, who has a degree in fisheries biology. "It's one of the few times that bass are especially predictable and you can easily locate them.

"Bass are all the same great gamefish no matter where they are located, and they will all react exactly the same way during the spawn. Biologically speaking, they are the same in every state. They're going to spawn at a water temperature over 63 degrees, and the biggest spawns will be around a full moon or new moon. The male will guard the bed after the eggs have been laid for two or three weeks, while the big female will not hang around long. But she will be on the bed for three or four days and then hang around the area for another week or so. But during the time she spends there, she is overly protective and most vulnerable to being caught."

Spawning season is one of the few times when surface lures can be effective throughout the day, Martin says, who reminds anglers to release the big spawners unharmed.

Spring & Grass

Like fellow Texan David Fenton, former Classic champion Tommy Martin's favorite topwater situation is built around hydrilla. But his favorite topwater times are during the spring when the water is clear and the hydrilla is submerged in 7 to 10 feet of water (and still about 3 feet below the surface).

The perfect day for this type of surface action corresponds with the dream day of most topwater enthusiasts- warm water, good clarity, on overcast sky and enough wind to create a slight ripple on the water.

Martin utilizes two surface lures for fishing over the top of the submerged hydrilla in the spring — the Pop-R and the Bomber Long A.

The Pop-R, which features a concave mouth, is worked quickly on the surface, while the Long A, which has a small plastic lip, is jerked more methodically, allowing it to dive slightly before returning to the surface.

"There is a time during the spring when both are extrememly effective," he explains. "I have found that early in the spring when the water is still cool, the bass seem to prefer a floater/diver-type lure that makes almost no noise like the Long A. But as the water warms up, the bass are more active and seem to be attracted to noise. That is when the chugger-type baits like the Pop-R outproduce other types of topwater baits."

Late Spring & Deep Water

Chris and Jimmy Houston's all time favorite topwater situation spans both late spring and through the summer (May through early July, depending on the location of the lake). The technique is most effective on timbered, clear-water lakes.

The Houstons concentrate on vertical structure (standing timber) in 15 to 20 feet of water — surprisingly deep for surface action. They utilize a Zara Spook, which is ideal for this type of clear-water fishing since it can be cast a considerable distance and easily controlled during the retrieve.

Their targets, Jimmy Houston says, are pre-spawn bass.

"This is a very overlooked pattern," he adds. "Unlike other topwater patterns, this kind of surface fishing is not limited to early and late because the fish are holding fairly deep. But you can sure bring them up to the surface with that Spook.

"A major reason why this is such a great time to catch bass on topwater baits is that pre-spawn fish are really aggressive and you have the luxury of accidentally running across some spawners in the process."

The Houston's deep-water topwater technique has paid off handsomely in lakes throughout the country. A prime example: Chris Houston won a Bass'n Gal tournament on Indiana's Lake Patoka with a final-day stringer of five bass that weighed 18 pounds, 7 ounces. She caught the fish on a Spook fished around a massive tree that stood in about 20 feet of water and was barely visible from the surface.

Summer & Weeds

The Houstons have discovered something that many northern bass anglers like Danny Correia have known for years: summertime topwater fishing can be outstanding.

Correia, a 24-year-old tournament pro from Marlboro, Mass., and runner-up in the 1986 BASS Masters Classic, says the calm, windless days of summer are his favorite topwater times. He enjoys the most success around lily pads, milfoil and other types of vegetation in water that is still fairly cool.

"The water is just starting to warm up and the fish are really just beginning to awaken and become especially active," explains Correia, the most successful Classic representative of the B.A.S.S. club federation system. "I take a twitch bait like a Bang-O-Lure and put a larger blade on the back of it for more noise. A lot of noise seems to be the key during this time of the year."

Summer & The Hatches

For tournament veteran Jerry Rhyne, the hottest part of summer often translates into the hottest topwater action of all.

Rhyne, a seven-time Classic qualifier from Denver, N.C., times his topwater attacks to correspond with the annual mayfly hatches found on many southern lakes during the summer. He enjoys his best success with the first mayfly hatch, which usually occurs in early June, and the final hatch in August.

"When the mayflies start to hatch, it creates all sort of activity on the surface of the water," he says. "The bream really feed on them and that attracts the bass, which will feed on both the bream and the mayflies. It's the ideal situation for the bass, which is a greedy, ambush-oriented creature, because during this mayfly activity he doesn't have to exert much energy to feed."

The mayfly hatch not only helps the average angler locate bass, it pinpoints the most active fish as well. To best take advantage of these active bass, Rhyne uses a Peco Pop, a small chugger that he modifies by adding a white bucktail trailer hook. He uses a split ring or snap in the eye of the Peco Pop to get the most noise from it.

"When the mayfly hatch activity is going on, you can stay on fish throughout the day," Rhyne adds. "That's not the usual situation with a topwater plug."

Summer-Fall & The West

Californian Rich Tauber's favorite topwater situation spans the summer and fall (May through October) in the clear reservoirs of the West.

The western reservoirs provide the two most important ingredients in topwater fishing, according to Tauber: clear water with temperatures that stay above 70 degrees during that period. During this time, he concentrates on submerged cover (vegetation, rocks or wood) in 4 to 12 feet of water (depending on the clarity), as well as cracks in the canyon walls and shadowy areas.

"I like real, real clear water for topwater fishing," says Tauber, perhaps the best known of the Western pros and a past Classic qualifier. "And the perfect topwater lure for clear water, in my opinion, is the Zara Spook.

"I consider the Spook to be the best surface lure of all for catching quality fish — 2 pounds and up. I almost always work it fast, trying to imitate a feeding fish. It's an impulse or reaction-type bait and there is almost nothing better for pulling bass out of deep water or heavy cover. And during this time of the year out West, the bass are particularly active. You will have days where you can catch fish all day long on a surface bait like the Spook."

While the favorite topwater situations of the pros cover a complete range of conditions, each shares a common theme: surface lures are not only the most exciting baits for catching bass, there are certain situations when topwater plugs are the perfect tool for capitalizing on active fish.

Chapter 20

Cochran's Topwater Tips

George Cochran is a walking, talking contradiction to the myths about topwater fishing that we have held dear for years.

You know the myths:

• Topwater fishing is just something you do in the early morning or late afternoon hours.

PROfile

• Surface lures only work in the spring and fall when the bass are most active.

• It takes a calm, overcast day for a topwater plug to be effective.

• With the ever-increasing fishing pressure, bass simply aren't fooled by surface lures like they once were.

Don't try to sell Cochran on these theories. The 1987 BASS Masters Classic champion and one of the sport's most consistent anglers, Cochran knows better.

Former BASS Masters Classic champion George Cochran is among the most consistent pros in the country.

"Although topwater baits have been around forever," Cochran says, "I think topwater fishing is maybe the most misunderstood type of fishing of all."

Surface fishing is easily the favorite universal technique for luring bass. Unlike all other types of fishing, topwater baits solicit a vicious predator-prey, life-and-death dance that is played out before our eyes. It is a visual confrontation that startles and overwhelms our senses in the amount of time it takes to blink an eye. It injects the adrenaline rush that most of us commonly associate with memorable fishing trips.

It is exhilaration re-defined.

Ironically, we, as fishermen, often deprive ourselves of the very excitement we crave, Cochran claims, by believing the myths that have been spread by the Joe Isuzus of the fishing world. Experiencing the thrills of topwater fishing doesn't have to occur as often as lunar eclipses if you believe Cochran.

Cochran has quietly become one of the country's true surface-fishing experts. His prowess with — and willingness to use — a topwater bait is largely responsible for his nine consecutive appearances in the prestigious Classic. As a result of his success with hard baits that work the water line, Cochran has developed an almost religious belief in their appeal, which has led him to refine his system of topwater fishing into something approaching an art form.

Allow the North Little Rock, Ark., angler to dispel the myths most commonly associated with surface fishing.

Myth No. 1: Topwater fishing is only effective early and late in the day.

"Anybody who believes that is really limiting the number of fish he can catch," Cochran counters. "To me, the ideal topwater time has nothing to do with what time of day it is. I've caught some of my biggest fish in the middle of the day when the sun was straight overhead. The ideal topwater times have more to do with the conditions than the time of day."

Cochran's largest stringer in a B.A.S.S. tournament (26 pounds) was caught throughout the day on two surface lures on Florida's St. Johns River.

Myth No. 2: Surface lures are most effective in the spring and fall when bass are most active and aggressive.

Following the Bassmaster Tournament Trail, Cochran fishes lakes and reservoirs throughout the country during practically every month of the year. And he can recall few tournaments in which a topwater bait did not play a role in his success. "The Classic was a prime example," Cochran explains. "I am one of the few people who have won the Classic on a topwater bait. It was one of my primary baits and it certainly helped me win the Classic."

The Classic is held in August of each year, a fact that should dispel the belief that surface lures are non-productive in the hottest portions of the summer. The only times when Cochran eliminates topwater fishing is when the water temperature drops below the 50-degree mark.

Myth No. 3: The conditions have to be perfect for topwater fishing to be productive. It is particularly important that the sky be overcast and the water be calm.

There is no doubt, Cochran says, that those are the ideal conditions for surface fishing, because bass have a tendency to be shallower as well as a little more aggressive in that setting. But some of the biggest fish he has caught were attracted to a noisy propellor cutting through a slight chop on the water. And he has caught countless bragging-sized bass in fairly bright conditions.

Myth No. 4: Bass don't hit surface lures as much as they used to.

Topwater expert George Cochran ties on a Zara Spook, which has long been a big-fish producer for him in both rivers and lakes.

"In this day and time, most people don't fish topwaters much," Cochran says. "But I catch as many fish right now as I did 25 years ago topwater fishing. People have gone away from topwater fishing, but that is a mistake.

"If the weather is favorable and you get on a good pattern, you will catch a bigger stringer on topwater lures than you will with any other lure. As long as I can remember, the topwater bait has been one of the No. 1 big-bass lures for me."

Although his surface system has been tested and proven on lakes and reservoirs throughout America, much of Cochran's topwater success has come on the Arkansas River near his home. River fishing, it seems, is the great equalizer when it comes to surface-fishing success.

The effectiveness of topwater lures seems to increase with river fishing, Cochran believes. The conditions don't have be as favorable. And the moving, heavily-oxygenated water seems to keep river bass in an active mode.

"Rivers are excellent for topwater fishing because most of the time on any kind of river, bass live in less than 5 feet of water," Cochran explains. "So most of the time, topwater baits will work in almost any situation on rivers.

"Some of my best topwater days have come on hot, clear, still days when the fish suspend on the Arkansas or Ohio or other rivers. The fish will suspend around vegetation or other cover. If you pitch a worm or jig around the cover, the only way the bass will hit it is while it's falling. They will be laying close to the surface and they don't go down to get a lure. They're more likely to come up to hit a lure, so topwaters are the best choice."

Cochran utilizes three types of surface lures, which he categorizes as darting baits (original Zara Spook, Zara Spook Puppy, Zara Spook Pooch and Cordell Boy Howdy), chugger baits (Rebel Pop-R, Tiny Torpedo, Heddon Chugger) and propellor baits (Heddon Dying Flutter and Cordell Crazy Shad). Each have a specific application depending on the situation.

Water clarity largely dictates lure selection for Cochran. In clear water, Cochran prefers lures that make little noise (the darting baits). In dingy water, he uses either chugger-type lures or prop baits, using the noise to attract bass that are not able to hunt by vision alone. To select the proper size of lure, Cochran attempts to match the size of the prevalent forage fish as closely as possible.

Cochran doesn't experiment much with various color schemes on his surface lures. He primarily relies on light hues and shad-colors.

"For river fishing, my primary bait is a prop bait like the Dying Flutter," Cochran says in reference to the twin-bladed stickbait. "The water is never clear, so you need to make noise to attract the fish. A lot of mornings, I will adjust the spinners on a Dying Flutter real loose and use it like you would a buzzbait. I throw it around weeds or brush and use a straight, steady retrieve. The bass will hit it like they do a buzzbait. With the two sets of treble hooks, you don't lose many fish like you do with a buzzbait."

Successful surface fishing begins with the equipment involved. Cochran stresses that the choice of rod is critical. Many of the so-called topwater rods on the market are much too stiff to handle a variety of surface plugs, he says, particularly the small lures. A good topwater rod should combine plenty of backbone with a limber tip.

Line size depends on the size of the bait — with no regard to water clarity. Cochran uses 10-pound test for the smallest baits and moves up to 14- or 17-pound line for the larger lures like the Zara Spook or Dying Flutter.

Pinpoint casting and the proper retrieve are the basic elements of topwater fishing that are obvious, yet overlooked by many anglers.

"With topwater fishing, you should cast the bait about a foot past the target," Cochran tutors. "It is important to bring it as close by the cover as possible. You have to really concentrate during that first a couple of feet of the retrieve. If you are around a fish, he will usually get it in that first foot of the retrieve. If I don't have a strike after the first couple of feet, I reel it in and make another cast elsewhere."

Cochran is asked to describe the most common mistake that fishermen make while topwater fishing.

"That's easy — not having enough patience," he says. "When the average fisherman thinks there is a fish around a piece of cover, he gets in too big of a hurry. But that's the wrong approach.

"When I throw a topwater bait, I usually let all of the ripples disappear and let the lure settle there for about 15 seconds in one spot before I ever move it. That gives the fish time to swim out of the cover and get under the bait about the time you get the slack out and begin to move it. I can't stress enough how important patience is with topwater fishing. Don't get in too big of a hurry because you only have to work the bait a foot or two before reeling it in and making the next cast."

Breaking the traditional rules of surface fishing helped pave the road to success for George Cochran. Follow his lead by not falling for the myths involved in topwater fishing.

Topwater artist Sam Griffin lands a Lake Okeechobee bass that was fooled by the movements of his Jerkin' Sam plug.

Chapter 21

America's Top Topwater Fisherman

Sam Griffin.

Few bass anglers know the name, except those in the south Florida and Lake Okeechobee region, who use his wooden lures.

But two of the sport's best-known fishermen know the name — and the man — well.

PROfile

Ricky Green of Arkadelphia, Ark., who qualified for 14 consecutive BASS Masters Classic appearances, believes in the man and his products. He credits the Griffin Lures' Wood Trap with enabling him to make a run at the Classic title in 1983 on the Ohio River, where he lost to Larry Nixon by just 10 ounces.

Roland Martin, who has no name-recognition problem, lives just 15 miles from Griffin's shop in Moore Haven, Fla.

And he openly admires Sam Griffin.

"Sammy Griffin is the world's premier topwater fisherman," Martin says. "Very few people know as much about the actions of topwater baits as he does.

Florida's Sam Griffin is an artist when it comes to surface fishing with the baits he makes by hand.

"That's because he designs them and spends a lot of time testing them. Plus, he's just a heckuva fisherman. There are other lure designers who have a good knowledge of top-water fishing, but they're not the fishermen that Sam Griffin is."

While Griffin dismisses Martin's praise out of modesty, his ability as a fisherman is demonstrated by his three top-10 finishes in Bass Anglers Sportsman Society tournaments on Lake Okeechobee. He also has a Red Man victory to his credit.

And he is a master at the finesse art of topwater fishing.

Spending a day in the boat with the personable Griffin is an education. Over the years, he has created a systematic approach to topwater fishing and has mastered its fine points. And he has enough confidence and skill in his ability that he can call his more inexperienced partners to the front of the boat and correctly call the action that's about to take place.

Griffin is simply a magician with a surface lure.

It all begins with confidence, he says.

"To be successful, you have to have confidence in the lure that you're throwing and the style of fishing you're doing," Griffin explains. "If you don't have confidence in a lure, whether it be a topwater plug or whatever, you're not going to keep it tied on long enough to catch fish.

"When you start swapping lures around, you might as well load your boat on the trailer because you're not going to have a very good day. You can't keep going from one extreme to another — switching from a topwater plug to a worm and throwing it five times and then going to a crank bait and trying two or three different colors of each. You won't accomplish anything doing this.

"With topwater fishing, you need to put in enough time on the water — or your swimming pool — so that you understand the actions of the bait and feel confident fishing it."

Griffin's system of topwater fishing utilizes five types of surface lures, as he defines them:

Twitch baits. "A twitch bait is basically a single-spin lure like a Creek Chub Darter. The pull-point is on top of the bait or underneath the throat and not straight out from the nose, which makes a difference in the action. If the pull-point is on top of the head, it slows the action down. If it's under the throat, it speeds it up. You can 'walk the dog,' a zig-zag pattern, with that type of bait usually. Usually, it has to have some weight in the tail to keep the nose up and be effective.

"But you can also twitch a twitch bait by just barely moving it, particularly if it has a spinner on it. When the fish are real finicky, I will sometimes take the screw-eye on the back of the plug and make two or three turns, which locks the spinner in place. It doesn't spin at all and when you twitch it with just a little bit of movement, it acts like a bug lying on the water and fluttering every now and then."

Stick baits. "There is a secondary type of twitch baits, which is the stick bait with no spinners on it. It sits straight up in the water, which makes it a little bit different from a twitch bait. When you pull it, the nose of it will actually flop on the water. Its attraction is that it will stay in one spot and you can work the strike zone around a piece of cover better. This is a good bait when the fish are holding tight to the cover because you can stay in the strike zone maybe 10 seconds longer. When you twitch it, it stays there. Plus, when that fish sucks a

stick bait in, you've got two-thirds of the bait under the water — because of the weighted tail — which means more hooking ability."

Chugger baits. "The chugger bait is a noise-maker, primarily. It's a better bait for deeper water. It can be just as effective in shallow water, but in deeper water, it will bring those fish up from deeper and muddier water. It gets their attention, like having rattles in a crank bait. So, your strike zone is increased in terms of distance away and depth below."

Skitter baits. "I think skitter-type baits, lures like the Dalton Special, are the best all-around bait. You can get a variety of actions out of it. It darts when you pull it one way and it's at an angle when you stop it, so the next jerk on it will pull it back the other way. It darts back and forth, which is a good type of action. And you can get noise from it. Some of the skitter-type baits, like the Woodchopper, have double spinners and can be buzzed across the surface like a buzz bait. It's a lot noiser than a twitch bait and, on some days, that's important."

Swimming minnow baits. "I don't use a swimming minnow lure very much, but that's just my personal preference. A swimming minnow bait, like a Rapala or Bang-O-Lure, is a good cold-water and a good slow-moving bait. Because it has a small lip on it, you can work it real slow, which makes it effective in cold water. It will stay in the strike zone two or three times longer than an ordinary bait would, which is important if their metabolism is slowed down by the cold water."

Griffin fishes surface lures under a variety of conditions, which might seem a little unorthodox to most bass anglers, who have been taught that topwater plugs are limited exclusively to early morning/late afternoon and overcast days. But the weather conditions are important, he says.

"When I go out in the morning, the first thing I do is evaluate the weather conditions, which will decide how I fish," he explains. "The conditions dictate the type of bait I use and my retrieve."

Griffin is asked to describe the absolute ideal conditions for excellent surface action.

TEMPERATURE: "I'd rather have a water temperature of between 65 and 72 degrees," he says. "Anything below 65, they get sluggish and you have to work the bait slower. The fish's metabolism slows down. Above 80 degrees, the amount of time you can effectively work a topwater bait decreases as the sun gets up and the day gets hot. With cooler water, you have more time to fish a topwater bait."

WIND: "The ideal wind would be a moderate wind, no more than 8 to 10 (miles per hour). But you want a little bit of wind because it makes the fish more comfortable and less likely to spook. Just as long as the wind isn't so strong that you can't work the lure properly."

SUNLIGHT: "A bright sun is fine, as long you've got wind. Most fishermen shy away from throwing a topwater plug when the sun gets up. That's

because all fishermen look down into the water. No fisherman is down in the water where the fish are looking up. The fish see the sky and the silhouette of the plug and when it's bright, he sees it much better from a greater distance."

Since ideal conditions come along about as often as Halley's Comet, topwater anglers are faced with weather conditions that require some on-the-water adjustment. Griffin is a master at such adjustments.

"Wind changes the type of topwater lure you should be using," Griffin explains. "As the wind gets up, you need to go to a smaller bait that makes noise. What happens is that the real big baits will dive through any type of wave on the surface of the water. But the smaller baits will ride the crest of the wave and you can still twitch it easily.

"If it's windy, I prefer to throw into the wind. If you concentrate on casting into the wind, you can soon establish a current pattern, which is determined by the direction of the wind. That current pattern will dictate where and how the fish will be positioned, which is important to keep in mind when topwater fishing. And remember to fish parallel to the waves and not across the grain of the wave."

An abundance of sunlight requires a change of tactics as well.

"It doesn't matter to me if it's overcast or not," Griffin says. "But you need to make an adjustment if it becomes a bluebird day and you're fishing crystal-clear water. In that case, you need to go to a lighter line and a heavier plug. That's not so much for the fish-catching ability of the plug, but for the extra distance you can cast it. You usually have to throw an extremely long ways because the fish tend to get real spooky in clear water. And you have to work the bait real slow.

"As the sun comes up, I think the shadow effect becomes a factor, too. A topwater plug is usually larger than most other types of baits and it has a distinct silhouette to the fish looking from below. You can take advantage of that. A lot of people want the sun behind them, but I prefer to fish into the sun. That way, the sun is behind the fish and he feels more comfortable with something coming to him from the opposite direction. They don't seem as spooky that way. Plus, the fish can't see your shadow."

Griffin is asked at what depth does he eliminate the use of a surface lure. "You can't fish it in real deep water, say 55 feet," he replies. "The only exception is that if the 55 feet of water is under a boat dock. The fish will be suspended under it, so it's immaterial how deep the water is in that case. You could catch those fish by working the lure fast along the edges of the boat dock, but you would have to present the lure several times to get their attention.

"Generally, you won't get much action with a top-water lure if you're fishing water more than 7 feet deep, particularly if it's clear water."

Sam Griffin somehow manages to understand both the complexities of topwater fishing, yet doesn't lose sight of its simpler side. But then, he's a magician with a floating piece of wood.

SECTION TWO
TECHNIQUES & TIPS

Chapter 22

Strategy for a 10-Pound Bass

It is the standard by which bass fishing accomplishments are judged.

It is fishing's equivalent to the undefeated season, a fisherman's crowning achievement. Some see it as an angler coming of age. Others see it as the dream of a lifetime.

There is truly something special about catching a 10-pound bass, the mark of excellence in terms of size. In this day and time, it is a remarkable feat for both man to catch a 10-pounder and a bass to escape fishing pressure long enough to grow to that size. In comparison, a 9-pound, 15-ounce largemouth may be a magnificent specimen, but in subsequent conversations and memories, it pales in comparison to a bass that weighs an ounce more. There is almost something magical about that 10-pound mark.

Nowhere is the thrill involved with catching a 10-pounder experienced more often than in America's big-bass states — Florida, California and Texas. Their status as the Big Three of trophy fishing is indisputable.

PROfile

A successful tournament pro, Texan David Vance also guides on the famed big-bass waters of Lake Fork.

So it makes sense that the big-bass experts from those states can provide an insight into the habits of these awesome fish and the techniques that produce so well for them. By sharing their knowledge and experience, these excellent anglers hope to improve your chances of experiencing a bass of a lifetime.

Consider the men and their credentials:

Doug Hannon, Odessa, Fla., the country's most renowned big-bass expert and researcher who has 511 bass over 10-pounds to his credit.

Roland Martin, Clewiston, Fla., nine-time B.A.S.S. Angler of the Year, and a big-bass specialist who has caught countless 10-pound-plus fish on both artificial lures and live bait.

Dan Kadota, San Pedro, Calif., recreational angler who has caught almost 50 10-pound-class bass in the last six years, including monstrous fish weighing 19.04 and 18.75 in the same year.

Bill Murphy, San Diego, Calif., a renowned guide who has more than 40 13-pound-plus bass to his credit over the past 20 years, including a 17-pounder.

Mark Stevenson, Plano, Texas, guide who gained national attention in 1988 by catching the state record 17-pound, 11-ounce largemouth, which has since been on display in the aquariums at Bass Pro Shops in Springfield, Mo., where it has grown considerably. Stevenson estimates he has caught about 35 fish that topped the 10-pound mark.

David Vance, Crandall, Texas, tournament pro and guide on famed Lake Fork, where he has caught 10 bass weighing 10 pounds or more in the past two years.

It is a star-studded lineup of trophy-bass experts that is well worth listening to.

"By their very being, 10-pound bass are special," Hannon emphasizes. "It is a special experience to catch one.

"I have always looked at fish of this size as different and tried to analyze what it took to become what they are. One of the biggest breakthroughs for me was getting beyond the idea that a 10-pound bass is smart, which is why it has grown that big. But that's not true. That fish has no more intelligence and is no harder to catch than anything else. What is difficult about it is figuring out how its environment has changed and how it has responded to our assault on big fish. We have selectively harvested the biggest fish and therefore, we can't think in terms of where the fish should be, but in terms of where man might allow it to still exist. That is the very basis of fishing for big bass."

"Catching bass over 10 pounds has to be approached as a science," Kadota adds. "Trophy fishing is not luck, it's hard work."

The experts from the big-bass states break their approach to trophy fishing down into four categories: understanding big-bass behavior, the habitats of big fish, trophy techniques and the intangibles involved in catching a bragging-sized bass.

BIG-BASS BEHAVIOR

Mark Stevenson guides on Lake Fork, a 27,000-acre Texas impoundment that is unique in that it was designed with some consideration to the biological needs of the fish. As a result of an abundance of wooden structure and vegetative cover, Lake Fork continues to re-write the big-bass standings in the Lone Star State on a consistent basis despite an enormous amount of fishing pressure. It is a lake that provides both Stevenson and Vance with a remarkable laboratory for coming into contact with trophy bass on a regular basis.

"I have come to believe that a 10-pound bass is a different creature," Stevenson says. "First of all, they seem to be solitary fish. And they tend to do a lot of things that are not the norm. Like on a blazing hot day when most of the fish are in the heavy grass or out deep, you can be casting out on a flat that has virtually no cover for schooling fish and stick a real big fish. There's no rhyme or reason for it."

From both his on-the-water experiences and observations of big bass beneath the surface, Hannon has determined that the largest members of the species are more territorial and seem to roam less than smaller fish. That aspect of their behavior is important, since trophy bass more vigorously defend their territory. That territory is usually a place that is difficult for fishermen to approach and exploit, which is the reason that a bass is able to grow to such a size.

One of the most important facets of big-bass behavior, according to David Vance, is realizing that, generally, a 10-pound fish will not aggressively pursue a baitfish as it darts through the water. That is one reason why a jig, worm or slow-moving spinnerbait produce so many trophy bass during the year.

Vance also believes that big bass have a tendency to feed in cycles. When targeting trophy fish for his customers, Vance tries to spend three or four days fishing the most likely area, while concentrating especially hard when the conditions are most ideal.

While most anglers assume that a 10-pound bass possesses a superior intellect to smaller fish, Hannon emphasizes that the trophy bass are only smarter in their selection of territory. Yet, bass, particularly the older fish, have the ability to learn and distinguish between live food and artificial offerings. "A 10-pound fish is a creature that has a certain degree of learning built into its predator make-up," Hannon says. "A big bass learns the most productive way of hunting and it is more difficult to fool with an artificial lure."

THE HABITATS OF BIG BASS

The days of catching trophy bass in shallow, shoreline cover are about over. Although it still occurs occasionally, bass fishing's trophy hunters have turned their sights to areas where the population is less disturbed.

For the California experts, that means deep water.

Bill Murphy, who fishes the heavily pressured San Diego lakes, has taught himself the difficult art of fishing offshore structure and, as a result, some of his trophy bass have come from as deep as 70 feet. Dan Kadota, a longtime saltwater captain, learned quickly in his newfound freshwater sport that he had to learn to probe the depths if he was to have any chance of catching a trophy in lakes Casitas and Castaic, which are bombarded by fishermen in the Los Angeles area.

As a longtime saltwater angler, Kadota has an advantage over most bass fishermen. Having learned to read bottom contour on the original fathometers a decade before freshwater anglers began using depthfinders, Kadota has spent as many hours reading the bottom of his home lakes as he has fishing it. He has also applied much of his saltwater knowledge and techniques to deep-water inland fishing with impressive results.

"My experience on the ocean has given me a tremendous advantage," Kadota claims. "Our perception and the way we conceive a spot is different. We look at bottom structure in three dimensions where as most guys read exactly what's on the graph. In finding and setting up on spots, I'd say guys like myself have an advantage."

For Kadota, the biggest breakthrough in terms of catching trophy bass was learning the importance of deep-water migration or access routes and how the fish relate to them as the water typically fluctuates in the California reservoirs. The key to locating fish on those impoundments is understanding the structure that the big bass move to as the water level rises and falls, he says.

The other crucial factor for pinpointing world-class bass is understanding the role of underwater current. "The basis for any fishing is current, whether it be bass or bluefin tuna," Kadota explains. "I would almost bet that the typical tournament fisherman who stays on the trolling motor has no idea which way the current is going. That seems ludicrous because current is the basis for the way fish feed and position themselves on a particular point. I work hard to position myself perfectly for fishing a particular structure on a specific spot with respect to the current, wind and access route to that structure."

The challenge of locating deep-water trophies may seem overwhelming to some anglers who are not adept with depth-finding equipment. There is an alternative — find the bass that the rest of the fishing neighborhood has overlooked.

Mark Stevenson has been able to locate an impressive number of relatively shallow trophy bass by fishing to the beat of a different drummer. "I fish a lot of places that are not typical bass spots," he says. "When I'm searching for a spot that might be inhabited by a 10-pound fish, I concentrate on spots that traditionally have a lot of baitfish and has deep water nearby.

"I'm like everybody else in that I need something to key off of, so I fish a lot of creeks and points. But the textbook places on creeks like bends and heavy brush get too much pressure, so I avoid them. I'll fish a long straight away that most people will pass up and catch a lot of big fish that way. It's the same with a point. I concentrate on the long, sloping points that are not obvious. It may just be a slight rise, but those kinds of places consistently produce big fish for me."

A shallow-water fisherman by nature, Doug Hannon concentrates on locating bass that are, largely, unmolested. To do that, he has followed an interesting progression over the years.

In early 1970s, intelligent fishing pressure was minimal in the weedy Florida waters that Hannon called home. He was able to catch big bass almost at will, so he simply concentrated on the areas that were easiest to fish — the edges of shoreline vegetation. In the mid-70s, the bass were not nearly as abundant in the emergent shoreline cover (a result of both being selectively harvested and moving to avoid fishing pressure), so Hannon moved out to submerged weed lines in 8 to 10 feet of water. In 1978, he began fishing lakes that had slightly off-colored water. The big bass in clear-water lakes had been plundered by the sight-fishing techniques of bed fishermen.

As the 1980s began, Hannon started fishing deeper vegetation, the kind of habitat that the shallow-water native Floridians despised. As a result, he was able to continue catching 10-pound fish. But that changed around 1985 when Florida fishermen began learning how to fish deeper hydrilla and other vegetation.

"Where I am right now is fishing the heaviest, thickest stuff in the lake — the places that other people avoid, which requires completely different techniques to fish it," Hannon says. "It has been a true evolutionary process for me as a fisherman to be able to continue to catch big fish over the last two decades."

BIG-BASS TECHNIQUES

Our big-bass experts can offer an insight into catching trophy bass on both artificial lures and live bait. Roland Martin and Doug Hannon have caught numerous 10-pounders on both lures and wild shiners. Bill Murphy's trophies have come on lures and live crawfish. In contrast, Mark Stevenson and David Vance exclusively fish artificial lures, while Dan Kadota relies on crawfish as his big-fish weapon.

Few will argue the superiority of using live prey for trophy bass. The golden shiner has produced more 10-pound bass over the last decade in Florida than anything and fishermen in both Texas and California are beginning to understand its allure. In some situations, a live crawfish is just as alluring, obviously, since it has produced 19.04 and 18.75 bass for Kadota.

The reason for that superiority, Hannon believes, are the natural behavioral cues that a frantic prey emits when approached by predators like bass. Those inherent, natural cues, which actually trigger the feeding activity, are the one element missing from artificial lures. Still, artificial lures, in the hands of a talented angler, will produce bragging-sized largemouths.

The key to selecting artificial baits for trophy bass is size, the experts agree. All emphasize the need for using a large bait, which can be seen from a greater distance and may be perceived as a bigger meal by the energy-conservative trophy bass.

Murphy's top artificial offerings for big bass are the Magnum Rapala and large plastic worms up to 16 inches in length. But the concensus is that the best big-bass artificial of all is the rubber-skirted jig with some type of trailer attached.

Vance and Stevenson use a large (1/2- to 1-ounce) jig with a No. 1 pork chunk trailer in colors that most resemble crawfish coloration (black-and-blue and black-and-brown color schemes). In the warmer months, both often switch to a plastic crawfish-like trailer.

"Jigs, in my opinion, are the very best big-fish bait," Vance says. "It has a bulky shape like a crawfish and you can move it similar to a crawfish. It's a slow-moving, bottom-hugging bait that can be finessed. The slower you move it, the better your chances are of catching a big fish."

An overlooked big-bass bait is a slow-moving 1/2- to 1-ounce spinnerbait with a large (No. 6 or 7) willow-leaf blade, according to Martin, who ignited a big-blade craze in several years ago by using tournament performances to dramatically illustrate that the giant willow-leaf bait will produce some impressive results.

Regardless of the lure, it takes more than simply retrieving a bait to entice a true trophy into striking. "It takes some skill and imagination in the way you work a lure," Hannon explains. "For example, the first thing I do when the bait hits the water is move it in a lifelike manner immediately so that the fish doesn't have to accept the splash down of an inanimate object and then have it come to life. That transition is where most fishermen fail to fool big fish. Big fish have seen so much. You have to actually convince him that it is alive upon inspection because he has banged on so many things that weren't alive. You'll catch fish otherwise, but that's the type of thing that would make a big bass respond to a lure that it would normally ignore."

THE INTANGIBLES

In this age of fishing pressure and declining big-bass stocks, it takes "the perfect combination of things to catch a 10-pounder," Hannon says.

"We've reached the point of turning off depth sounders to avoid alerting the fish and not running the trolling motor at any time during the cast. We're having to cast more accurately and make the lure enter the water a lot quieter. We're having to leave the bait in a likely spot longer. Everything has to come together to catch a 10-pound bass in this day and time."

The numerous intangibles involved in trophy-bass fishing include maintaining well-functioning equipment, re-tying knots and sharpening hooks regularly, keeping a low-profile in the boat in clearer water, making a quieter approach, anchoring properly to fish a piece of structure and countless other details that may seem insignificant to some. But Roland Martin reminds us that "10-pound bass magnify even the slightest mistake."

An important intangible, according to Dan Kadota, is selecting the time to fish. Anglers fishing at night and on weekdays stand a significantly better change of tangling with a trophy than the typical weekend fisherman. Kadota caught the 19.04 giant on Jan. 8, 1989, the day after the historic appearance of snow in the Los Angeles area. As a result of the unusually cold weather, normally hectic Lake Castaic had just five boats fishing its waters.

Kadota's beliefs are supported by telemetry studies of Dr. Loren Hill, which indicate that bass behave differently on weekend days when the fishing pressure is the heaviest.

Florida guide Dan Thurmond with a 13 1/2-pound trophy.

The most critical intangible of all is mental, according to the experts. All insist that the angler who longs to catch a 10-pounder must adjust his attitude, tempering his enthusiasm with patience and understanding that those who seek trophy fish will more often go home skunked than their fellow fishermen.

Martin takes the mental aspect a step farther. "One thing I do all of the time that I'm on the water is imagine that there is a 10-pound bass around every target that I'm about to cast to," he says. "I actually conjure up the image of that old bass and I visualize him every time I cast.

"This does a couple of things for me. First of all, it gives me a good positive attitude. And secondly, this silly little mental game forces you to think about that bass and how it should be positioned to ambush a lure as it comes by. It makes you note the shady side of the cover or the direction of the current or the point of the cover that provides the very best angle to ambush a baitfish that is being swept by. All of those things are important because when you are dealing with big 10-pound bass, your first casts are critical."

For a bass to grow to 10 pounds or greater is an accomplishment in its own right. And catching such a trophy demands the ultimate in angling skill and dedication. For those who are able to achieve this lofty goal, the big-bass experts of Florida, Texas and California remind us of the importance of carefully releasing trophy bass to continue to live, spawn and pass on those magnificent genes to other future 10-pounders.

Chapter 23

Stalking Visible Bass

It can be the most exciting and frustrating fishing of all.

Sight-fishing for bass, the way the guides in the Florida Keys stalk bonefish on the flats, ignites an adrenalin rush like no other type of bass fishing. Visual fishing has the same allure as topwater fishing with one major difference — this game is played out before your eyes from cast to hook-set.

But it is this visual element involved in clear-water fishing that makes it such an intimidating and frustrating experience when the fish don't cooperate. With other types of water clarity, you rarely ever know where a bass will be located; your only clue is the available structure and weather conditions that should place fish in a fairly predictable position. But with visible bass fishing, you see almost all of the fish that you cast to. In terms of nerve wear-and-tear, it is the difference between thinking that a bass should be holding in that submerged bush and actually seeing how it is positioned as you approach it.

Shaw Grigsby is one of the masters of the specialized art of catching visible bass. His prowess with catching bass he can see has paved the way to much of his tournament success, which includes qualifying for the prestigious BASS Masters Classic on three occasions.

Two prime examples: En route to winning the 1988 Texas Bassmaster Invitational on Sam Rayburn Reservoir, Grigsby used light line and finesse lures to coax heavily-pressured clear-water bass into biting and then wrestled them from some bad places. Grigsby first spotted every bass he caught, both spawning and pre-spawn fish. An impressive opening-round five-fish stringer weighing 26 pounds, 3 ounces, paved the way to his first B.A.S.S. victory.

Although he finished as the runner-up in the 1989 MegaBucks event on Florida's Harris Chain, Grigsby ran away with the four qualifying rounds, slight-casting to bass in the tannic-tinted clear waters of a canal to catch more than 60 pounds.

The 33-year-old Gainesville, Fla., angler is among the most versatile of the touring pros, but his forte — and favorite method — is visible fishing.

"I like clear-water bass fishing because it's a challenge," Grigsby says. "It's real exciting to see the fish ahead of time, work the bait just right to get it interested and then watch it charge the bait. It's a neat feeling to sit there and watch it bite the bait before setting the hook. To me, it's the ultimate.

"I prefer to see my prey before I catch them. But most people — even the top tournament pros — are just the opposite. They automatically look for dirty, stained water because the fish there are probably going to be a little more aggressive. But I tend to find fish that are a little larger, a lot of times, and almost untouched. Other people don't fish for them in real clear water because they are a little harder for most people to catch. Because they are not fished for much, it gives me a little advantage because I will often have an area to myself, rather than having to share stained-water areas with other fishermen."

Fishing for visible bass intimidates even some of the best tournament pros?

"Definitely," Grigsby replies. "A lot of people get psyched out because you may see a lot of fish, but you may only catch one out of 100 if you're not real adept at this type of fishing. It's intimidating to see fish and not be able to catch them. So they tend to shy away from this type of fishing."

Contrary to popular opinion, visible-bass fishing is more than just bed-fishing for spawning bass. That certainly is a productive time for sight-fishing, but it is by no means limited to spawning season. Grigsby and others including 1988 Classic champion Guido Hibdon, have proven that along the national tournament trail. Grigsby seeks out clear water and visible bass in his travels throughout the year, with the exception of the coldest times when most bass migrate to deeper water.

As with other types of fishing, the conditions dictate when sight-fishing will be most productive.

Obviously, good water clarity is required. Through years of fishing the crystal-clear waters of Florida's spring-fed rivers, Grigsby has developed an uncanny ability to spot bass that would not be visible to most anglers. In the process, he has learned to read shallow water that is slightly off-colored or has a slight tint to it.

The ideal conditions for chasing visible bass are a bright, overcast day — enough clouds to hide the sun, but plenty of sunlight penetration for seeing beneath the water's surface — and little or no wind. The cloud cover makes

Shaw Grigsby shows off a 6-pound bass that he spotted in a Lake Harris canal during the final qualifying day in the 1989 MegaBucks tournament -- part of a 60-pound-plus catch. Ken Cook looks on.

clear-water bass slightly less wary, Grigsby says. The exception to his preference for cloud cover is spawning season when bright, cloudless days are best. Bass that are protecting a nest are more likely to hold in that position and less likely to spook under sunny skies.

"Spawning bass are a whole different game from regular visible fishing," Grigsby explains. "Bedding fish don't want to bite, so you have to really work those fish. Generally, they're harder to catch. They're finicky because they are not feeding, they are protecting. It takes a whole different style of fishing to catch them."

Grigsby utilizes a variety of lures for catching visible bass, including minnow-type surface plugs, tubejigs like the Fat Gitzit, small worms, a downsized jig-and-pork combination, in-line spinners and noisy surface lures such as the Zara Spook and Rebel Pop-R.

His most productive lure choices are the G-2, a tubejig made by Lucky Strike Manufacturing, Inc., and a 4-inch Gillraker, a small-diameter plastic worm. The G-2 is fished most often on a 1/16-ounce jighead, but Grigsby uses more weight depending on the water depth (1/8-ounce for 5 to 10 feet and 1/4-ounce for below 10 feet). The tiny worm is impaled on a 1-0 hook and coupled with a 1/16- or 1/8-ounce bullet weight. Grigsby sometimes fishes the worm without a weight, which slows its descent, for unaggressive bass.

"The G-2 is an outstanding lure for catching visible bass — probably the best of all," Grigsby explains. "I think that's because it resembles a minnow when its floating and a crawfish once it hits the bottom, especially when you pop it and it darts backwards like a crawfish. With that bait, you can represent two major food sources of the bass.

"For sight-fishing, it is important to use a lure that you can keep track of easily. You need to be able to watch the bait so that as you're working it, you can see what triggers a strike. Then you can duplicate that later with other fish."

Catching visible bass demands using light tackle and line. Grigsby uses a 6-foot medium-action Quantum Quartz-Lite rod and a Quantum Brute 4W reel, which features a wide spool. The wide spool is important, he says, because it will handle a variety of line sizes. Most of Grigsby's visible bass fishing is done with 6- to 10-pound test DuPont Magna Thin, a small-diameter monofilament line, that he believes is practically invisible to the fish.

One of the most important pieces of equipment for sight fishing, Grigsby says, are quality sunglasses. The most important considerations when selecting sunglasses for fishing are polarization and ultraviolet blockage. Grigsby utilizes two different models made by Hobie Precision Optics: an amber-colored pair for low-light conditions and a dark blue pair for brighter skies.

Perhaps the most crucial aspect to stalking visible bass is the initial approach. Unlike a camouflaged hunter in the woods, an approaching angler has a good chance of being seen by clear-water bass. "You have to present a bait to the fish before it can see you because once it sees you, it gets real tough to catch that bass," Grigsby says. "You can still catch them, but it's difficult. I think that's the toughest part of sight-fishing."

Although there are some obvious aspects of enhancing your chances of sneaking up on a clear-water bass such as avoiding wearing brightly-colored clothing, boat positioning may be the most important consideration of all. Sight-fishing requires being positioned at an angle and distance to both see and then cast to the bass, without being easily detected by the fish.

In a current situation, Grigsby approaches visible bass by positioning his boat downstream of the fish and casting his lure well upstream. Bass holding in current are most likely to be facing the flow, watching for baitfish to be swept by. This positioning allows Grigsby to keep his boat behind the bass, while his lure is carried downstream in a lifelike manner.

Still-water conditions require a different approach. One way to sneak up on a clear-water bass is to keep the structure or cover between man and fish. But that is not always possible. Grigsby, who catches many visible bass that are cruising instead of holding tight to cover, emphasizes the importance of making a long cast and a quiet entry into the water.

Grigsby is a master at working clear-water bass and enticing strikes from finicky fish. Watching him manipulate a bass into a frenzy with a tiny finesse bait is a thrilling experience. He has developed a true understanding of bass behavior in a clear domain and an amazing ability to match the posturing of an individual bass with the proper subtle bait movements to trigger a strike.

The first step in this process is choice of lure. The bait must be alluring enough to get the bass' attention. Finding that lure, for Grigsby, is usually a matter of experimenting with several baits each day on the water, although the G-2 tubejig seems to have the most universal appeal.

"Once you have a bait that's enticing to them, you then have to present it in the most lifelike manner," Grigsby adds. "People tend to move baits too fast in clear water. If you move a bait real slow, you tend to get more strikes in clear water.

"I see that over and over with my G-2. Most people think that you are supposed to throw a G-2 or Gitzit-type bait and and hop it through the water. The bass may notice it, but it moves too fast to appear lifelike. It should be moved slowly and smoothly. I even let it set on the bottom for a second before I move it each time. That tends to get a fish's attention a lot more than rapid movements. They will move up on a slow, sporadic-moving bait and examine it more closely. Then you can get even more subtle with your movements, which will usually make them strike it. With this type of fishing, you need to finesse them into striking."

Shaw Grigsby has a mastery over the type of fishing that most of us avoid. But his success is evidence that you can catch visible bass — once you overcome the intimidation factor.

A small rattle chamber adds the dimension of sound to a plastic worm, a somewhat subtle bait.

Chapter 24

Pro Bait Modifications

The coolness of the recently departed summer night lingered in the air as professional bass angler O.T. Fears brought his boat off-plane and drifted toward a shallow flat dotted with old stumps.

This had the makings of a buzzbait morning, a surface celebration that is universally revered by all bass enthusiasts. The weather was stable, the bass were shallow and locked into an aggressive mode.

Reaching into his huge tacklebox, Fears grabbed several buzzbaits still in their packages. After freeing the safety-pin-like baits, he took a pair of pliers — and cut the lure in half.

"You'll find very few tournament pros — or even experienced fishermen — who fish a bait exactly the way it comes out of the package," Fears says in response to an astonished look. "I modify baits a lot of different ways — some in little ways and and some in major ways. I guess you could say this would be a major way."

PROfile

North Carolina pro Guy Eaker is an eight-time BASS Masters Classic qualifier.

Although the country's lure manufacturers have refined the technology necessary to supply the average angler with a ready-to-go, sure-fire fish-catcher, years of experience have enabled the tournament pros to develop an insight into largemouth, smallmouth and spotted bass that most of us will never attain. They have discovered small behavioral quirks and sure-fire methods of taking advantage of them. And they have found ways to modify artificial lures to make them more effective and productive.

Tricks of the trade, so to speak. And every top bass pro will tell you that it is the little things that separate the best from the rest.

In many cases, these lure modifications are only a slight, enhancing twist that makes the bait perform better. In others, the lures undergo a complete personality change. But all have a common result — they produce more bass under a wider variety of fishing situations.

O.T. Fears, a three-time qualifier for the prestigious BASS Masters Classic and past Red Man All-American champion, certainly understands the value of bait alteration. And he vividly demonstrated it on that calm summer morning.

BUZZBAITS

Most people wouldn't abuse a buzzbait the way Fears routinely does with his pliers. But this is a man with a definite purpose.

Fears calls it "hinging the bait." That involves cutting the buzzbait wire in half about a half-inch above the leadhead. He then attaches the two ends to a split ring by twisting the ends of the wire. It looks like a buzzbait from hell, but Fears sings its praises.

"What this does is allow the bait to ride lower in the water, which gives you a higher percentage of the fish that you hook than you will with a standard buzzbait," he explains. "The split ring works like a hinge and allows the hook to swing free. That gives you another advantage. If a bass ever wraps you up in a bush with a regular buzzbait, he has a lot of leverage to use to his advantage. I'd say that 99 percent of the time a bass will use that leverage to twist free. But that is practically impossible with this bait."

The Oklahoma pro went on to prove his case convincingly to his skeptical fishing partner, who insisted on throwing a conventional buzzbait.

These noisy surface lures are routinely modified by knowledgeable anglers — though not as drastically as Fears. While buzzbaits are among the most exhilarating lures to fish because they produce a senses-startling assault that is played out before your eyes, it can be a frustrating lure as well. It is often not a very efficient lure for actually hooking bass.

For that reason, most of the modifications done to buzzbaits are meant to increase their hooking ability. Most bass pros bend the wire of the bait to make the hook and leadhead ride lower in the water. And if the hook is bent precisely, the blade will tick the shaft as it rotates, making a louder noise.

CRANKBAITS

In the realm of artificial lures, crankbaits are among the most likely to be altered, despite the fact that these baits have few components. Although wooden baits are far easier to alter, plastic crankbaits don't escape from the pro's tendency to give it his personal touch.

The most common modification involves exchanging the factory hooks for larger, stronger versions. Although the manufacturers have made major strides to improve the hook quality on their crankbaits in recent years, almost all of the top tournament pros prefer to replace them with hooks that are a size larger, which increases the percentage of bass that they are able to boat. And many insist on using a wide-throated hook like VMC model.

Losing fish is a major consideration with crankbaits and the object of much modification. But it might surprise some to learn that crankbait expert Joe Hughes believes he actually improves his hooking ratio by closing the barbs on the hooks. And he has had the success to prove it.

Veteran Virginia pro Woo Daves routinely clips off the barbs when fishing heavy timber and brush to reduce the number of times it gets hung. In especially heavy cover, Daves will remove the treble hooks and replace them with a single 3-0 worm hook.

Although he is not a tournament pro, noted big-bass authority Doug Hannon has developed a novel way of making lipless, vibrating shad-shaped lures (like a Rat-L-Trap and Cordell Spot) considerably more weedless. Hannon removes the rear treble hook and strategically inserts a tiny piece of a magnet into the belly of the bait. This keeps the remaining hook tight against the body of the lure, allowing it to come through junglelike vegetation. And it doesn't seem to significantly effect its hooking ability.

You can change the track of a crankbait by turning the line-tie slightly.

Anglers have weighted diving baits for years to gain a little added depth. Wooden baits, in particular, have been weighted down, usually by drilling a hole and inserting lead. Some fishermen gain extra depth by using a large bullet weight in front of the line-tie on the bait.

Perhaps the most common way that crankbaits are modified is referred to by the pros as "maltuning the bait" for the times when they don't want the lure to track true. Using pliers, you can alter the course of the bait by slightly turning the eye (line-tie) of the lure. "I often maltune a crankbait to run off to one side or the other," says Guy Eaker, a top touring pro from Cherryville, N.C. "If you're fishing a boat dock with a crankbait, you can make it run well up under the dock where the fish hide. I've seen that make a difference between catching fish and not catching anything with the same bait on a dock or around a tree."

Veteran tournament pro and Tennessee guide Bill Bartlett reveals an unusual treatment to plastic, slab-sided vibrating baits that makes the lure move slower through the water. It involves actually boiling the bait in hot water to make it expand, creating a bait that will slowly rise to the surface and can be fished in a foot or so of water. But be advised that you can also ruin some perfectly good crankbaits this way by overcooking them.

Fears removes the split ring on the eye of his crankbaits, claiming it is impossible to tie a decent knot to those connectors. "And a split ring has two sharp edges on the opening of it," he adds. "If you tie a knot there, it will soon cut your line. A split ring can also pinch your line and you will eventually have a weak knot." Instead, Fears uses a No. 3 Berkley Cross-Lok snap, which he claims does not hamper the action of the bait.

SPINNERBAITS

Every angler, from the novice to the money-maker, fools around with spinnerbaits, changing the size and color of its skirt and blades. The difference is that the tournament pros have a definite purpose when they make a change.

For example, top pro Charlie Ingram of Columbia, Tenn., has a sure-fire solution to short-striking fish. He simply reverses the color of the blades on his tandem spinnerbait.

For some unknown reason, that seems to enable the bass to better home in on the bait. "It's amazing how well that works," Ingram says. "but I can't really explain why."

Georgia tournament pro and B.A.S.S. winner Tom Mann, Jr., has a different answer for short-striking bass that also tends to attract fish in muddy-water conditions. He puts about a 1/8-inch bend in the end of a No. 3 or 5 willow-leaf blade (at a 90-degree angle). That alteration gives the blade more vibration and a slightly different wobble, yet retains its reflective quality.

Renowned spinnerbait specialist Guy Eaker doctors the blades to get different actions out of them. For example, he sometimes cups an Indiana-style blade to get more vibration in off-colored water. For clear-water situations where he prefers more flash and less vibration, Eaker flattens the blade slightly. Another trick that has produced in situations where his tournament spot was enduring heavy pressured involves drilling a 1/8-inch hole through the middle of a Colorado blade. This gives the bait a different look and sound as it comes through the water.

Many spinnerbait alterations are designed to enable the lure to better penetrate heavy brush and vegetation.

Former Classic champion Jack Hains of Many, La., makes a spinnerbait more weedless by bending the blade arm closer to the hook. "Not only will this help the spinnerbait come through thick cover, it will also fall a little quicker," Hains explains. "I'll use that to make the bait run a little deeper at times, too."

Missouri pro Johnnie Borden's answer to heavy cover is to extend a small rubberband from the line-tie to the barb of the hook. The fine rubberband protects the hook, yet breaks away on the hookset, he says.

PLASTIC WORMS

The biggest trend on the national tournament trail over the past couple of years involving plastic worms has been to spice up their attractiveness by inserting a plastic rattle chamber. The small chambers contain several tiny BBs that vibrate and create a sizeable sound that seems to produce especially well in vegetation.

"Rattles are great because they add the dimension of sound to a plastic worm," says Shaw Grigsby, a Florida-based pro and two-time Classic qualifier. "I'm a big believer in them. I even sometimes glue one to the back of a spinnerbait blade to get more sound and a different sound."

Although many anglers insert the rattle in the body of the worm or near the tail, Grigsby positions it near the hook.

Most pros prefer to position a bullet weight against the top of a worm when flipping or pitching, a practice commonly referred to as "pegging the sinker." This enables the bait to better penetrate heavy grass or thick brush. And it also reduces the risk of the sinker interfering with the hooking process.

The traditional way of pegging a sinker is to insert a toothpick through the weight (beside the monofilament) and then clipping off the ends. But Tom Mann, Jr., believes he has a superior method. He replaces the toothpick with a small rubberband. The result is a securely-fashioned sinker without the risk of abrading the line (a common problem with the toothpick method).

After rigging a worm, Mann does, however, put a toothpick through the eye of the hook and then clips the ends away. That keeps the worm from sliding down the hook as often.

Alabama's Jack Chancellor, 1985 Classic champion and maker of the Do-Nothing Worm, has a couple of neat little tricks that have paid big dividends for him on occasion. The Do-Nothing is a 4-inch straight worm with exposed hooks that is rigged Carolina-style and attached to a 1-ounce bullet weight. The sinker drags the bottom, while the worm floats above it on a leader of about 3 feet.

When searching for big bass, Chancellor sometimes replaces the Do-Nothing with a huge, 10-inch ribbon-tail worm. The worm, which is rigged Texas style, drags the bottom as it follows the sinker — a combination that, apparently, is irresistible to big bass.

During the times when bass are schooled tightly on open-water structure like a drop-off, Chancellor adds a three-way swivel to the Carolina rig and uses a pair of Do-Nothing worms on separate leaders of 2 1/2 and 5 feet. This often results in double hook-ups and Chancellor dreams of rigging up seven Do-Nothing leaders to see if he can catch his limit on a single cast.

JIGS

The rubber-skirted jig has emerged as perhaps the top big-bass bait of all on the national tournament circuit. It is also among the most heavy modified.

Knowledgeable pros begin by shortening the wire weedguard that protects the hookpoint. Most trim the fiberguard to about a 1/8-inch above the hookpoint. This allows the bait to retain its weedless quality, yet doesn't interfere with the hooking process.

To make the jig even more weedless, some pros fan the wireguard out to cover a wider path. And others trim the skirt significantly to make it bellow out more and expose the trailer as it descends through the water. These might sound like minor considerations, but they can mean the difference between encountering fish and enduring frustration.

Jigs are most often fished with pork trailers, which add to the bulky appearance of the bait, creating a lifelike creature that resembles a crawfish, a universal bass delicacy. These guys have even developed little tricks for making the pork a more effective and alluring trailer.

Johnnie Borden trims some of the fat off of a No. 10 pork chunk to make it drop faster as it moves through the water. Another alteration that pays off regularly involves inserting a rattle chamber into the body of the pork. Borden uses the hook point of the jig to creates a tiny hole where the rattle is then inserted, giving the bait an entirely different sound as it moves through the water.

SURFACE LURES

Most fishermen would never consider modifying a top-water plug. If there was ever a bait that would seem perfect right out of the package, it would be a surface bait.

Would you believe:

• On a Zara Spook, Woo Daves files a tiny nick inside of the line-tie, which enables him to keep his knot on the bottom of the eye.

• Former Classic champion George Cochran of N. Little Rock, Ark., tunes the propellors on his top-water baits so that they make plenty of noise and leave a trail of bubbles — similar to a buzzbait. "It's easy to tune them," he says. "Take a propellor in each of your thumbs and twist it in opposite directions enough that they move freely. I like them so loose that they move in the water with the slightest motion."

• Massachusetts pro Danny Correia makes a significant modification to both a Zara Spook and Rapala. With the Spook, he places a split ring between the hooks and the hook holder. The result is a more free-swinging hook that eliminates any leverage that a bass might use to tear the hooks loose. Correia also files the underside of the lip of the Rapala (reducing the thickness of the diving plane), which enables it to dive deeper when pulled through the water. "I always feel like I have to do certain things to get a bait to work properly once I take it out of the package," he says. "A good fisherman will always find a way to modify a lure."

• Veteran pro and Oklahoma guide Tommy Biffle gets extra depth out of minnow-shaped diving baits like the Smithwick Rattlin' Rouge by drilling a hole and inserting a small lead weight between the front hook and the lip. He then uses glue to seal any water out. The result is a bait that will run a little deeper, cast farther and has a slow-suspending quality similar that approaches neutral buoyancy.

• Guy Eaker tunes a top-water lure to make it run off to one side or the other. By turning the line-tie of a bait like a Zara Spook, he can make it run well up under a boat dock or walk behind a tree.

TUBEJIGS

With the ever-increasing popularity of light-line fishing and the so-called "sissy baits" on the tournament trail, it was inevitable that the pros would develop a few tricks for getting the most out of tubejigs like the Fat Gitzit.

Californian John Bedwell, one of the top western tournament anglers, scores well by Texas-rigging a tubejig. He pinches the bait together and cuts a tiny slot for the hook of the jighead to penetrate. That allows the bait to remain weedless, but significantly reduces the resistance the hook point faces when it has to be pulled through the lure body on the hookset.

In addition, Bedwell makes a point to dull the jig heads (and all other lead) when fishing the clear-water reservoirs that dominate the West. The shiny, metallic flash of the lead can spook fish, he believes. So Bedwell drops the lead into hydrogen peroxide until the flash fizzles away.

Most pros replace the factory hooks on crankbaits with a larger version.

Bill Bartlett has enjoyed good success by fishing a Gitzit on a Carolina rig and inserting a small piece of Styrofoam inside of the jig body to make it float higher in the water. "I believe the fish can see the bait a lot better because it no longer drags the bottom," he says.

Perhaps the most bizarre tubejig trick belongs to 1988 Classic champion Guido Hibdon. Through his years as a guide on the clear waters of Missouri's Lake of the Ozarks, Hibdon found that he could entice particularly stubborn bass (as well as spawning fish) into striking by irritating them. He accomplishes this by inserting pieces of an Alka-Seltzer tablet into the body of his Lucky Strike G-2 tubejig. The bubbles and fizzle coming from within that piece of plastic usually prove to be more than a nearby bass can stand.

Whether they border on the bizarre or the mundane, the pros have shared secrets for modifying lures that should enhance the success of anglers on all levels. They have demonstrated that successful fishing begins well before the first cast.

Flipping remains the most popular big-bass technique of all.

Chapter 25

Flipping Made Easy

Jimmy Rogers' introduction to the technique called flipping took place in the mid-1970s on the famed big-bass waters of Florida's Lake Okeechobee.

Fishing a national tournament, Rogers was catching fish next to a stand of bulrushes. About 50 yards ahead of him, he watched in amazement as a little-known California angler actually drove his boat inside of another patch of reeds and began fishing in what they then considered "no-man's land."

For three days, Rogers watched the quiet Californian pull in big bass after big bass — without even casting the bait. "He was sort of dipping the worm into little holes and openings in the reeds right next to his boat," remembers Rogers. "All he seemed to pull up was 5-pound-plus bass."

The angler was Dave Gliebe, who won the tournament with more than 90 pounds of bass. And his technique would revolutionize the sport of bass fishing.

PROfile

Missouri's Basil Bacon, an eight-time BASS Masters Classic qualifier, was one of the eastern pioneers of flipping.

Gliebe was one of the pioneers of this new technique of flipping, along with fellow Californian Dee Thomas and others. It was Gliebe who brought the new heavy-cover technique East, where it quickly caught on and today ranks as the most universal of all bass-fishing methods.

The significance of the introduction of flipping was not lost on Jimmy Rogers, who returned to his Lakeland, Fla., home, bought a 7-foot surf rod and began experimenting with fishing's version of hand-to-hand combat. And it would pay off handsomely for him in years to come. In one Bass Anglers Sportsman Society tournament, flipping produced nine bass weighing more than 45 pounds for Rogers, paving the way for his appearance in the prestigious BASS Masters Classic in 1980.

"Flipping changed everything for all bass fishermen," claims Rogers. "It opened up a whole new world for us."

The birth of flipping provided bass enthusiasts with a combination of attributes not found with any other technique.

The mechanics of flipping, along with the lack of distance involved, provided a much greater degree of accuracy than conventional casting. Basically, the bait would fall where the rod was pointed. Suddenly, fishermen were able to put a lure into the smallest of openings in vegetation or up against a tree trunk or rock wall with impressive accuracy.

Perhaps its most important attribute is the quiet lure presentation that it provides. Because the bait is propelled just a few inches above the water's surface, it enters the water without the noise and splash associated with casting. For the first time, this allowed you to move close enough to cover or structure suspected of harboring bass and present a lure without spooking them.

The combination of increased accuracy and soft lure presentation provided anglers with a way to fish for hard-to- reach bass — particularly big-bass — that had largely been ignored in the past. As the technique was perfected and refined, fewer bass would be able to go unmolested by simply burying up in junglelike cover.

And flipping became particularly important during times when the fishing was tough, such as bright days and cold-front conditions when the bass held especially tight to cover and were inactive. Here was a technique that allowed you to penetrate their shelter and place a lure right in front of them.

It didn't take long for flipping to become the primary weapon for tournament fishermen and weekend anglers alike.

"If a man wants to consistently catch fish, particularly big fish, he has to learn to flip," claims Basil Bacon of Springfield, Mo., an eight-time Classic qualifier and one of the first eastern anglers to master and promote the technique. "No other technique allows you to keep your bait in the strike zone (in and near cover or structure) as long as flipping does.

"With other types of bass fishing, your lure may be near where the bass should be maybe 10 percent of the retrieve. But with flipping, the bait is in the area where the bass are likely to be 90 percent of the time. Flipping is just a way of putting the percentages in your favor."

No type of cover or structure is immune to this tight- to-cover target-fishing technique, which is done using long, stout rods, heavy line and weedless lures. It was designed with the heaviest of cover in mind.

Like any technique, learning to flip takes practice, but it is surprisingly easy to learn. In fact, it may be easier to do than to explain.

First of all, understand that flipping is a two-handed technique, unlike other conventional fishing methods. One hand works the rod, while the other simultaneously manipulates the line. The two hands work at a rhythm that sends the bait across the top of the water to quietly enter the target area. For explanation purposes, our fisherman in this demonstration is right-handed. So he works the rod with his right hand and the line is in his left.

The basic steps involved in flipping:

Begin by holding the rod tip up and letting out about 7 feet of line. With the left hand, pull an arm's length of line from the reel (which is in free-spool). To put the lure in motion, lower the rod tip slightly and then raise it upward, which creates a pendulum motion with the lure.

The lure will swing out slightly and then return toward you. As it nears you, lower the rod tip a second time, which will propel the forward with increasing momentum. At this point, the rod tip is held low and pointed at the target.

As the lure begins to move forward, begin feeding the line through the guides with the left hand. The left hand should reach the reel about the same time that the bait enters the water. At that point, feed a little more line out to ensure that the lure falls vertically into the cover and is not pulled away accidentally.

From that point, many fishermen differ in how they work the bait. Some keep a length of line in their left hand and work the lure by manipulating the line. But this can cause some anglers to lose fish on the hook-set, which then must be done with both hands — a la fly fishing. Most of the tournament pros work the lure with their rod tip and both hands stay on the rod for optimum hook-setting power.

Flipping isn't overly complicated and can be mastered indoors on a cold winter's day. It just takes a little practice to develop a rhythm.

The most common mistake that fishermen make while flipping is not working to penetrate the most difficult parts of cover or a piece of structure, according to Bacon. Many are content to flip a worm or jig beside a fallen tree, for example, rather than working it through the tangled intersections of limbs and branches. Or they will flip into a small opening in a floating mat of surface vegetation, rather than finessing the bait through the thickest portions of the weeds.

And those are places where bass, particularly the largest of the species, often hide.

"Flipping is an art," adds Jimmy Rogers. "With enough experience and practice, you begin developing little tricks that make flipping even more deadly. For example, I don't always drop a worm in a spot and allow it to go zooming to the bottom. I will often throw it over a blade of grass or cattail or piece of brush and just slowly feed line out with my left hand. That lets the bait to drop at a rate of speed that I can control. And I can jig it up and down without moving it away from that spot. That's often a lot more effective than just dunking the worm and letting it go."

Missouri's Denny Brauer, a highly successful touring pro and one of the modern-day masters of flipping, emphasizes the need to be as quiet as possible with this close-quarters form of fishing. That includes using a quiet trolling motor (which runs only when necessary) and not talking loudly.

"You should look at flipping for big bass like you would trophy whitetail deer hunting," says Brauer, the 1987 B.A.S.S. Angler of the Year. "You just don't get close to a great, great big buck by stumbling through the woods. And it's the same with flipping for bass. It's almost a game of trying to slip up on them. The quieter you can be moving up to that cover to flip it, the better the results are going to be."

The advent of flipping first brought the importance of boat control and proper positioning to the forefront for most tournament fishermen, according to four-time world champion Rick Clunn of Montgomery, Texas. Here was a technique where you were practically on top of the fish and any mistake with boat control was greatly magnified.

Boat positioning is the most crucial aspect of flipping, according to Basil Bacon. And in determining the proper way to approach a piece of cover or structure, the two most important considerations are the direction of the wind and sun.

"Obviously, it is impossible to flip with the wind at your back," Bacon explains. "You ease up to a log in front of you, make a flip to it and before you even complete that flip, the wind will have pushed the boat right on top of the cover. So you have to move the boat into the wind, regardless of how slight it is.

"The sun works to your advantage because you know it will position the fish on the shady side of that log. But you have to take the direction of the sun into consideration as you approach it. As you move up to the log facing the sun, the fish will often be able to see you moving in. If you put the sun at your back, he will not be able to see you, but you have to be careful ot to get your shadow too close to that section of the log. You have to play the angles just right."

Bacon was one of the first fishermen to realize the importance of boat positioning with flipping and, as a result, equipped his boat to enhance his ability to control it. Several years ago, Bacon built the first flipping deck on his Ranger (many boat manufacturers now offer flipping platforms) by constructing a 14-inch raised deck that attached to the nose of his boat.

To keep his hands free for flipping, Bacon uses a hand-operated trolling motor, which he steers with his leg. Two switches are mounted in the makeshift deck — an on-and-off button and a switch to change from 12 to 24 volts — and Bacon rarely uses his hands to position the boat. He believes that foot-operated trolling motors create problems for anglers while flipping because they spend much of the day fishing on one foot and running the trolling motor with the other.

Flipping is a big-bass technique as Guido Hibdon demonstrates.

"Because you are fishing so close to the fish, it is important to leave your trolling motor on the lowest speed possible and leave it on constantly," Bacon adds. "Don't turn it off and on anymore than you have to. That spooks the fish more than anything."

There are times when flipping can work against the angler, though. This is particularly true when the water is clear or the bass are especially spooky. It was for these times that innovative fishermen developed an extension of the flipping technique known as pitching.

Pitching is, primarily, a form of long-range flipping. It provides the angler with the attributes of flipping (accuracy and a quiet lure presentation) along with greater casting distance.

Learning to pitch is relatively simple. It begins like conventional flipping with the reel in free-spool and a rod's length of line hanging free. The fishermen then grasps the lure in his free hand and holds it even with the reel. He then drops the rod tip toward the water and quickly snaps it upward, while simultaneously releasing the lure. The lure swings forward, traveling along the surface of the water toward the target. As the lure begins pulling line from the reel, it is important to begin lowering the rod to control its height above the water. As it reaches its target, the fisherman simply stops the spool with his thumb.

"So many people have turned to pitching and sometimes it is necessary to pitch because the fish are so spooky that you can't move up on them," Bacon contends. "But flipping has some real advantages over pitching that you need to be use whenever possible, particularly when dealing with heavy cover.

"If you pitch to a spot 30 feet away and let the bait fall into a bush, the odds of you setting the hook and getting a big fish out of there aren't very good. That is because you have to get that fish up and over the structure. But if you are flipping, the boat is closer and you only have about 10 feet of line out, so line-stretch is not a factor. The odds are in your favor because you are in a position to pull him straight up and out of the cover."

The best anglers are able to distinguish the situations that allow flipping or demand pitching, Brauer says.

Flipping remains today the most consistent producer on the top tournament trails, but it is just as viable for the weekend angler. It is a technique well worth learning and perfecting.

Chapter 26

Denny Brauer's
Big-Bass Bonus

The creature Denny Brauer specializes in stalking is different.

But then, so is Brauer.

Brauer, a professional bass angler by trade, is a big-fish fisherman, perhaps the best in America. There certainly were no better big-bass catchers during the 1986-87 Bass Anglers Sportsman Society tournament season when the Missouri pro broke into the most elite club in all of sports by becoming one of only nine men to win the Angler of the Year title.

PROfile

In the professional ranks where the latest trend revolves around light line and finesse (some call them "sissy") baits, Brauer stands out. Although he will occasionally turn to spinning tackle and small lures out of absolute necessity, Brauer's entire gameplan is built around big bass. Tournament trophies. The kind of bass the weekend angler dreams of.

Big-bass expert Denny Brauer is a five-time B.A.S.S. winner, past Angler of the Year and eight-time Classic qualifier.

And, more often than not, Brauer's big-bass tactics payoff. In addition to his Angler of the Year crown, Brauer has won five stops on the B.A.S.S. trail and his average winning weight was slightly more than 8 pounds ahead of the field — an impressive difference in a league where ounces often separate the champion from the also-ran. (To better understand the significance of that, consider that on the 1986-87 B.A.S.S. circuit, the average winning margin — excluding Brauer's 1987 win — was 3 pounds, 3.5 ounces).

Brauer won three B.A.S.S. tournaments by a whopping 9 pounds or more. "I consider myself a big-bass fisherman," he says, "because of a lot of the baits and techniques I prefer to use are tailored toward catching big fish.

"I really think I relate to big fish better than I do to little fish. I get more fired up and it's a lot more thrilling to go fish for that kind of fish. Schooling fish are fun if that's all that is available. But if I'm on a lake that has a reputation for holding good numbers of big fish, I just cannot slow down or speed up or do whatever it is to catch those limits of little fish. I'm going to spend all of my time trying to find those big fish and win the tournament. That's just my style of fishing.

"And the weekend angler would rather fish for big fish, too."

As a result of Brauer's zeal for catching trophy bass, he has developed a tournament-oriented system for locating and landing big bass that fishermen of all skill levels can learn from.

Big bass, Brauer believes, act differently from their smaller counterparts.

"Big bass are more predictable, at least to me," he explains. "There are so many variables to consider in trying to locate big bass, including water color, time of year, water depth and type of cover, but, usually, you can pretty much predict where the bigger fish are going to be, while little fish have a tendency to wander more. I believe big bass are a little more territorial."

Brauer's No. 1 rule for locating big bass states that heavy cover is the starting point. From that point, he concentrates on heavy-cover areas that have a combination of cover types (for example — two types of aquatic vegetation or a log laying in a grassbed). His next two steps involve water clarity and depth. Slightly off-colored water is usually more likely to be the liquid medium in which a big bass will stay. And any change in the depth (caused by an irregular feature in the bottom contour) is a prime location.

In several tournaments that Brauer has won, his winning spots met all of the above criteria for harboring big bass.

Big-name pros like Denny Brauer and the average weekend angler share a common problem — fishing pressure. Just like Brauer may have to share the best spots on the lake with 250 of the top tournament pros in America, the average fishermen on large, heavily-pressured southern reservoirs face competition each weekend for the better places.

Brauer's secret to eliminating his competition is one that will work for the weekend angler willing to put in the necessary effort.

"Perhaps the biggest key to locating big bass is looking for obscure places that aren't obvious to the average fisherman," Brauer says. "Those big fish didn't get to be big by being stupid. They're a little more cautious.

"They will often utilize places that the average person is not going to fish. That usually means areas that are hard to get to and spots that aren't obvious. I look at what types of areas that everybody is passing up. Those types of areas often hold a school of fish that have been able to reach above-average size

Denny Brauer has an almost magical ability to bring big bass and a jig-and-pig together on a regular basis.

because they haven't been hit on as much. And a lot of our lakes get a lot of fishing pressure, today.

"Still, some of the big lakes have a virgin population of big fish that has gone, largely, untouched. So it becomes a matter of being able to key in on them and figure out where they're going to be during this particular time of the year. You're not going to find these populations of big bass on the perfect point on Lake X, the chalkboard perfect example, because it looks perfect to every other fisherman, too. So, I don't bother to stop and fish that place because I know half the people on the lake that day are going to fish it. But you can bet that I will check this little stretch of bank that looks so ugly that it should not hold a school of fish. I spend a lot of my practice time exploring unlikely-looking places."

Brauer emphasizes that these obscure, not obvious places vary greatly. Some can be found visually, while others require some skill with electronics.

Three of Brauer's recent tournament victories prove his contention that big bass often hold in areas that are difficult to get to and somewhat obscure.

Brauer's prowess with a jig produced an impressive 72 pounds en route to winning the 1990 B.A.S.S. Tennessee Pro-Am. His jig proved to be deadly on both spawning bass and post-spawners holding in dingy-water buck bushes, willow trees and flooded grass along a 3-mile mid-lake section of Chicka-mauga. Fishing water that ranged from 6 inches to 9 feet in depth, Brauer concentrated his efforts in protected areas that had an abundance of cover at a variety of depths. The shallowest cover held the big spawning females, while the deeper cover served as a resting point for post-spawners.

A key to winning the $91,000 top prize in the 1987 Bassmaster Super-Invitational and securing his first Angler of the Year title was Brauer's deter-mination to fish an area on Lake Barkley that seemed inaccessible. Brauer nursed his 17-foot Ranger across a shallow mud flat — which included plowing the bottom for several yards — to reach an isolated area filled with stumps, buck bushes, logs and waterfowl nesting boxes. That spot produced most of his 61 pounds, 12 ounces, of bass.

In winning the 1985 Chattanooga Invitational Tournament on Chicka-mauga Lake , Brauer found a textbook combination of cover, structure and water depth. But the area was anything but obvious. Brauer had located an area where a ridge along the channel of the Tennessee River joined the Hiwassee River. The area, which was lined with vegetation and scattered stumps, featured a breakline where the water dropped from 5 to 30 feet.

In this case, locating the fish wasn't the problem. Brauer's vast experience and his extra-sensory ability to read lake maps told him this was a prime spot and his depth finder confirmed it. But the fish were suspended out in the main river channel and "seemed impossible to catch," he says.

On the final day of the tournament, Brauer's most productive area had run dry and he noted that the wind had switched and was now blowing in the right direction to bring those bass up onto that textbook-perfect ridge. In the last couple of hours of the tournament, Brauer cranked up three bass that weighed 16 pounds, 9 ounces, off of that ridge.

"That spot was good, but the weather conditions are what made that spot so productive," Brauer explains. "The weather made those fish catchable. The fish were suspending under schools of baitfish and the change in wind direction blew the baitfish up onto that ridge, which brought the bass into a more catchable position and a mood to feed."

Brauer's winning spot in the 1986 B.A.S.S. stop on Sam Rayburn Reservoir in Texas featured the same type of bushes most of the tournament field was concentrating on. But Brauer had located a spot where some of the bushes were adjacent to deeper water and when a cold front came through, it was an area where a sizeable population of bass re-located.

"One of the real keys to winning the Chickamauga tournament and the '86 Rayburn tournament was map study," Brauer claims. "I don't think people spend enough time studying maps to start with. It's something we all get a little lax on."

Utilizing his years of experience both as a guide in Missouri and as a highly-successful tournament pro throughout the country, Brauer offers these seasonal starting points for locating big bass:

WINTER: "The main thing is hunting for baitfish. The fish are naturally going to be in deeper areas. The bass have moved to deeper depths and you are going to find them along rock bluffs and creek channels. To pinpoint them even more, you can chart big swarms of baitfish and the bass will always be nearby.

"To me, winter starts in late November when the fish start their transition to deeper water. That can be a real tough time to catch fish. But by mid-December, it starts to pick back up. The fish will be schooling real tight and this is the time for good jigging-spoon or grub fishing."

SPRING: "Spring begins at different times in different states. In Texas, spring starts in February, but here in Missouri, it's April. Water temperature dictates the beginning of spring and triggers the migration of bass to shallower water. When the water temperature reaches 47 or 48 degrees, the bass start moving up and a good migration begins. You'll be able to locate them next to deeper breaklines.

"This is the best time of year for catching big bass — from the time they start to move shallow through their spawning mode. The reason, I believe, is that there are more big bass shallow and therefore more susceptible to being caught. Plus, they haven't been exposed to much fishing pressure. Not many people will fish during the coldest part of the winter, so they aren't bothered much. I've found that these bass are easier to catch after a few months of inactivity."

SUMMER: "You'll find fish in the same places as in the winter in the clearer lakes. They will be in deeper water. But in lakes with off-colored water, I have the most success by staying shallow and fishing heavy, heavy cover during the summer."

FALL: "The fish will be moving shallower, up onto creek channels from their summertime holes. A lot of big fish can be found on the flats and in the backs of creeks. And the bigger bass will usually be found on the edges of those areas during this time of year. You need to look for shad concentrations to better pinpoint the big bass."

Denny Brauer's Big-Bass Primer. Armed with some of his knowledge, locating and catching big bass doesn't seem such a mystery.

Brauer's Best Big-Bass Bait

Although his fishing prowess with a plastic worm, spinnerbait and crankbait has contributed to national tournament victories, Denny Brauer is almost fanatical when it comes to the big-bass allure of the jig-and-pork combination.

"Without a doubt, I think it's the best big-bass lure there is," says the Camdenton, Mo., pro. "It's a bait that I have a lot of confidence in.

"It is a compact bait that you can get into places that are hard to penetrate with other lures. I can put a jig-and-frog into places where you cannot put a plastic worm. And another big advantage of a jig-and-frog is that it allows you to do so many things with its speed of fall, which is important to adjust according to the water temperature."

Most bass pros believe that the jig-and-pro combination resembles the bulky shape of a crawfish, which is a highly-desirable food source for bass. Brauer believes that the pressure waves produced from the water displacement of the bait as it falls attracts the attention of big bass more than other types of lures.

Brauer selects jig size in accordance with the water temperature. When the water is warm enough to indicate that the metabolism of the fish will be active, he uses a 5/8-ounce jig with a No. 11 pork chunk that falls quickly. For cold-water situations when the bass are less active, his choice is a 1/4- or 3/8-ounce jig and a big piece of pork, which has enough buoyancy to slow its fall.

"Don't be afraid to experiment and adjust the jig size," he advises. "During the course of a tournament, if the water warms up 5 degrees, you might be catching them on a 1/4-ounce jig and big pork frog that falls real slow at the beginning of the week. But as the water warms up, in order to continue to get as many strikes, you may have to switch to a bigger jig that drops fast."

Color isn't a particularly important consideration, though. Brauer uses a black-and-blue combination in clear water and black-and-chartreuse in off-colored water. "Most of the time, I don't think color is the key," he says. "I think jig size and speed of the fall are a lot more important."

Because the rubber-skirted jig and impaled pork chunk is such a productive big-bass combination, Brauer fishes it on a flipping stick with heavy line. Some heavy-cover situation demands 25- to 30-pound test line. "Too many people try to get by with the lightest line," he says.

Chapter 27

In Pursuit of Trophy Smallmouths

Mention the name Bill Dance and the American fishing public thinks "television."

That is understandable. After all, the personable Tennessee sportsman has been educating anglers for more than 15 years through his Bill Dance Outdoors series, which ranks among the most successful outdoors shows of all time.

Few fishermen realize what an outstanding tournament competitor Bill Dance was before retiring in 1980 to pursue his true love — television and educating fellow anglers.

PROfile

One of the pioneers of the fledgling sport, Dance is one of only three anglers to ever win the coveted Bass Anglers Sportsman Society Angler of the Year title twice, qualified for the prestigious BASS Masters Classic on eight consecutive occasions and won seven B.A.S.S. tournaments.

After retiring from tournaments, Dance poured the same determination and effort into his television production. In an age when television fishing shows are plagued by tanked bass and artificial action,

Legendary Bill Dance is best known for his television show, but he is a two-time B.A.S.S. Angler of the Year as well.

Dance displays his ability to locate and catch fish on a consistent basis in lakes, reservoirs and rivers across the country.

Without the restraints of a tournament schedule, Dance now spends as much time as possible pursuing his favorite sport — stalking giant smallmouths. With or without a television camera over his shoulder, Dance can regularly be found probing what he considers the best trophy smallmouth lair in the country — Pickwick Reservoir on the Alabama, Mississippi and Tennessee borders.

As anyone who has ever experienced the sheer fury of a big smallmouth will attest, Dance is obsessed with 5-pound-plus bronzebacks. And, as a result, he has developed a system that produces huge smallmouths on a consistent basis.

"There is nothing like a big smallmouth," Dance says. "And I have been fortunate to catch some magnificent smallmouths. But it certainly isn't an easy task.

"In all my years of fishing for these special fish, I've only boated three in excess of 8 pounds and a dozen or so over 7 pounds. I can also brag that I had one fish on that weighed over 10 pounds, but that's a story in itself. I honestly believe that if I had to catch a 7-plus pound bass, I could do it, but it would require lots of work and time.

"There are just so many factors involved — the lake, location, depth, water temperature, lure presentation, time of day and, most importantly, the time of year."

Allow Bill Dance to guide you to the smallmouth bass of a lifetime.

The Ideal Lake: In choosing a lake that is likely to produce a trophy bronzeback, Dance recommends selecting a body of water that has excellent water quality and a tremendous forage base. Your chances are best with one of the more renowned smallmouth lakes in the South where the growing season is considerably longer than their northern counterparts.

The Ideal Location: Dance concentrates on points, slopes and ledges that have irregular features and are adjacent to deeper water. The bottom composition should be hard with sand, gravel, black shale rock or red mud mixed in.

The Ideal Depth: It depends on the lake, reservoir or river, Dance says. The ideal depth also depends on whether it is a lowland, midland or highland body of water.

The Ideal Lure: This is dictated by the depth and clarity of the water, as well as the time of year.

The Ideal Presentation: This depends on the lure, water temperature and season.

The Ideal Conditions: For shallow smallmouths, overcast conditions from an approaching front with a falling barometric pressure is best. With deeper fish, Dance prefers an overcast day with stable barometric pressure and a calm or light chop on the water.

The Ideal Time of Year: Dance targets mid-November through mid-April as prime time for catching a bragging-sized bronzeback when the water temperature is below 70 degrees.

"During that period, there is normally a period of two to three weeks when you stand a greater chance of catching a trophy smallmouth," Dance adds. "I think this has a lot to do with falling temperatures and forage movement. During this time, an angler must set his mind to fishing many, many hours and getting out on good places and beating the thunder out of them.

Light line and a quiet approach produced this nice smallmouth.

"It's extremely important to know the terrain you are fishing and being at the right place at the right time. What kills your soul is knowing there are so few days when you can be there at the right time."

The key to scoring big during this time of year, Dance claims, is locating the "setting up house-keeping banks" that smallmouths use for spawning. These banks have small chunks of rocks, pea gravel or black shale rock intermingled with either red or tan clay. Such cover attracts the smallmouth's favorite delicacy — crawfish.

Water temperature and moon phase have a major influence during this time of year. Normally, a major migration occurs on a new moon phase and is followed later on a full moon.

"I've taken good fish shallow in 58- to 60-degree water," Dance explains. "But I have seen the water in these areas warm 6 to 10 degrees in less than a week, especially when the nights are above 45 degrees for several nights. Several days of warm rains will also raise the water temperature drastically.

"Just keep in mind that once the water temperature drops into the low 60s and the moon is in its proper phase, the smallmouths are ready to spawn."

When it comes to enticing trophy bronzebacks, Dance is a big believer in big lures. It is his form of matching the hatch.

"There are some very good reasons why bigger baits attract big smallmouths," he continues. "Bigger baits create a bigger image. There's more room for contact and less room for error.

"And I think big fish are very selective in their feeding. They don't want to exert more energy than necessary to eat. They're not going to do the hundred-yard dash after a hundred 1-inch threadfin shad when they can eat one big shad and fill up. I've been on schools of fish when a 10-inch worm was a noticeable preference over a 6-inch worm."

By large baits, Dance means 1/2- to 1-ounce spinnerbaits, 3/4-ounce jigs and 10-inch-plus plastic worms. This is obviously not what most anglers consider normal fare for catching a bass named for the size of its mouth.

Although some fishermen may not realize it, smallmouth bass prefer slow-moving lures most of the time, according to Dance's experience. He believes that big smallmouths conserve their energy as much as possible, gauging the amount of effort it will take to catch a certain prey against the reward (the nourishment) it will result in. A large, slow-moving lure seems to provide an easy, yet full meal.

Locating trophy-class bronzebacks varies considerably depending on the type of lake or reservoir. But, generally, Dance catches more big fish on slopes than sharp drop-offs. Some of his most impressive catches have occurred a sloping shoreline or secondary bank or point that has a change in the bottom composition — where clay turns into chunk rock or a gravel line and sandy stretch converge. These transitional zones are where the trophy members of the species seem to congregate.

"Smallmouths and running water go together," Dance says in discussing bass location. "However, as great a fishery as moving water is, it's not as good an environment for a monster smallmouth as a reservoir would be."

Dance outlines his approach to the different types of smallmouth waters:

LOWLAND LAKES AND RESERVOIRS

On lowland lakes, the smallmouths relate to shallow structure and the majority are caught in depths of 15 feet or less. These waters are extremely fertile and productive for growing smallies into impressive sizes. Dance pinpoints shell bars and sloping hard-bottom ledges that are lined with stumps or brush.

"Wheeler, Wilson, Pickwick and Kentucky Lake are four good examples of this," he says. "Three of these TVA waterways have always been known as brown bass hotspots, but the one that has really come on strong in the past few years is Kentucky Lake.

Smallmouth were native to this region of the Tennessee River prior to the creation of Kentucky Lake. After the Kentucky Lake dam was constructed, the rich riverside bottom land was flooded and the smallmouths disappeared from most of the new lake. I believe one of the key reasons for their absence was that the new lake lacked good holding areas like rocky points and gravel bars and ledges, which these fish select and use. Today things have changed. The smallmouths are back and there are some good-sized ones, too. That's because Kentucky Lake has aged. The points, bars, flats and ledges have gradually lost their earthen cover, exposing the underlying bedrock and creating ideal smallmouth habitat."

Dance's Tips For a Trophy Smallmouth

√ Be very selective in the lakes you choose.

√ Pick key areas and work them well.

√ Be particular about your equipment, lures, colors, rod, reel and line.

√ Check your hooks for sharpness and your line for fray.

√ If you're catching small fish, fish deeper; big smallmouths stay deeper than small ones.

√ Repeat key locations.

√ Set your fishing times around prime times, seasons and moon phases.

√ Be motivated, have confidence and be patient.

√ Approach each area quietly and from deep waters.

√ Keep records of the lake, location, time, depth, lake elevation, lure color, presentation, moon

MIDLAND LAKES AND RESERVOIRS

On midland lakes like Tims Ford, Woods, Percy Priest and Watt's Bar reservoirs, the larger smallmouth bass typically select and use both the shallow and deeper structure. But the most productive structure will be found at a depth of between 15 and 25 feet.

Dance emphasizes stratification on these lakes is a consideration when there is no current present. So pinpointing a pH breakline or thermocline can be important.

HIGHLAND LAKES AND RESERVOIRS

In highland lakes like Cumberland, Dale Hollow, Norris and Smith Mountain, the trophy bronzebacks seldom stray from deep water, according to Dance, who says that the fish even spawn in 10 to 15 feet of water.

The most productive depth on lakes of this type is 25 to 40 feet.

Dance is a big fan of the highland reservoirs along the Tennessee River, particularly Pickwick, where many smallmouth experts believe the next world record is swimming.

"If I wanted to catch a trophy smallmouth, I would go to the Tennessee River, which has excellent water quality and is located in the southernmost range of the species," he says. "That is also the northern boundary of the threadfin shad. The type of bottom composition, the water quality and the predator-prey relationship is well in balance.

"There are gigantic smallmouths that thrive in these waters."

When listing the reasons why most trophy smallmouths are lost, Dance mentions improper tackle, incorrect drag settings, line that is too light, inexperience, over-excitement and overpowering the fish during the fight.

"Hooking a big smallmouth is hard enough to do, but that's only half of the battle," he explains. "Just because you can get him on doesn't mean you'll get your thumb over his bottom lip. Most folks who hang a fish like this have never been exposed to such an experience and don't realize what's really involved. These fish are so strong — they pull like a late freight train. The pressure they apply is really hard to believe and their will to live and never-give-up determination is something to see."

Dance experienced that first-hand several years ago when a huge (he estimated it to be over 10 pounds) Pickwick bronzeback put up a valiant battle that required counterpunch after counterpunch. Finally, Dance worked the magnificient fish to the side of the boat and was mapping out a strategy for landing it when his line suddenly went slack. The topwater plug, its two treble hooks solidly embedded moments before, had somehow released its grip on the frantic smallmouth.

Dance returned to the same spot for several months, hoping for a rematch. It never occurred.

"There's just nothing like big old smallmouth," Dance says, grinning. "Nothing like 'em."

Chapter 28

The Light-Line Trend

Professional bass fishing has endured its macho era.

The '70s and early '80s was the era of brute force where telephone-like flipping sticks and winching monster bass out of nightmarish cover was standard operating procedure.

But times, as they do, have changed.

PROfile

While flipping sticks and heavy cover are still a part of today's tournament fishing scene, the days of the one-dimensional pro are over. And more than ever, the nation's top tournament pros have discovered the value of a new game, a totally different type of fishing from the days of wind and grind.

Today's most successful pros have learned that their heavy-handed ways of old are not the answer to every situation. More and more have discovered the value of the finesse game, where light line and a skillful touch can be the ticket to qualifying for the prestigious BASS Masters Classic.

Californian Rich Tauber is a past U.S. Open champion and BASS Masters Classic qualifier.

The trend toward light line, smaller lures and scaled down tackle has been especially evident in the last two years or so. Suddenly, it seemed that the very men who had earned their reputation in past B.A.S.S. wars had traded in their cannons for water pistols. But they were wise enough to know that they had to conform to continue to conquer.

The transition to light-line finesse fishing has been the biggest trend on the Bassmaster Tournament Trail during the past few years. And the top pros are a trendy bunch. It isn't a fad if it produces fish on a regular basis, in their eyes.

It is largely because of this trend that the last two Classics have been dotted with new faces and fresh names. And most of those first-time Classic qualifiers quickly credited their ability to catch limits of bass — the forte of light-line bassin' — with enabling them to secure a spot in competitive fishing's biggest event.

It is largely because of the new trend toward light-tackle angling that the poundage it has taken to qualify for the last few Classics has soared. Quite simply, finesse fishing produces the numbers of fish that make it more profitable to seek limits instead of big bass.

"Light-line fishing is the thing of the future," says Arizona's Greg Hines, one of several western anglers who helped ignite the light-tackle trend on the predominantly-eastern Bassmaster circuit. "And I don't mean just as far as tournaments are concerned.

"As the fishing pressure gets heavier and the fish get fished harder on public lakes and reservoirs, light line and smaller baits will continue to produce more and more fish."

"There's a definite trend toward gearing down for the '80s, adds Californian Rich Tauber, one of the most successful of all western pros after winning the U.S. Open and qualifying for the 1986 Classic. "The pros throughout the country are starting to realize that the future lies in the light finesse stuff.

"It's the newest trend in fishing, particularly in the East. I think the key to being successful on a consistent basis in the next 10 years will be light tackle, small baits and gearing down your whole attack."

This trend toward finesse fishing is the most prevalent example of the western influence on the nation's top tournament circuit. There seems to be plenty of reasons to dislike California, but the ingenuity of its fishermen (and those of other western states) has to be appreciated, when you consider that both the heavy-handed art of flipping and the soft-touch tactics of light-lining originated there.

The light-tackle finesse techniques were devised for fishing the deep-clear lakes and reservoirs of the West that are often practically void of cover. In a region where a shady crack in a canyon wall may provide the only inviting place for a bass to hide, small baits like Bobby Garland's Fat Gitzit and 4-inch plastic worms have become the most productive of all weapons.

It takes light line (4- to 8-pound test), light-weight spinning tackle and a sensitive touch to fish these tiny lures properly, which is a major reason why most eastern anglers were slow to make the transition. But the better fishermen have taken the time to learn this radically-different approach to bass fishing.

"We've been fishing this style for a long, long time, but it's only been in the last two years or so that fishermen in the eastern part of the country have started to apply these techniques," says Hines, another former U.S. Open champion. "And you'll see the popularity of light-line fishing grow more and more in the next few years. Especially on the clear-water lakes, where light line will simply catch more fish."

Once a western tool, tubejigs like the Fat Gitzit have become standard tackle for anglers in all parts of the country.

The awakening of eastern bass anglers to the productivity of light line and finesse lures can be attributed, largely, to one Guido Hibdon, a veteran Missouri pro, who was one of the first to prove the power of wielding a small stick in this region of the country. After fishing with Gitzit inventor Bobby Garland in a western tournament, Hibdon became enchanted with the tiny, hollow-bodied jig with an exposed hook and had the foresight to see some applications for it east of the Mississippi.

Hibdon brought the bait East and promptly finished fourth in the 1985 Super B.A.S.S. Tournament on Florida's St. Johns River. A few weeks later, he won a national tournament in Georgia with an amazing 51 pounds of fish in just two days of fishing.

All on the Gitzit. And his competitors took note.

Orlando Wilson was one of the few easterners who was not caught by surprise by the tournament trend to light-line fishing.

The Woodstock, Ga., pro and host of a long-running nationally-syndicated television show, had long known the value of fishing light fishing Lake Lanier, a man-made reservoir in the foothills of the western Georgia mountains that has many of the same characteristics of the western reservoirs — notably, deep, clear water and little cover.

"The trend toward light line has been much more noticeable on the tournament trail in the last couple of years than any time before," Wilson says. "The pros are no dummies and they will eventually come around to any technique that produces fish on a consistent basis.

"I think people are starting to realize that you don't need 20- and 25-pound test under 90-percent of normal fishing conditions. They're also starting to realize that you'll get more strikes with light line than you can with heavy line. That's been proven time and time again.

"I think I'm living proof of that. I attribute a lot of what success I've had in fishing to my ability to fish light line and the confidence I have in that style of fishing."

Much like the dilemma that the average angler faces during the weekend on many heavily-pressured public reservoirs, the tournament pro not only competes with the bass — he competes for that bass with other competitors. This is when light-line fishing pays its biggest premium.

Finesse fishing and small baits are most valuable when faced with heavily-pressured bass, according to those who know.

"In national tournaments these days, it can become an absolute circus around one particular point or a certain grassbed that has been holding fish," Tauber explains. "In that situation, you have to do something a little bit different to get strikes. That's when light line and the smallest lures really stand out.

"I think the weekend angler should understand the value of this type of fishing far more than a tournament fisherman. He faces as much pressure and competition for fish as the tournament anglers do in some of the southern reservoirs. The way to best combat pressure and competition is to gear down. Use light tackle and they can better compete on those weekends and catch more fish."

Few men understand the finesse game as well as Tauber, who at 33 is one of the sport's rising young stars.

He was among the first to bring his favorite finesse tools to the East and try them in tournaments, which was unheard of. His favorite finesse lures are the 1/16- and 1/8th-ounce Gitzit and two styles of small plastic worms. The "shaking" or "doodling" worm is a 4-inch straight-tail worm that has almost little action. The angler provides the action with his rod tip by lightly shaking the worm as it falls or hopping it along the lake bottom. The Dart-head worm is a 4-inch curl-tail worm impaled on a bullet-shaped jig head (the hook is exposed). The best way to fish the Dart-head rig is to slowly slide it down banks, canyon walls, rocks and points.

Rich Tauber knows little baits and light line will catch giant bass.

One of the best ways to fish the Gitzit and Dart-head worm is to slowly drift it along the bottom in areas of the lake where the aging process has removed all cover. The biggest drawback to fishing these light-line finesse baits is they are ineffective and often aggravating in most heavy-cover situations because of the exposed hook.

"But in most fishing situations, it is no handicap to fish light line," Orlando Wilson claims. "People realize that light line gets more strikes, but I don't think people fully realize that small baits can actually translate into more successful hook-ups as well.

"With a small worm, you're using a small hook, which means using a light diameter of wire that is easier to penetrate a fish's jaw. You can stick a 1-0 hook in a fish's mouth fairly easily, but the diameter of the steel in a 5-0 hook is so big that it is much tougher to make it penetrate. That's a real plus that light-line fishing provides."

Another disadvantage with these small lures is that they are most productive in clear water. Although the Gitzit has produced in some off-colored water situations along the tournament trail, the finesse baits are usually not the best choice when fishing dingy water.

One pro who has resisted the light-line trend is four-time Classic champion Rick Clunn, who coined the phrase "California sissy baits" in ridicule of the finesse lures.

"I will admit that these baits have paved the way to the Classic for quite a few people," Clunn says, "but almost no tournaments have been won on these baits. They just don't usually produce tournament-winning fish.

"I don't like to fish these baits, so I have avoided them. This may be hurting my performance because every bait and every technique has a place in a fisherman's arsenal. But I just don't like to fish the sissy baits."

Greg Hines understands the reluctance of Clunn and others to make the light-line transition. "This style of fishing is slow and it's conducive to staying in one area catching a lot of little fish," he explains. "It is a technique that will enable you to place in a tournament, but there usually seems to always be a better way to catch bigger fish, which you need to win tournaments.

"But light-line provides consistency and that's what it takes to make the Classic."

Tournament fishing (and weekend angling, to some degree) demands that bass enthusiasts be versatile and learn all styles and techniques. While light-line, finesse fishing isn't the answer to every fishing situation, it is definitely worth the effort to learn.

"Fishing is really a game now where you've got to learn to play with all of the clubs," Rich Tauber says. "These days, you can't just say `I'm a jig man.' `I'm a topwater man.' `I'm a flipper.' If you are, you're a loser."

Chapter 29

Desperation Tactics of the Pros

It is the final afternoon of the Texas B.AS.S Invitational and Sam Rayburn Reservoir has begun to rock and roll like only Big Sam can.

The wind is howling now, sending many of America's best bass pros scurrying for cover — or at least a sheltered place to fish. But Roland Martin has more on his mind than just the weather.

It is now crunch time for the nine-time B.A.S.S. Angler of the Year and 16-time tournament winner. Time is short before he must leave the Black Forest section of Rayburn and run back to the weigh-in site. Empty-handed.

Martin faces the prospect of being skunked, a fact of life that no angler — pro or amateur alike — embraces. And he knows that without some sort of fisherman's miracle, he has no chance of making a run at his 17th national title. A good opportunity would slip quietly away.

PROfile

Gary Klein, the 1989 B.A.S.S. Angler of the Year and a five--time winner, is one of fishing's brightest stars.

While others may have yielded to the weather and his own bleak personal prospects, Martin concentrated hard on his final precious couple of hours of fishing. And in the last-minute, go-for-the-glory style that carries his name, Martin put a 7-pound, 15-ounce bass in the boat (the largest of the final round). A few minutes later, he boated a 6-pounder and soon two more good keepers found their way to his livewell.

In just 20 minutes, Martin had caught 18 3/4 pounds of bass and made an impressive charge from 35th to second place. It doesn't matter that he fell a little more than a pound short of Rayburn expert David Wharton. What is important here is Martin's perseverance and drive to avoid being branded with the skunk.

In Martin's remarkable performance, the average angler can find reason not to abandon ship on days when a shutout seems inevitable.

"The biggest thing that the weekend angler has to overcome is the mental side of a bad day if he is going to avoid getting skunked," says 10-time BASS Masters Classic qualifier Jerry Rhyne of Denver, N.C. "Usually, if a guy has been out there all day without catching a fish and he calculates that he's only got an hour or so left, he will usually forfeit the last hour and go home.

"That's the wrong attitude. If you're going to take your time to be out there and go fishing, fish all day long. Set your time before you go and fish hard right up until the last minute. In that last hour, you usually have to remind yourself to slow down and concentrate on the job at hand. That last hour is when you start thinking about how hungry you are, how miserable you are. It's too hot or too cold or the wind's blowing too hard. That's when you really have to bear down and keep your composure.

"That's the difference between a good fisherman and an excellent fisherman. Roland has been one of the world's best at this — keeping himself psyched up. A lot of us can psych ourselves up and make ourselves believe that we're going to catch a big string of fish before the day begins. But when it doesn't go as planned, we start to lose that confidence. Roland never gives up until he walks onto the weigh-in stand. That's why he is the best at what he does."

When questioned about their desperation tactics to avoid getting skunked, some of America's best bass pros offered interesting, thoughtful and even conflicting answers and techniques. But all agreed that the mental side of fishing is never more critical than the situation that we've all faced: the sun sitting behind the horizon and you're sitting with an embarrassingly empty livewell.

The travelling pros have a decided advantage over even the better amateurs. That advantage includes a wealth of experience in a variety of fishing situations in all geographic regions of the country. More importantly, that advantage includes a strong mental approach to fishing that enables them to persevere and succeed when others would fold and fail.

"Everybody faces the prospect of being skunked, regardless if he is Ricky Clunn or the average weekend angler," explains Gary Klein, a talented California native who now lives in Irving, Texas. "The reason a Ricky Clunn succeeds when the average Joe doesn't is largely mental. It's all in his ability to maintain a confident attitude and concentrate intensely on what he has to do to catch fish on that day.

"And being skunked or shutout is, in some ways, harder on the average angler than it is a pro. Sure, we make a living by catching fish in tournaments,

Perhaps the most versatile of the top pros, Gary Klein rarely faces a desperate situation on the water.

but that weekend fishing trip or that single day's outing is just as important to the average angler. I'm very fortunate in that my profession gives me the opportunity to fish virtually any time I want to. So if I go fishing and spend a couple of days without catching a fish, before finally finding them, it's no big deal. But the weekend guy is actually fishing just like he's fishing the BASS Masters Classic. He's got one day that month and he has to do well on that day. That's why getting skunked is a little harder for him."

In addition to concentrating harder and attempting to maintain a good attitude, Klein's last-ditch desperation tactics include a little mental trick that may well pay good dividends to the weekend angler in the future.

The nine-time Classic qualifier recommends selecting a lure and style of fishing that you have confidence in and "going back to the basics." In tough fishing situations, Klein pauses to re-gather his thoughts and then proceeds to concentrate on the smallest basics in the style of fishing he has selected for that tournament day.

Predictably, the top pros polled on their desperation, shutout-avoiding tactics aligned themselves with one or two basic schools of thought regarding strategy.

The question that emerges is one of whether it is better to run and cover a great deal of water quickly or to slow down and fish the same area more thoroughly and efficiently. If you quizzed 100 of America's top tournament pros on that question, they would probably form a 50/50 split.

Still, such conflicting ideas of desperation strategy provides good food for thought and a majority of the pros questioned agree that perhaps it would be best if the average angler solved the strategy question by selecting the tactic that best suits his style of fishing.

Orlando Wilson of Woodstock, Ga., faces the painful dilemma of avoiding a shutout both in tournaments and during filmwork for his nationally-syndicated Fishing With Orlando Wilson television show. He quickly aligns himself among the strategists who prefer to run and gun in desperate situations.

"Nobody likes to get skunked, particularly on a tournament day, but we all are faced with it from time-to-time," says Wilson, a three-time Classic qualifier. "If I'm going into the last day of a tournament without having any success, I start with a brand new approach just as if it was the first day of practice.

"I start running and gunning. I fish anything and everything I can see. When it gets to that point, I'm more or less fishing visible cover because you don't have time to look for deep-water cover and structure, unless you are really familiar with the lake. I just see how many places I can fish and cover a lot of water with a bait that is conducive to fishing fast. Sometimes this approach really works."

Wilson also advises fishermen to attempt to glean information from other anglers when the situation gets desperate. By learning how deep the fish are positioned or what type of cover the bass are holding on, you can make some quick and productive adjustments, he says.

Nineteen-eighty-two Classic champion Paul Elias of Laurel, Miss., agrees with Wilson's strategy of saturating large areas of water with a fast-moving lure, but differs when it comes to the water depth and type of structure he fishes.

Typically, Elias ties on a large, deep-diving crankbait, put his trolling motor on "high 24" and works a deeper type of structure such as a ledge or river channel edge.

"In a desperate situation, like when you're just trying to keep from getting skunked, it's my opinion that you have to choose a quick method of fishing just to cut into the law of averages," Elias explains. "The more casts you make, the better shot you have at catching a fish."

Two-time B.A.S.S. Angler of the Year Jimmy Houston of Cookson, Okla., is renowned as a spinnerbait specialist and a proponent of the cast-saturation philosophy that says the more casts you can make and the more water you can cover, the more fish you can catch.

When faced with a desperate situation and the looming specter of a shutout, Houston considers two strategies. First, he considers tailoring his gameplan so that he can spend his remaining fishing time stalking a big bass. "The philosophy behind that is that if you're not going to catch anything, you would rather not catch large ones than not catch small ones," Houston says, smiling.

But more often, Houston takes the exact opposite approach.

"If it is 11 or 12 o'clock and I haven't had a bite, what I will normally do is go to a small spinnerbait, like a 1/4-ounce Strike King Houston model with a single blade," he explains. "I automatically go to a small spinnerbait, because a smaller bait will catch about any fish in a lake. A small bait doesn't eliminate any size of fish and a spinnerbait allows you to cover water quickly.

"Another thing about a small spinnerbait is that you can really work it in heavy cover and you can really finesse it better. So it allows you to make better presentations into the water and it allows you to get into some areas that maybe you couldn't work with a larger bait. It gives you an opportunity to get a little bit tighter to the fish. Usually, when you can't catch fish, they are tighter to the cover. So you have to use baits that get in tight to the cover."

In desperation situations, Houston routinely will run points and fish quickly. He selects points as his main targets because all lakes have this structure, which Houston calls "the most natural structure in any given body of water for a bass to be on."

Veteran Texas pro and former Classic champion Tommy Martin agrees with Houston when it comes to down-sizing lures when times get tough, but the pair are diametrically opposed when it comes to the run-and-gun or stay-all-day debate.

When fishing is especially difficult and few bass are being caught, Martin concentrates on slowing down and fishing each piece of structure or cover as thoroughly as possible. Many anglers "tend to get in too big of a hurry when fishing is tough. I automatically slow down."

In cold-front and other conditions that dictate frustrating fishing days and inevitable shutouts, Martin routinely down-sizes his approach to a 4-inch worm with a 3/16-ounce sinker on 10-pound test line. "When the bigger lures are not working and you're not able to catch any fish, just out of desperation to avoid getting skunked, I go to that rig and fish slowly," Martin says. "And it usually pays off for me."

Jerry Rhyne agrees with Martin's slow-fishing in heavy cover approach.

"To avoid getting skunked, I go flipping," the North Carolina veteran pro says. "I find some of the thickest cover on the lake and I flip a worm or jig in it. Usually, you can connect on a fish doing that.

"Today was a prime example. I was literally skunked late into the day and my partner was beating the socks off of me. I knew of a canal where I thought I could catch a few fish flipping. So to straighten my mind out a little, we ran to that canal after my partner had limited out. I knew my last shot was flipping up a fish in that canal. And I did. I flipped up one fish that saved me from getting skunked.

"I think flipping in heavy cover is the quickest and best way to save a skunk."

Roland Martin is a proponent of Rhyne's flipping philosophy, saying "as a last-ditch stand, my flipping technique is one I can rely on."

But Martin's versatility and willingness to make radical changes in his strategy is a major reason why he has been so successful. So when fishing a lake where flipping isn't much of a consideration, Martin takes an entirely different approach.

In desperate situations on deep, clear lakes, the Clewiston, Fla., pro takes a real departure from the heavy-handed technique of flipping. He arms himself with a 5 1/2-foot spinning rod, 6-pound line and a finesse lure like a Fat Gitzit on a 1/16-ounce jig head. "The slow, slow fall of the Gitzit is enticing, particularly to reluctant fish," Martin says.

The last-ditch desperation tactics of America's best bass pros take on varying perspectives, but share a common theme. Confidence, concentration and a never-say-fail attitude will — more often than not — keep being skunked a problem that only the other guy has to worry about.

Chapter 30

Boating for Bass

You don't hear much about it on the victory stand of major tournaments. It isn't a lure, pattern, technique or piece of tackle.

Yet, many time world-champion Rick Clunn credits it for playing major in all three of his BASS Masters Classic championships. Paul Elias remembers it as a fundamental key to his Classic victory in 1982. Gary Klein cites it as the most crucial aspect of his victory in the 1988 B.A.S.S. Arkansas Invitational on Bull Shoals. Basic Bacon attributes his eight qualifying tickets to the Classic, largely, to it. And Lake Lanier guide and budding young tournament star Doug Youngblood swears it is a major reason he can stay at the front of the competition on his home lake and elsewhere.

Yet not a single headline has ever been written about it in the tournament reports in major fishing magazines.

Boat positioning.

"I think boat positioning is the most overlooked part of fishing there is by fishermen of all skill levels," claims Clunn, America's premier tournament pro with four Classic titles, two U.S. Open championships, nine B.A.S.S. victories, the 1988 B.A.S.S. Angler of the Year title, a Red Man All American Championship, 17 Classic appearances and a million dollars in earnings to his credit. "It is the single aspect of bass fishing that can make or break you, yet even some of the top pros don't put enough emphasis on boat control."

PROfile

Doug Youngblood is a talented guide on Georgia's Lake Lanier and a past BASS Masters Classic qualifier.

On the national tournament trail where the competition is so fierce, it is the more subtle aspects of fishing that usually separate the winners from finishers. And although you don't hear much about it, boat control and positioning is just as crucial as any facet of the sport.

Boat control is the ability (or inability) to approach a piece of cover or structure from the position that best allows you to take full advantage of the situation. It is the ability to position yourself to create the best possible casting angle to both work the cover or structure, as well as present the bait properly to its inhabitants. It also involves the ability to maintain that proper positioning as Mother Nature works against you with unfavorable winds or currents.

Good boat positioning is necessary to properly fish every type of cover or structure, both visible and submerged. It is just as important with fishing a main-river ledge as it is working a weedline; casting to the bank or "doodling" a worm over a deep-water hump; flipping a fallen tree or vertically jigging a brushpile.

The best tournament pros understand that. So do the better guides and non-competitive anglers. It is an overlooked aspect of fishing that is well worth a little extra consideration.

"I can't emphasize enough that a bass boat is a part of your equipment that is as important as a rod, reel or anything else," says Gary Klein, a nine-time Classic qualifier from Texas. "And you aren't getting everything out of your boat if you aren't concentrating on boat positioning.

"There are so many different things that boat positioning does for you. Boat positioning determines how you cast and your lure retrieve, but I think beyond that. Each cast is planned and, at our level, we're thinking several casts in advance. Not only that, but I'm thinking about the fight back to the boat after I've hooked the fish. So you have to try to control the boat so that everything is to your advantage, whether it be deep water or shallow water, light line or heavy line, big fish or small fish."

Klein is one of five of America's top pros who share their secrets and experience on the subject of boat positioning.

Rick Clunn's Book on Boat Positioning

For the vast majority of bass fishermen, boat positioning is a subject relegated to their subsconscious thoughts. All conscious thought on the water is usually reserved for what they consider to be the most crucial aspects of catching bass — casting, retrieving, interpreting electronics and paying close attention to the area they are fishing.

"Because your conscious is occupied, your subconscious is in control of operating the boat," Rick Clunn explains. "That is the way it is with almost all experienced fishermen.

"When you first start getting serious about bass fishing, most people are much more conscious about boat positioning. Through experience they get their subconscious fairly well programmed about what they should be doing with the boat. And although it becomes mostly a subconscious effort after that, you should still allow your conscious thought to double-check your boat positioning from time to time while fishing. That's the biggest mistake — never giving boat control any conscious thought."

Boat positioning while on mental autopilot.

"Boat control determines so much about your success," Clunn continues, "and it's not so much what most people usually think about — spooking the fish.

"What really brought this into focus for me was the technique of flipping. Here was a technique where you brought your boat close to the target, so boat control suddenly became more critical. You had to be more conscious of how you could keep the boat just the perfect distance away, keep it at the perfect speed and keep it at the perfect angle. I gradually translated this into what I was doing even when I wasn't flipping."

Perhaps the most single important aspect of boat positioning is finding the perfect range and maintaining it, according to Clunn. The perfect range means being able to reach the target with an accurate presentation and from the proper casting angle. That is easier than it sounds, however. Frequently, most of us find ourselves too far away to make that pinpoint cast or so close that the next breeze blows the boat over the cover.

Proper boat positioning begins with your boat's equipment, Clunn emphasizes. That includes being comfortable enough with either a foot- or hand-operated trolling motor to use it without giving it any thought. It also includes using a trolling motor with enough power to fight a steady wind or the proper prop for invading jungle-like vegetation.

Above all, there is one main enemy of proper boat positioning — wind.

"Boat control is a very critical part of fishing and it, more than anything, determines the enjoyment of fishing," Clunn says. "When we buy a boat, most of us visualize good-weather fishing. We don't visualize the normal fishing trip. That's when the wind is blowing you around and it blows you in too close. Or it blows you away and you've really lost control of the boat. On those days, boat control is even more important to your enjoyment.

"Good boat control means trying to work with the elements — the wind, the current, the grass — to catch fish. For me, that means not trying to fight the wind, in most cases. That is just a rule of thumb. There are all levels of wind, but I usually will work with the wind and try not to let it bother me mentally. There are certain situations and techniques, though, where you need to go against the wind. But if you get to the point where you stop and your mind says `Wait a minute, trying to fight this much wind is stupid,' listen to your instincts and try something else. Find a better way to approach the situation, even if it means letting the wind blow you through an area and then cranking the big motor and running upwind to make another drift."

Basil Bacon on Boat for Flipping Fish

Veteran Missouri pro Basil Bacon is one of the eastern pioneers in the technique of flipping. After its introduction by western pros in the mid-1970s, Bacon has developed his system of flipping into an artform. It is largely responsible for his eight Classic appearances.

"Boat positioning and control is probably as critical as any aspect of flipping," Bacon says. "I give it so much importance because you are so close to the fish the entire time."

When flipping, Bacon's two most emphasized considerations are the sun and wind, which he tries to use to his advantage.

The sun will usually help a fishermen pinpoint the areas to fish on a piece of flipping cover or structure like a fallen log, tree top, stump or willow tree because bass, generally, prefer the shady spots. The bass, usually, will be not be positioned toward the bright sunlight.

But that sun and shade can work against the angler in this close-quarters approach to fishing if your shadow falls close to the fish, warning it of your presence. Bacon approaches such structure with the sun to his back, but not from an angle to drops his shadow near the bass. With the sun at his back, Bacon can approach the bass (which is facing the opposite direction) without being spotted, being careful to watch the direction of his shadow. If you approach the tree with the sun at your face, the fish will often be able to note your presence, Bacon claims, and will spook.

"There usually is no easy answer to fishing in wind," Bacon explains. "Obviously, you cannot flip with the wind. You just can't do it.

"You start easing up to this log in front of you, make one flip and before you can actually complete that one flip, the wind has pushed your boat right up on that log. So you have to move the boat into the wind, regardless of how slight it is."

Gary Klein on Fishing Submerged Grass

Nowhere is the practice of boat positioning more critical than with fishing a submerged patch of aquatic vegetation that is not visible to the eye.

As exotic visitors like milfoil and hydrilla invade our reservoirs and lakes, creating improved fishing for many, it is forcing many of us to change our tactics to be consistently successful.

One of Gary Klein's favorite fishing situations involved sumberged vegetation with a well-defined edge. Klein treats that edge the same way he approaches fishing other vertical breaks. Again, boat positioning is crucial to following that edge and taking the correct casting angles to achieve the proper lure presentation.

To illustrate Klein's approach, we will use this example: a large section of milfoil sits in 15 feet of water. Its top is 5 feet below the surface, hidden from the human eye. Only the advancements of our electronics allow us to get an accurate picture of its dimensions.

"First of all, most anglers are going to pull up on this grassbed and because they usually have a short attention span, it won't be long before they'll be drifting across the grass," explains Klein,. "At this point, they're lost, basically.

"The top guys run a grassline by constantly reading their electronics and paying close attention to the line and the little subtle details. I'm going to be constantly thinking about the edge and the angle of my cast. The edge of the grass is the key with grass fishing."

Where Klein positions the boat and what casting angles he uses depend, primarily, on the type of lure involved. Every lure dictates a slightly different approach, he says.

"But most of the time, I usually put my boat out slightly off of the edge and make angle casts over the grass, but always involving that edge during my retrieve," Klein continues. "If the fish have been hitting a crankbait that runs 8 feet, I obviously can't get it up on top of the grass, so I parallel the edge of the grassline.

"If I'm fishing a Rat-L-Trap-type bait, I position the boat a little tighter to the edge and cast across the grass, bring the bait back to the edge. Or if I'm fishing a jig-and-pig or worm, I'll often drop it right down through the grass, being sure to keep the grass edge directly beneath my boat."

Paul Elias on Fishing Ledges

Allow 1982 BASS Masters Classic champion Paul Elias to select a favorite fishing situation and he would quickly select a well-defined reservoir ledge, either along a creek channel on the main river. These are areas that traditionally hold good concentrations of bass, yet go unmolested by fishermen unskilled at using electronics and fishing deep structure.

Although the elements often dictate otherwise, Elias takes the same basic two-pronged approach to boat positioning for properly fishing ledges. Generally, he marks the perimeter of the breakline with buoys and then positions his boat on its deeper side and casts his lure to the shallower side of the drop. If that doesn't produce, Elias moves his boat tighter to the ledge and parallels it as closely as possible. This is a particularly productive way to fish a deep-diving crankbait, he says.

"In nine situations out of 10, I'll position my boat in the deep water and cast to the shallow side," Elias adds. "The main reason for that is that on our reservoirs, I'm usually fishing around some type of cover on a ledge, like stumps or brush. When you try to pull a bait from deep water into shallow water, you just constantly stay hung up in the cover. Plus, I just think you get more bites fishing the shallow side and casting from the deep.

"There are certain times when you have to approach it differently. For example, if I am fishing a river-channel ledge, I fish the flow of the river. I position my boat so that I can cast and then pull the bait with the current. If there is any flow at all — whether it be on a TVA reservoir where they're pulling water or just current from the wind — you need to be positioned in the opposite direction so that you bring the bait with the current."

Doug Youngblood on Deep-Structure Bass

Georgia's Lake Lanier is a deep, clear reservoir where the spotted bass is king. Guides like Doug Youngblood know that if they are to be consistently successful, they must learn to fish deep-water humps, brushpiles, rockpiles, standing timber and subtle bottom-contour changes.

About 75 percent of Youngblood's fishing year on Lanier is spent fishing deep-water for spots. For water 20 feet and deeper, Youngblood prefers to fish vertically, whether he is jigging a small spoon or doodling a tiny worm. For this type of finesse fishing, the proper boat positioning is at a premium.

"The best way to catch fish in water that deep is fishing straight up and down," says Youngblood, a past Classic qualifier. "You just get more strikes with a vertical presentation than you do staying off of the cover and casting to it. And you certainly land a lot more fish because you get a much better hook-set from straight overhead and you can control the fish better once he is hooked.

"There are two important aspects to boat positioning with this type of fishing. The first is that you have to be positioned directly over the brushpile or whatever cover you're fishing. That means reading your flasher to stay in the proper position and not drift a few feet off of it, which often means not getting bit. The second key is the installation of your transducer for that flasher. It has to be mounted on the trolling motor, so that you — the fisherman — are always directly above the signal. A transducer mounted anywhere else in the boat will kill your chances of catching fish with this type of fishing."

The ingredients of proper boat positioning are various, ranging from strategic to the equipment involved. Upon examination, it is a subject with more depth than most of us ever expected. But it is an aspect of bass fishing that separates the elite fish-catchers among us. And a part of fishing that is well-worth a conscious effort.

Chapter 31

Hot Lures for Cold-Water Bass

Mercifully, Guido Hibdon brings his Ranger boat off of a plane and allows it to settle to a stop along a creek bank in Bull Shoals Lake. The agonizing, 15-minute run up the lake has caked Hibdon's mustache and beard in ice. His flotation vest is encased in an even thicker layer.

The thought is inescapable — there has to be a better way to spend a bitterly cold winter day than bass fishing.

Simultaneously tossing down the trolling motor and picking up a spinning rod with more dexterity than a man in a bulky snowsuit should be capable of, Hibdon pitches out a small, feathery jig and begins to slowly hop it 20 feet or so below the boat. Two casts later, he boats another keeper, his fourth on this freezing morning. Within 20 minutes, Hibdon has completed his limit, a stringer that most fishermen would be proud of during any time of the year.

And this is the winter.

PROfile

Texan Michael Dyess is a jig-fishing expert and past BASS Masters Classic qualifier.

"I'm not surprised," the veteran Missouri angler says in reference to a fine frozen morning of fishing. "Just because it gets cold doesn't mean the fish will quit biting completely. There's actually some real good wintertime bass fishing to be had, but the problem is that most people don't want to have to fight off the cold to experience it."

Hibdon should know. The Ozark region of Missouri and Arkansas can feature brutally cold winters. And Guido Hibdon will still fish for bass through the month of January, when winter is at its height. He will consistently catch fish, too.

The coldest water temperatures of the year don't signal an ending to decent bass fishing, although it certainly won't be as comfortable as other seasons. But the bass are still around and can even be cooperative with the right lures and techniques.

Five types of artificial lures stand out as prime wintertime weapons. Call them hot lures for cold water.

But all share a common denominator in that each has to be presented to the winter-weary bass as slowly and precisely as possible. The cold water temperatures drastically slow the metabolism of the bass, transforming this normally aggressive predator into a sluggish shadow of itself. Cold-water bass are the most inactive of the species and feed only sporadically because their slow metabolism makes digestion a lingering process.

Still, with the right lure and a methodical presentation, you can get either a feeding or reaction strike from both largemouth and smallmouth bass during the absolute coldest times of the year

THE JIG-AND-PIG

If you don't think it gets cold in northeast Texas in the winter, then visit this little corner of the Lone Star State some January day when just running a boat is a masochistic experience.

Michael Dyess knows. He also knows just how good the fishing can be during the coldest days of the year.

"The coldest time of the year can be the best jig fishing of the year," says Dyess, a former BASS Masters Classic qualifier and jig-fishing expert. "While everybody is out deer hunting, a few determined fishermen are catching some of the biggest bass of the year.

"It is the greatest jig time there is because during the coldest times, the bass are staged on cover, whether it be grass or wood. Instead of being suspended, you will find them related to structure that is obvious. You can then work that piece of structure completely and if you are slow and precise enough, you can catch some big fish without a lot of finesse."

To illustrate his point, Dyess recalls a recent late January day when a tournament on Lake Conroe produced some of its finest fishing of the year. The weather was so miserably cold that the guides on their rods were accumulating ice, but the tournament AVERAGE was almost 4 pounds. The secret, Dyess, says, was loading the jig with a pair of large No. 11 Uncle Josh pork chunks to slow its descent as much as possible.

That is an important tactic because an agonizingly slow fall is the secret to scoring with a jig-and-pig in the cold times. Dyess also fans out the bristles on his weedguard to get more resistance and slow the fall even more.

Dyess' main winter weapon is a 3/8-ounce black Stanley jig with a large black pork chunk, fished on 14- to 20-pound test line with a heavy-action flipping rod.

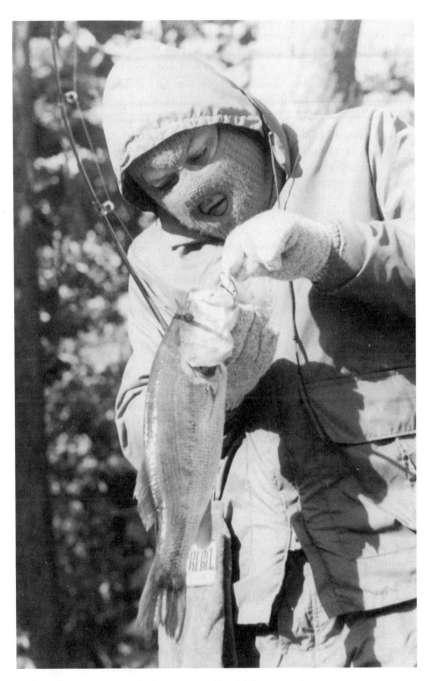

Lead sinking lures are excellent tools for cold-water bass.

"I look for cold-water fish in the textbook areas — sloughs where they can move up as the water warms, creek channels and along the edges of deeper points," Dyess adds. "They aren't hard to locate."

Dyess cautions that the nonaggressive strike of these sluggish bass is often undetectable and recommends watching your line at all times. Most of the strikes come on the fall of the jig.

A Crappie Jig for Bass

The standard cold-water lure in the deep, clear Ozark lakes for as long as anybody can remember as been the simple marabou crappie jig.

Guido Hibdon's father passed that knowledge on to him and his 21-year-old son Dion has come to learn its value. Both Hibdons, one of the few father-and-son combinations to ever qualify for the BASS Masters Classic, consider it their prime wintertime lure and it has rarely let them down.

"I saw my dad catch a ton of bass on that crappie jig in the winter," Guido Hibdon says. "He would fish it all the way through December, which is really cold in our part of the country, and he would catch limit after limit of bass on that crappie jig."

The jig is a brightly-colored marabou version of a standard crappie tool, equipped with a fine-wire hook. The Hibdons have their best cold-water success with two sizes —1/8- and 1/4-ounce. It is fished on light line (4- to 8-pound test) because the water is typically deep and clear. The small diameter line slices through the friction of the water and allows the jig to reach its target a little quicker, Dion Hibdon says, which is important when you consider how deep they are fishing during this time of the year.

The Hibdons concentrate on water depths of 20 feet and greater, both casting and vertically jigging to brushpiles they have planted or natural lake structure such as points and bluff banks in the back half of creeks. They toss the jig out, count it down until it should be in position and slowly work it across the top of the structure.

"You have to fish it slow because it is so cold that the fish are almost in a dormant stage," Dion Hibdon says. "Everything else is moving slow in the water, too, so you have to fish slow to imitate anything that they might eat."

"We catch some hellacious fish this way in the winter time," Guido Hibdon adds. "But it's not easy for the average guy because it's light-line, deep-water fishing, which the average guy isn't accustomed to doing. To the average guy, 10 feet is deep, but not to us."

A Surprising Winter Choice

It is a type of lure often referred to by different names, including jerk bait, rip bait, top-water minnow bait and even a crankbait. In essence, it is a minnow-shaped plastic lure that features a slightly-angled plastic lip and its members include the Spoonbill Rebel, Bomber Long A and the Rouge.

Rarely is it ever referred to as a cold-water lure.

But it is Joe Hughes' No. 1 choice for bringing the sluggish winter bass to life. In addition to being an executive with PRADCO, Inc., parent companies to several lure manufacturing companies, Hughes is an extremely knowledgeable bass fisherman and considered one of the country's foremost crankbait specialists.

Hughes was given a valuable cold-water lesson about the allure of such baits in 1976 while fishing on Toledo Bend Reservoir with an old and veteran guide named Luther White. White's fish-producing ability was somewhat overshadowed by the high-profile of other Toledo Bend guides like big-name tournament pros Tommy Martin and Larry Nixon, but he held his own, particularly in the winter, using a Spoonbill Rebel.

On the blustery February day that Hughes hired White, the Spoonbill Rebel produced four bass weighing between 5 and 7 pounds. Hughes never again underestimated the wintertime value of the Spoonbill.

"It is a bait that a lot of the professionals have in their tackle boxes, especially for the winter and early spring months, but they don't say much about it," says Hughes, who lives in Fort Smith, Ark. "I start using it when the water temperature is anywhere from 39 to 44 degrees.

"A lot of guys don't use it then, but I have found that it works extremely well because of the pattern of the fish. They are not aggressive and won't chase something to kill it, so this is the perfect lure. The key is you can fish it slow."

Few lures are as versatile as these types of plugs. Lures like the Spoonbill Rebel can cover depths from the surface down to about 7 feet, which is important because winter bass often suspend. It can be fished atop submerged vegetation and along vertical wooden structure such as stumps and standing timber as well as cranked down to bottom-contour irregularities.

Perhaps the bait's most effective feature is its ability to be cranked down to a certain level and then stopped, where it will almost suspend before slowly rising upward. Hughes has enjoyed great success with cranking the Spoonbill down to the structure, stopping it where it momentarily suspends and then twitching it as if it were a topwater minnow bait. They key, he says, is making the lure act erratic once it has been pulled down to the structure.

"The Spoonbill is a bait that will actually back up," Hughes adds. "Few people realize it, but if you pull it slightly and then pop it, the Spoonbill will back up four or 5 inches. That is a hell of an action to put on a bait when you can get it to back right into the fish's face."

Hughes, primarily, fishes the 4 1/2-inch Spoonbill in the unique G-Finish color on the lightest line possible. He cautions that the lure is difficult to cast into the wind, which is a reason why more winter fishermen have not discovered it.

Grubs for Sluggish Bass

Few bass fishermen truly understand cold-weather fishing as intimately as John Hunt. There is almost no day too cold to keep Hunt from venturing out on

Tennessee's Kentucky and Barkley lakes.

Although the weather is anything but comfortable for humans, Hunt concentrates his efforts in what he calls the "comfort zone" of the bass. Generally, Hunt finds that comfort zone to be 10 to 20 feet deep by marking suspended bass on his depth finder along creek channels and points, as well as main-lake points. The bass will often be suspended 4 feet or so off of the bottom.

The ideal tool for catching these sluggish suspended fish, Hunt believes, is the plastic grub, which can be slowly floated down to the bass and then methodically worked along the bottom. He uses a light jighead (1/16- to 1/4-ounce) and 4- to 8-pound test line to ensure a slow, enticing fall.

Hunt emphasizes the need to concentrate during this type of fishing because the strike is often difficult to detect. Watching the line is mandatory, along with a quality, sensitive graphite spinning rod.

"I can't stress enough that because this is cold water, you have to fish extremely slow," Hunt explains. "You have to fish the grub slow to keep it within their very small strike zone and get them to hit it. These fish are not going to move very far to hit a lure, so you have to barely move the jig once it reaches the strike zone."

SECTION THREE
PATTERNS & CONDITIONS

Doug Weir caught this 14-pound, 1-ounce beauty on a cold, rainy Florida morning.

Chapter 32

Foul-Weather Bass

It's a familiar scenario.

You've endured that punch-clock mentality for another week, surviving on a few well-placed daydreams of quiet coves and fiesty bass. You've spent Saturday rigging tackle, lining rods, readying the boat, preparing a gameplan and just generally drooling with anticipation of what tomorrow will bring.

Then Sunday arrives.

PROfile

Arriving at Big Bass Lake, your enthusiasm is dampened by the relentlessness of a torrential morning rain shower that threatens to make this a miserable day-long affair. Or you taxi your boat down the launch ramp only to find that gusty winds have transformed your local lake into a mini-ocean.

Sound familiar?

Confronted with those situations, a large portion of even the most avid bass fishermen will turn around, head for home and pray for better weather next weekend. But foul weather doesn't have to make your precious weekend trip a washout.

Dave Gliebe, perhaps the most successful western pro of all, is a three-time BASS Masters Classic qualifier and pioneer of the technique of flipping.

Nobody knows that better than the nation's legions of tournament pros who face a wide array of foul weather during their travels across the country. And the cast-for-cash boys simply can't call their fishing trip off on account of bad weather.

"Rough weather should almost never ruin a fishing trip," insists North Carolina's Hank Parker, one of America's best bass anglers and a two-time BASS Masters Classic champion "You simply have to adjust to it and try to use it to your advantage. And some times foul weather will play to your benefit."

Other knowledgeable pros agree that only extreme weather conditions should drive you off of the lake.

"I wouldn't let the weather ever ruin a fishing trip, except for lightning or severe storms or stuff like that," adds Missouri's Denny Brauer. "There are foul weather conditions that will improve the quality of fishing if you make the proper adjustments."

"You would be surprised what rough weather — wind and rain, particularly, will often do to the kind of action and success you're having," says California's Dave Gliebe, three-time Classic qualifier and one of the pioneers of the flipping technique. "There are many times when I look forward to it."

Parker, Brauer, Gliebe and Ken Cook, a former fisheries biologist and five-time B.A.S.S. winner, agree on another point that might surprise weekend fishermen — foul weather (notably wind and rain) consistently improves your success rate. All say they have caught more impressive stringers of fish when the weather was less than ideal than when the conditions were closer to perfect.

"I've caught more big fish when the weather was stable, but it seems like the masses of fish, which are smaller, are very active under those poor conditions," Cook says. "Bad weather just generally makes the fish more active.

"The thing about those kinds of conditions is usually if you have a good warm water temperature, you'll have active fish during this rough weather. Even though the weather is bad, if you can get to a place that you know holds fish and figure out some way to catch them, you can catch plenty of fish. I've caught good numbers of fish in weather so bad that I couldn't hardly see the water."

The biggest adjustment to foul-weather fishing is usually a mental one rather than some change in tactics. "I like to fish in nasty weather," Brauer claims. "The nastier the weather, the more it effects a lot of my competitors mentally in a tournament. They get disgusted with the weather and don't concentrate as hard on their fishing.

"I don't necessarily like being out in the rain, but I got conditioned to it from guiding in all types of the elements all through the years and I know what can happen on those rainy, bad-weather days — big stringers are often caught. So you just have to do your best to ignore the wet conditions and concentrate on catching fish."

"The average fisherman probably has the hardest time making the mental adjustment to foul weather," Cook adds. "He has the hardest time trying to stay prepared to catch fish and keep trying under those conditions.

"The average guy is out there to have a good time, which brings up another point: you have to weigh in your own mind whether having a good time means

184

getting out of the nasty weather or catching fish because, really, some of the best fishing occurs during the nastiest weather."

Parker advises anglers to "psyche themselves up for foul-weather fishing," which means concentrating on catching one bass at a time, instead of "worrying about trying to catch 20 pounds. Your concentration is put to the test."

The two foul-weather conditions the pros encounter (and must counter) most often are rain and wind. While a bass fisherman has never met a wind he ever liked, knowledgeable anglers usually welcome rain — except in hurricane quantities.

A steady rain can benefit both fish and fisherman in several ways. First, it often cools the water temperature, which makes bass more active. The accompanying cloud cover often encourages fish to move out of some impenetrable spots and cruise for a meal.

"Rain usually enhances the fishing and actually makes it easier to catch fish, even the bigger fish," Brauer explains. "For one thing, it helps cover up the sounds and noise you're making. It puts the fish a little more at ease and they are less on guard and overall just easier to catch. I think the activity of the rain beating on the surface of the water excites them and puts them in a little more of a feeding mood."

All of the pros agree that a steady rain usually encourages bass to move to shallower water where they are more accessible to an artificial lure or live bait. That's the biggest tactical adjustment fishermen must make, they say, when the rain begins — look for bass in shallower cover and structure.

"You'd be surprised how far rain will normally bring fish up," adds Gliebe, a veteran of the clear, deep-water lakes of the western United States. "It will move a lot more fish into shallow water and I think most fishermen would agree that shallow-water fish are often the easiest to catch.

"Another thing it does in lakes out here like Lake Mead, it causes off-colored water (from hillside runoff) to come into the lake and color up an area, which will also bring fish up to shallower water. Then, I automatically consider tying on a top-water bait or a shallow-running crankbait."

A consistent rain calls for another adjustment — switching to lures that will cover a considerable amount of water (a spinner bait instead of a plastic worm) since the rain often makes the fish more active and they won't be holding as tight to the cover or structure as before the rains began.

"If you've patterned the fish tight to the cover while the sun is shining bright and all of a sudden the rain brings a heavy cloud cover, the fish don't need the shelter of that dense vegetation or whatever the cover might be," Brauer explains. "You might have been able to flip to the fish before, but now you'll have to go to a spinner bait or a buzz bait to cover more water because the fish won't be tied to the cover."

The exception, Brauer adds, is when heavy thunder is present. The noise usually drives bass to the heaviest cover available and actually puts them in a "negative feeding mood." With thunder present, Brauer advises returning to heavy-cover techniques like flipping, working the bait slowly and keeping an eye out for lightning.

Wind probably drives more fishermen off of the lake or river than any other condition. An angler's misery barometer usually relies heavily on the strength and direction of the wind that day.

There is no getting around the fact that wind can ruin a trip on some occasions. At best, it can make you change tactics and locations and, at worst, it can send you scurrying for safety ashore.

En route to winning Super B.A.S.S.-IV in 1985 in Florida, it can safely be said that Hank Parker endured the worst physical beating of his career. Casting a spinnerbait to a submerged, shallow-water grassbed in a completely exposed area of the St. Johns River, Parker battled constantly to keep his boat in position to work the grass as his boat took waves over the bow and stern with increasing regularity.

"I think if I had been fishing for fun today and I would have known that the fish were where they were and the wind was like it was, I wouldn't have fished for them because they weren't fun to fish for," Parker moaned a couple of hours after coming off of the water after the tournament's second round. "It was too much work.

"My back hurts. I'm tired. I could not stand up in the boat at times. I took waves over the front and the back of the boat all day long. Where I caught my fish was the roughest place on the whole lake and that wind beat me up pretty good."

Most fishermen would not want to endure the torturous treatment that Parker handled, even with $100,000 at stake. But Parker's performance makes an excellent case for foul-weather fishing — he took advantage of what the 20-mile-per-hour-plus wind was doing to the fish and put almost 69 pounds of bass in the boat.

Parker believes his success would have been limited considerably without the steady wind for two reasons. The current caused by the strong wind stood the eelgrass up enough for Parker to easily run his spinner bait (equipped with the giant willow-leaf blade) through it. And "even with the big rollers crashing through there, the wind stirred the fish and the baitfish up and made them active when they wouldn't be normally. With all of the bait stirred up and the grass stirred up around them, the fish really couldn't sit still. They roam and it tends to make them feed a little better."

While Parker's performance involves extreme conditions, Parker, Gliebe, Cook and Brauer agree that it's best not to try to fight the wind. Instead, let the wind work to your advantage.

A good example of working the wind to your advantage involves Super B.A.S.S.-II winner Mickey Bruce of Buford, Ga., who took advantage of a gusty Lake Okeechobee wind to finish in second place in the 1986 B.A.S.S.

event there. Bruce caught more than 40 pounds of bass by flipping a worm into the holes and pockets in thick patches of peppergrass. He simply allowed the wind to drift him over the submerged grass until he reached a likely-looking spot and dropped a worm into it.

Bruce found that the technique was much more productive than when he used his trolling motor, so even when the wind had died down, he would back off of the grassbed and get a running start with his electric motor before turning it off and drifting over the vegetation.

"I've always found that it's best that you not try to fight the wind," Gliebe adds. "Just join it and go with it. Instead of trying to fight a tough wind and fish a particular cover, you've got to give it up and go with the wind and work the shoreline that the wind allows you to fish."

"You really have to weigh each situation before deciding how to approach it," Cook says. "I like to fish in an area that's windy within reason.

"Not to where the waves could sink the boat, though. I prefer to fish into the wind, but when you get to the point where your trolling motor can't hold the boat, you'll have to change and fish downwind. Sometimes if I'm in an area that's fairly windy, I turn the boat into the wind and let the boat drift backwards, while holding it as best I can with the trolling motor. Often you can use your trolling motor to slow down the drift and fish that way. That's a helpful thing to do and you can also drag an anchor if you don't mind dragging it through the area you just fished."

Several knowledgeable Florida fishermen like Chuck Faremouth combat Lake Okeechobee's legendary winds by borrowing a tool from their saltwater counterparts. They use a sea anchor, a funnel-shaped piece of plastic-coated canvas (which is open at both ends) that allows you to drift at a more fishable speed. "It's perfect for drifting and fishing," Faremouth says. "Most people don't use it because they think it would get tangled up in the weeds, but it just collapses when it goes through the grass and opens up again when it reaches clear water. Weeds are no problem."

A steady wind can provide fishermen with an advantage that most don't consider, according to Brauer. It positions both the baitfish and the bass.

"If you have a wind that's not too strong, but steady, it's possible to predict the most likely spots that are holding bass," he explains. "Look at the area and try to imagine in your mind what it's doing to the baitfish; how it's positioning and moving the baitfish. Imagine the baitfish roaming around in open water. Where is that wind going to push them?

"Then, where have the bass been holding in the past and how will the direction of the wind have them positioned? Once you make a guess at answering those questions, try to figure out where the baitfish and the bass are likely to collide. And concentrate on drifting through and making a good cast at those possible collision points. If you figure out the collision points and throw your bait there, you're going to catch a bunch of them."

The pros agree that extremely windy conditions dictate a change in lures from finesse-type lures like worms and small jigs to a spinnerbait or crankbait — lures that provide more contact for the angler. Windy conditions create current that deafens most fishermen's feel for finesse-type baits.

Combating unpleasant weather conditions is part of the job for men like Hank Parker, Dave Gliebe, Ken Cook and Denny Brauer. But they are the first to recommend avoiding dangerous situations like lightning or severe temperature changes. Cook can easily recall the bitter cold he endured during a national tournament on Lake Mead in mid-July when a violent thunderstorm sent the normal 110-degree temperature plummeting into the 70s in less than an hour and hypothermia became a real threat for the rain-soaked competitors. Cook, like past Classic champion Larry Nixon and others, bobbed in the waters of Lake Mead for several hours to ward off the bone-chilling air temperature.

In that case, the rugged mountain conditions and sheer bluff walls kept them from seeking shelter ashore. But they recommend always knowing where coves and creeks offer nearby shelter on your favorite lake instead of sitting out in the lake waving a graphite rod. That could give the brand name Lightning Rod a whole new meaning.

But, generally, a little foul weather endurance will pay off in limit days.

"You just have to gear yourself up for the rough weather," Denny Brauer says. "It's not going to be pleasant out there fighting the conditions and bouncing around in a boat through rough water. A lot of times you have to force yourself to go that extra mile rather than sit in some sheltered cove. You've got to brave the elements to succeed on a consistent basis."

Chapter 33

Temperature and Bass

The most overlooked and underutilized instrument on most bass boats is the easiest to operate and, the experts say, the most beneficial piece of equipment of all. This tiny gauge can tell you where the bass should be located; how deep they should be; when they should be most active and likely to feed; even recommend a lure and how it should be manipulated.

PROfile

No, this is not some new high-priced bass-fishing computer capable of digesting mega-bytes of information and spewing out on-the-water alternatives. This inexpensive instrument registers and reports a single piece of data, information that biologists and knowledgeable fishermen claim is the most telling detail available about the habits and habitat of bass.

Water temperature.

Most boats have a temperature gauge that was factory-installed, but these simple meters suffer from a serious case of neglect. Yet, knowing the temperature of the aquatic homes of largemouth

Former fisheries biologist Ken Cook is a five-time B.A.S.S. winner and nine-time Classic qualifier.

bass provides an element of predictability rarely available in this sport.

Listen to the experts:

• **Doug Hannon, renowned naturalist, bass researcher and trophy authority with 511 10-pound-plus bass to his credit:** "Temperature, oxygen levels and to some degree pH are all interrelated. But temperature is the one factor that you can distill out of every factor and predict what will happen when it changes. If it goes up or down, we know what will happen. It's a variable that we can react to in a definite way. In the sense that the rules don't change, it's one of the most important things a fisherman needs to understand."

• **Dr. Loren Hill, chairman of the University of Oklahoma's Department of Zoology and noted expert on bass biology:** "Temperature is a very controlling factor with fish behavior. It is the controlling factor of metabolism, movement, feeding activity and every other behavioral function."

• **Ken Cook, former fisheries biologist and one of the country's top tournament bass pros:** "Water temperature is a major consideration anytime you are fishing for bass or any animal that's cold-blooded because it dictates what they are doing. It dictates the metabolic rate, which tells me a lot of about how fast they are moving on a minute-to-minute basis and what percentage of bass in a population is going to be active."

• **Bill Dance, former tournament great and perhaps America's best-known angler:** "Water temperature plays a major role in my fishing because it is such a major factor in dictating fish behavior. Fish use it to make their major moves and fishermen should, too."

• **Roland Martin, all-time tournament great and nine-time Bass Anglers Sportsman Society Angler of the Year:** "Water temperature gives us the most predictable and reliable element of all."

• **Shaw Grigsby, past Red Man All American champion and two-time B.A.S.S. winner:** "I don't use any piece of equipment as much as I do a temperature gauge. To me, that's the most important consideration."

Convinced?

Given such high praise and lofty status, it is obvious that those in the know realize the importance of monitoring water temperature and utilizing that information to its fullest potential. But the average angler doesn't seem to understand that a temperature reading can provide the answer to many fundamental tactical and technical questions ranging from where the bass should be holding to how fast you should bring a lure past its underwater lair.

And, although it might surprise some, understanding the role of temperature and using that knowledge to catch more bass doesn't require brushing up on your old high school biology lessons. The principles involved are really quite basic and easy to comprehend. It is more a matter of being aware of the make-up of the bass' environment and the predictability that temperature provides.

Water temperature is a basic element that neither man nor fish can manipulate. Instead, both must adjust to it and, by doing so, hopefully improve their plight.

"It is important to understand that you can't separate temperature and oxygen, which is the bass' top requirement," says Bill Phillips, a respected fisheries biologist, avid angler and senior writer of bass biology for *Bassmaster Magazine*. "Both go hand-in-hand, but it is far easier for the average fisherman to monitor water temperature. And knowing the temperature of the water will

Ken Cook checks the water temperature using a Combo-C-Lector

tell you a lot about the oxygen content and other indications such as how active the fish are likely to be."

Water temperature can provide useful information on a seasonal basis, as well as an hour-to-hour and even minute-to-minute basis in certain seasons. It is most often relied on seasonally as the basis for determining a starting point for locating bass. Knowledgeable fishermen use water temperature to follow bass throughout the year as the majority of the population makes its migration back-and-forth from deep and shallow water.

As the water begins to warm and approaches the mid- to upper 50s, largemouth bass begin to move shallower from their deep winter homes in preparation for the spawning ritual. In the pre-spawn stage, they will position on any type of structure located in moderately deep water adjacent to shallower water where they await nature's signals — water temperature and sunlight from the lengthening day — to make a spawning bed. At about 60 (and up to around 72) degrees, biologists say that bass begin to spawn and will remain in the shallow nursery flats for some time. As spring ends, post-spawn largemouth bass generally move out to locations similar to those used just before spawning. Although some bass will stay shallow throughout the year, the general consensus among biologists is that the majority of the fish then move off into deeper (and cooler) water to spend the summer.

As the temperatures cool in the fall, bass move shallow again, before returning to their deep sanctuaries to endure the coldest times of winter. The migration cycle is completed. And you can follow that migration route by monitoring the temperature of the water.

Spring may be the time when knowing the water temperature is most valuable. Actually, spring is three seasons in one — pre-spawn, spawn and post-spawn. Temperature readings provide the key to knowing where bass should be during each of those phases.

Knowledgeable anglers use temperature to allow them to utilize their favorite style of fishing for the longest amount of time — as much as a month or more on some lakes and reservoirs. For example, Ken Cook believes that pre-spawn bass are the easiest fish to catch. So in early February, he concentrates on likely pre-spawn areas near the protected northern coves and creeks. The water in these areas warms the quickest because of its positioning to catch the sun's radiation, making it a spot where every part of the bass' food chain is likely to be most active. Taking temperature, readings, Cook simply follows the temperature trend around the lake as the pre-spawn bass appear later and later in other parts of the reservoir.

Four-time BASS Masters Classic champion Rick Clunn of Montgomery, Texas, prefers fishing for post-spawn bass. He takes the same approach as Cook. "The key to finding bass in the spring is understanding the heating cycle of your own lake — the areas that heat up the earliest and the latest — and then following that heat cycle around the lake," Clunn explains.

Shaw Grigsby is an expert at sight-fishing for spawning bass, so he uses a temperature gauge to move from bedding site to bedding site. He will often spend a tournament practice day running from spot to spot to take temperature readings. Temperature, he believes, is an excellent way to eliminate water.

Summer may be the season when water temperature provides the most predictability.

As the days get hotter, the bass are often more difficult to locate for the majority of bass anglers in this country, who are shallow-water oriented. But a temperature gauge with a long probe cord and a chart-recorder or liquid crystal depth-finding unit can pinpoint the exact positioning of schools of bass. Simply look for the thermocline.

In the summer, water has a tendency to stratify and both bass and baitfish will seek the layer of water that offers the most comfort in terms of sufficient oxygen and coolest temperature. A thermocline, which is visible on a depth-finder, will be the level that harbors the most bass. To take advantage of it, determine the depth at which the thermocline exists and then look for any structure in the area — brushpile, point, drop-off, creek channel edge. The bass will move back and forth from that structure to feed, according to Phillips.

"People don't take advantage of the predictability that the thermocline provides," Phillips claims. "And it is so easy to take advantage of. All you have to do is lower a temperature probe down until the temperature quits changing. Then back up to the last point where it changed — that's the bottom of the thermocline. The thermocline is generally very predictable and stays about the same throughout the summer. You can eliminate so much of the lake in mid-summer by using the thermocline."

Winter is the season when Bill Dance most relies on his temperature gauge. Using the long probe cord of a Combo-C-Lector, Dance looks for water that is 2 to 3 degrees warmer than the prevailing temperature, which can be the difference between a sluggish bass and a feeding fish in the winter, he says. One of his most reliable spots on Dale Hollow Reservoir, a favorite Tennessee River chain impoundment, is an old spring that has been long forgotten since the river was dammed. Dance was told of the deep-water spring's existence by an old farmer and spent several days checking water temperatures until he found it.

That spring, which provides water that is significantly warmer in the winter and cooler in the summer than surrounding areas, harbors a large population of bass throughout the year, Dance says.

You can begin to understand the seasonal value of water temperature. But temperature readings can provide important input on an hourly basis as well. Grigsby utilizes his temperature gauge throughout the day in the spring as approaching or passing fronts can change the temperature drastically from morning to afternoon. Such temperature changes can trigger a feeding frenzy or eliminate any action entirely.

Hourly changes occur because of fluctuations in the metabolic rate of bass caused by temperature changes. That is the most important concept involved in the role of temperature in bass fishing for anglers to understand.

Most anglers know that temperature controls the metabolic rate of bass, which regulates its activity level. It is basically understood that bass in extremely cold and hot water can be sluggish, even dormant. In those extremes, bass tend to conserve energy and rarely feed. But they don't stop eating entirely and can be caught with the right approach.

In his experiments, Dr. Hill has found that the ideal temperature for optimum largemouth bass growth, activity and feeding is around 80 degrees. In laboratory tests, he found that bass rarely ate in water below the 45-degree mark. Feeding frequency increased rapidly from 47 to 70 degrees, but showed a marked decline at around 90. Eighty degrees, Dr. Hill contends, is the "magical temperature" when bass are the aggressive, responsive creatures that we know and love. Unfortunately, we must contend with more extreme temperature variations, which forces adjustments on the part of the angler.

One of the facets of the metabolic rate that most controls a bass' activity level is digestion, according to Ken Cook. "Understand that hunger is the primary reason that bass strike a lure," he explains. "Down at the 40-degree mark, which is about as cold as I can catch fish, their metabolic rate is so slow that it takes about a week for a minnow to be digested. So I know from that information that a small percentage of the bass at that temperature are going to be hungry. They aren't hungry, so you have to tempt them with something small and slow your retrieve down enough to make it easy for them to get it.

"As the water warms up to 50, it still takes about five days for digestion. At 60, there is a significant increase in digestion time — about two-and-a-half days. At 70, the digestion efficiency is starting to peak out. Between 70 and 80, it takes only 18 to 24 hours for a food item to be digested. But once you get into the upper 80s — depending on the acclimatization of the particular strain of bass involved — their metabolic rate begins to slow down because the water reaches an oxygen saturation point. The bass become lethargic and it takes longer for its food to digest."

"There is an old scientific dictum called Vant Hoff's Law that states that for every 20 degrees you raise the temperature, you increase the metabolic rate and oxygen demand by 300 percent," Doug Hannon adds. "So you can see that temperature really is a predictor of activity levels."

Understanding the metabolic cycle that bass endure from season to season, Cook and others use small baits during the coldest times, while altering the presentation and retrieve depending upon the activity level of the fish. To illustrate that point, Cook singles out the jig-and-pork combination and plastic grub as lures that will catch bass in 40- to 90-degree water.

During the coldest times (40 to 50 degrees), Cook slowly drags these lures across the bottom, simulating the sluggish movement of the bass' food sources.

As the water approaches the 60-degree mark and the fish become more active, he works the lure in a more erratic fashion, shaking it as it falls and using a more vertical approach. In the 70- to 85-degree range, Cook begins using larger lures, swimming and hopping the baits along the bottom. And in the hottest water, he returns to a slower presentation.

The metabolic rate (dictated by the water temperature) can significantly inhibit the swimming ability and speed of largemouth bass, Dr. Hill says. His research has shown that bass swim fastest at a temperature between 78 and 80. "Below and above that, they are not as fast and anglers can use that concept to catch more bass," he says. "For example, if you are fishing a crankbait real fast in the spring, a lot of times the fish simply can't catch it. So you can see where temperature has an effect on speed and different types of lures and how they should be presented."

Roland Martin agrees with Dr. Hill's findings and uses water temperature to eliminate some types of lures, while suggesting the size and speed of others (see accompanying chart).

Using the results of stomach-content analysis, Dr. Hill makes a convincing case that bass are most likely to consume large baitfish when the water is between 78 and 82 degrees, making that an ideal time to use sizeable lures like a Zara Spook or 5/8-ounce jig with a pork trailer. Hill, an enthusiastic bass angler, downsizes below that point.

It should be noted that there is no simple rule that governs all areas of the country. Different strains of bass have different tolerances toward extreme water temperatures. In other words, the northern strain of bass is better suited genetically for cold-water conditions than the sub-tropical Florida strain. As a result, the activity level of the northern strain doesn't diminish as much in cold water as their Florida cousins. It is also true that Florida bass are more adapted to warmer climes and aren't as susceptible to the warm-water doldrums as the northern strain.

"That could be useful knowledge in a lake that has a mix of northerns and Florida bass like the Texas lakes," Hannon says. "You could target the larger Florida bass in the summer by fishing shallow in hot vegetation. The size of fish you would catch — the percentage of Florida bass — would go up as opposed to fishing for a mixture in water temperature that was comfortable for both strains to be in."

Fishermen who sincerely understand the value of water temperature in bass behavior don't rely on a surface temperature gauge. They utilize meters with probe cords long enough to allow them to reach most fishable depth. Martin checks water temperature with a sophisticated Sentry Oxygen Monitor, while Dance uses the temperature gauge on his Combo-C-Lecter. A typical dash-mounted surface temperature gauge is limiting in the information it can provide.

Understanding the role that water temperature plays in the bass' environment is an engraved invitation to consistent success on a year-round basis. A temperature gauge can open up a whole new world, while solving some of its greatest mysteries.

Temperature and Vision

A recent study of cold-blooded creatures shows that the vision of fish improves as the water gets colder.

That information should have a far-reaching impact on bass fishermen, according to Doug Hannon.

"The study found that the colder the eye, the greater the visual acuity and sensitivity of the vision becomes," Hannon explains. "That allows the fish to go to deeper, darker water and still retain good vision, which is important because bass are very much sight feeders."

The study, which centered around frogs (which have eyes with the same physical composition as bass) tested water temperatures down to 39.5 degrees and showed that the animal's visual acuity doubles with a drop in temperature of just five or six degrees. The study also showed that cold-blooded creatures like bass have difficulty seeing in warm water.

The eye of both fish and frogs has a cluster of sight cells on the retina that discharge when struck with light, sending a nerve impulse that carries a visual pattern to the brain. The warmer the eye gets, the more sensitive it is to light penetration (the difference between 70 and 95 degrees is about eight times more light sensitivity). Extremely warm water sets off a spontaneous discharge of the sight cells — creating a snowy picture similar to that of a poorly functioning television set — and significantly hampers the fish's visual acuity and contrast level.

As the water (and subsequently the temperature of the eye) cools down, the spontaneous discharges decrease and the vision clears.

"This is scientific information that fishermen need to react to," Hannon says. "This implies that you can get away with using smaller lures in deep, cold water. And for better results with these winter fish, you should use lighter line because scientific evidence shows that the fish are seeing better than we ever thought at those depths."

Roland Martin's
Temperature Guide to Lure Selection

Clear Water

Water Temperature	Lure Speed	Lure Size	Lure Choices
90	fast	large 3/8-5/8 oz	buzzbaits, topwater plugs, crankbaits, weedless spoons, jigging spoons, night lures
85	fast	large 3/8-5/8 oz	buzzbaits, topwater plugs, crankbaits, plastic worms, weedless and jigging spoons, night lures
80	fast	large 3/8-5/8 oz	buzzbaits, topwater plugs, worms, crankbaits, jigging and weedless spoons
75	fast	large 3/8-5/8 oz	buzzbaits, topwater plugs, worms, crankbaits, jigging and weedless spoons, Carolina-rigged worms, jerkbaits
70	medium	medium 1/4-3/8 oz	topwater plugs, rubber-skirted jigs, worms, crankbaits, spinner baits, jerkbaits, weedless spoons
65	medium	medium 1/4-3/8 oz	topwater plugs, rubber-skirted jigs, worms, crankbaits, spinner baits, jerkbaits
60	medium	medium 1/4-3/8	topwater plugs, rubber-skirted jigs, worms, spinnerbaits, crankbaits, jerkbaits
55	slow	small 1/8-1/4 oz	rubber-skirted jigs, tubejigs, spinnerbaits, crankbaits, topwater plugs (worked slowly)

		small	
50	slow	1/8-1/4 oz	mini-jigs, tubejigs, jigging spoons, spinnerbaits, crankbaits, rubber-skirted jigs
45	extremely slow	ultralight 1/32-1/8 oz	rubber-skirted jigs, tubejigs, spinnerbaits, crankbaits, topwater plugs (worked slowly)
40	extremely slow	ultralight 1/32-1/8 oz	mini-jigs, tubejigs, small spoons
35	extremely slow	ultralight 1/32-1/8 oz	mini-jigs, tubejigs, small spoons
30	extremely slow	ultralight 1/32-1/8 oz	ice flies and jigs

Bass Activity: pre-spawn -- 40 to 60 degrees; spawn -- 60 to 72 degrees; post-spawn -- 75 to 90 degrees

Muddy Water

Water Temperature	Lure Speed	Lure Size	Lure Choices
90	fast	jumbo 5/8-1 oz	topwater plugs, buzzbaits, worms, spinnerbaits, crankbaits
85	fast	jumbo 5/8-1 oz	topwater plugs, buzzbaits, worms, spinnerbaits, crankbaits
80	fast	large 3/8-5/8 oz	topwater plugs, buzzbaits, worms, spinnerbaits, crankbaits
75	fast	large 3/8-5/8 oz	topwater plugs, buzzbaits, worms, spinnerbaits, crankbaits
70	medium	large 3/8-5/8 oz	buzzbaits, worms, spinnerbaits, crankbaits, rubber-skirted jigs

65	medium	large 3/8-5/8 oz	worms, rubber-skirted jigs, spinnerbaits, crankbaits
60	slow	large 3/8-5/8 oz	rubber-skirted jigs, spinnerbaits, crankbaits
55	extremely slow	medium 1/4-3/8 oz	rubber-skirted jigs, spinnerbaits, crankbaits
50	extremely slow	medium 1/4-3/8 oz	rubber-skirted jigs, spinnerbaits, crankbaits
45	Minimal Activity In Muddy Water		
40	Best Advice -- Look For Warmer Water		

Bass Activity: dormant -- 35 to 45 degrees; pre-spawn -- 50 to 59 degrees; spawn -- 60 to 72 degrees; post-spawn -- 75 to 90 degrees

Joe Thomas releases proof that suspended bass can be caught.

Chapter 34

The Dreaded Suspended Bass

WARNING: What you are about to read is rated PG (parental guidance is suggested) and not for the faint of heart. It may be wise to put the children to bed, secure all windows and double-check the lock on the door. Enter at your own risk.

The wind is practically howling across the surface of Lake Lanier on this devilishly cold December day, the backdrop a ghoulish gray. And nothing is moving about.

It is obvious that the tension has worn on the nerves of one Tom Mann Jr.

His boat comes off plane and settles down into the middle of a large cove. He steps on the front deck, drops his trolling motor into the water and switches on his depthfinder. Almost immediately, he wheels around, startled, with terror in his eyes.

"No, no . . . not this," he shrieks. "I can't take it anymore."

Nightmare on Lanier Street.

He refuses to look back at his depthfinder, where the picture of horror is painted. And we begin to understand his terror.

For the electronic portrait shows that 50 feet below the surface — in the middle of this enormous cove — sits a school of bass. And they are holding below a school of shad, with nothing around them to relate to.

Suspended bass.

PROfile

Past Classic qualifier Joe Thomas scored his biggest victory in 1990 by winning the Red Man All-American Championship.

While it doesn't really elicit any blood-curdling screams, the term "suspended bass" is the stuff that nightmares are made for bass fishermen throughout the country. For a great many anglers, the mere mention of those two words is reason enough to surrender.

That is understandable. Not only can suspended bass be difficult to locate at times, the greater horror for fishermen is that they can consistently be almost impossible to catch.

But suspended bass can be caught.

Suspended bass are more of a problem in the winter and dogdays of summer, according to famed biologist and fishing tackle innovator Dr. Loren Hill. But bass will occasionally suspend in the spring and fall, as well.

Why Bass Suspend

The first key to learning how to coax bass into striking during these dreaded times is understanding why they suspend away from cover. By nature, bass are an efficient predator with a penchant for using cover or structure for ambushing position as well as shelter. But there are several factors that prompt this unnatural behavioral change in both largemouth and smallmouth bass.

Low metabolism. "Bass suspend most in the winter and the hottest part of the summer, which has to do with the conditions they are in," Hill explains. "Because of the conditions, their metabolism is low and they become fairly sluggish. Dormant. They don't have any major activities to complete in their life-cycle at these times, like reproduction. And they're encountering conditions that are difficult for them them to survive in."

It is during those times that bass will pull away from cover and structure, repositioning themselves at the depth that has the most comfortable temperature and oxygen level (referred to as the thermocline and oxycline). If there are no underwater objects at that level, the bass are — just as the term implies — suspended.

Cold fronts. The arrival of cold fronts can trigger a move by bass offshore and into deeper water, according to Ken Cook, a highly successful tournament pro and former fisheries biologist for the state of Oklahoma. During the passage of a cold front, bass will often lose contact with shoreline or the bottom, opting for a position deep enough to provide overhead protection from both the elements and predators, such as birds.

Following baitfish. During almost any season, a considerable portion of the bass in a lake or reservoir will concentrate faithfully on schools of baitfish, most notably shad, even to the point of following the food source around. They will suspend under a school of bait anywhere, regardless of the submerged terrain beneath them.

Drawdowns. Veteran California pro Rich Tauber has watched in horror on several different occasions as western reservoirs endured severe drawdowns, which instantly creates suspending bass. "The fish will generally pull off of where they have been holding and re-position at the same comfort level elsewhere in the lake," Tauber says. "If they've been holding on the shoreline at the 15-foot level, they will then pull off of the shoreline and find that 15-foot level farther out in the lake. When they do, they can be difficult to locate and extremely hard to catch."

Weekend boat traffic and fishing pressure. From extensive tracking studies of bass living in reservoirs that are heavily used, Dr. Hill firmly believes that bass behave differently on the weekend, as a result of fishing pressure and surface commotion that increases significantly. Using telemetry units implanted inside of bass, Hill has noticed that the fish tend to move off and suspend more on the weekends.

"I've never had anybody ask me about and I've never really talked about it, but bass in some bodies of water behave differently on the weekends," he explains. "I believe that.

"When the boat traffic elevates, their behavior changed (in the studies). They moved out down to here on Friday and then on late Sunday or Monday, they would come back up and have a different pattern — move around in a different manner. It's amazing how much their basic (behavioral) patterns changed when the weekend arrived."

Locating suspended bass that are not relating to cover or structure isn't nearly as difficult as it once was, thanks to modern-day advancements in marine electronics that are easier to learn and use. The result is more involvement in electronics by anglers than ever before.

In times when fishing for suspended bass are inevitable, knowledgeable pros like Ken Cook use those underwater eyes to search for those fish near the same areas where they had been before the conditions moved them. For example, if the bass had been positioned on the shallow side of a channel ledge, they should still be somewhere in the vicinity — probably in the deeper water.

Experienced bass anglers know, though, that locating suspended bass isn't the hardest task they face.

Why Suspended Bass Are Difficult to Catch

Suspended bass are more difficult to catch for a variety of biological and behavioral reasons, including:

• Dormant, sluggish stages. In the most extreme portions of winter and summer, bass in most lakes and reservoirs simply aren't active, eager feeders.

• Not related to cover or structure. "Suspended bass are less likely to bite because they aren't object oriented," Tauber claims. "They're not using the cover or structure for a point where they can ambush something. They're out in open water and not in an ambushing posture. You almost have to bump your lure right into the fish's nose to get a reaction strike."

"A lot of people don't realize it, but cover gives us a tremendous advantage as fishermen, because it keeps bass in an ambushing position most of the time," adds Joe Thomas, a top touring pro from Cincinnati, who studied fisheries biology in college. "A lure popping past a tree or hopping over a log or limb and falling into a strike zone is a lot more effective than hopping a spoon or dragging a crankbait past a bass sitting in the middle of nowhere."

• The baitfish competition factor. When the bass are suspended under a sizeable school of shad, it is simply difficult for the angler to compete with his single bait imitation, Thomas believes. Many times, there are simply too many shad in the area for a bass to give his attention to a single, isolated shad-like lure moving through the water.

Those are the major reasons why suspended bass give even the most experience fishermen fits of frustration. Suspended bass call for an immediate attitude adjustment on the part of the fisherman, who must realize that the number of strikes will be limited, demanding the utmost concentration.

But there are some methods for enhancing your chances of getting strikes out of suspending bass. And it involves more than simply vertically hopping a jigging spoon or absentmindedly retrieving a deep-diving crankbait.

To Thomas, the key is determining the exact depth at which the bass are staged. He uses his electronics to get a ballpark figure of the depth and then pays close attention to his crankbait as it comes through the water to pinpoint their location even further. A single strike can indicate that exact depth of the bass, telling Thomas where to slowly work a finesse lure like a plastic worm or small jig with a pork trailer.

Keeping the bait working at the same level as the bass is much more difficult than it sounds, according to Ken Cook. "Depth control is the whole key to catching suspended bass, but it is hard to keep a bait in the proper position when the fish may in 15 feet below the surface and 30 feet above the bottom," he explains. "Fishing vertically, it is easier to have some type of depth control — more than you would have if you backed off and ran a crankbait down to that depth."

The depth of the suspended bass can severely limit the choice of tools available to anglers. Since only a relatively limited number of fishermen can coax a crankbait down to 20 feet, vertical fishing becomes the only option past that point.

The standard tools for deep vertical jigging are a lead spoon, plastic grub and heavy jig. But two gifts from western fishermen have become some of our best hopes for turning on these suspended bass.

A Fat Gitzit tube jig, fished on a 1/16th-ounce leadhead and 6-pound line, is Rich Tauber's most effective weapon for catching suspended bass. The Gitzit has a slow, tantalizing fall that can be irresistible to the fish, but painstakingly methodical to the fisherman.

Another effective tactic involves the "doddling" technique with a small diameter plastic worm. Doodling involves lightly shaking the rod tip to impart

Rich Tauber relies on a small-diameter worm for suspended bass.

action on the worm as it descends through the water or is being dragged across the bottom. Again, this is a slow, methodical method of fishing, but one of the best ways of being able to maintain a lure at a desired depth level.

With bass that are suspended at levels where crankbaits can reach them, Tauber recommends working the fish over with a fast-moving lure like a vibrating crankbait (Spot or Rat-L-Trap) or jerkbait like a Bomber Long A. "I always bring a fast-moving bait by them first in an attempt to get a reaction strike out of one of them," he says. "If that doesn't work, I'll then go to the finesse baits."

In the summer and winter when the thermocline (and/or oxycline) has positioned the bass at a certain depth, Joe Thomas uses that knowledge to search for bass that are not suspended away from cover. In other words, if there is a uniform thermocline at 28 feet, Thomas searches the lake for brushpiles and other structure at that exact level, knowing those bass will be more likely to strike.

It is important to emphasize that not all bass will suspend away from cover or structure. In the mid-summer and fall, bass in the Ohio River and midwestern lakes suspend above the tops of large hardwood trees, predictable positioning that Thomas actually takes advantage of. But, again, this isn't the same creature as the Lanier monster. A deep-diving crankbait will usually entice some strikes from those bass.

Bass will often suspend in deep water (20 to 50 feet) off of the ends of major points. For these bass, Tauber has enjoyed good success with a fast-moving top-water bait like a Rebel Pop-R or Heddon Zara Spook, making a 45-degree cast to ensure that the lure comes across the top of several depth levels along the long point.

When it comes to the open-water variety of suspended bass, though, many anglers take a similar approach to six-time BASS Masters Classic qualifier Ken Walker.

"I've spent a great deal of time scuba diving and seen tremendous numbers of bass that were suspended," Walker says. "They weren't feeding. They weren't swimming around. They were just there killing time. As a fisherman, when I see that on my depthfinder, I get the heck out of there."

But even those dreaded suspended bass can be caught with enough finesse and determination.

Chapter 35

Big, Bad Junkweed Bass

Jimmy Rogers lowered his boat into the water, started up his outboard and began cruising through what looked like the best bass waters in Florida.

And, after all, it was a private phosphate pit, the best of many privileged fishing spots that Rogers had access to. While central Florida's phosphate pits are renowned for producing trophy bass, Rogers had remarked that this one had a reputation all its own.

PROfile

We motored past some of the best looking sections of lily pads, mouth-watering stumps, even fallen trees that had been fished by only a handful of men since the pit was dug some 30 years ago. I couldn't believe what we were passing by.

Or what we were heading for.

In the distance, the water from bank to bank was covered with a solid limegreen carpet. Surely, this wasn't what Rogers had meant when he said we were in for some of the most bizarre — and successful — fishing I'd ever experienced.

Jimmy Rogers, host of a syndicated television show, is a former BASS Masters Classic qualifier.

The thought that this guy had spent too much time in the sun came to mind as Rogers lowered the trolling motor and made his first cast.

"Just wait and see," Rogers replied to my obvious skepticism as he cast a chrome-colored Bagley Bang-O-Lure toward the densest part of this floating green matter that surrounded us. Heck, you couldn't even see the water.

Rogers made three casts and each time he completed his retrieve, the Bang-O-Lure would come back covered with this foreign green stuff. Without even looking at it, much less cleaning it, he would cast again toward his target, oblivious to my laughter.

On the fourth cast into this mass of green, I finally saw the color of the water as a huge bass blew a hole in the floating green cover and inhaled the Bang-O-Lure. With more brute strength than finesse, Rogers boated the fish, an 8-pounder, released it and turned to snicker at me.

"Are you a believer now?" he asked, but I was too busy flailing away at that funny-looking green cover to answer.

As the morning went on, we would catch about two-dozen quality fish, all 2 1/2 pounds or better. And Rogers would get his limit of snickering in.

Welcome to the bizarre world of junkweed fishing, one of the most unusual techniques known to man for catching bass, both big in size and numbers. Rogers had let me in on a secret.

We were fishing water covered with duckweed, a thin layer of floating vegetation common in many lakes. But the technique is one that Rogers has scored well in lakes throughout the country, on a variety of floating vegetation. It's a time-proven winner.

And Jimmy Rogers has the kind of credentials that make you take notice to any secrets he decides to let you in on. Rogers, who hosts the Anglers in Action nationally syndicated television show, is a retired tournament pro who qualified for the 1980 BASS Masters Classic. In addition, Rogers was the runner-up two consecutive years in the American Bass Association World Championships.

And he's had good success along the B.A.S.S. circuit, where he has put his patented junkweed technique to work time and time again. A prime example is the 1980 B.A.S.S. Champs Tournament on Lake Guntersville in Alabama. Rogers robbed the milfoil for nine fish that weighed a whopping 45 pounds to finish fifth.

In the process, Rogers set a B.A.S.S. three-fish record for his trio of milfoil bass that weighed 19 pounds, 15 ounces.

"I first discovered it in 1971 when I was fishing Tenoroc (fish management area near Lakeland, Fla.)," Rogers says. "I had this pass that I always liked to fish whenever I was going in or coming out because it's right near where I put my boat in.

"I came in one day and it was covered with duckweed, covered over solid. So, I cussed a little since I wanted to fish there badly. So, before I put my boat up, I just threw a topwater plug right up in the middle of it. I snatched it about two or three times real hard when one about 8 pounds came up and ate it.

"I said 'Oh, my God, I've learned something.' So I caught two or three more good fish out of it, but it got dark quickly and I had to quit. The next time I went fishing, the only thing I looked for was duckweed."

But Rogers has been able to adapt this strange technique to other types of vegetation found throughout country.

With a bloom of duckweed creating a carpet on the surface of the water, Jimmy Rogers coaxed this bass into hitting a Bang-O-Lure.

"Duckweed is ideal because you need a floating type of vegetation that will hang on to the bait, but keep moving," Rogers explained. "If it's anything that's stationary, it's going to hang up.

"It will work in vegetation like milfoil or floating hyacinths, where the Bang-O-Lure can still pull a little bit at a time. I've had that Bang-O-Lure hung up in the hyacinths and kept twitching it because the tailspinner kept moving and had bass bust right through the hyacinths to get it.

"I've had excellent results using this Bang-O-Lure technique in the milfoil at Guntersville. The lure will hang up, so you have to drag a little with you and it will make a motion that attracts fish. A lot of people fish milfoil by using a weedless frog. That will work across the top of the milfoil and it doesn't make any noise. It will just create a little wake on the surface. The fish will actually blow a hole in the milfoil to get to it."

But the 5-inch Bang-O-Lure is much more effective because it makes noise and has three sets of treble hooks, so the success rate is higher than the frog that has one set of hooks.

Rogers claims the technique is ideal for the big southern reservoirs.

"It's a unique way to fish and there's different kinds of cover all over the United States that people can use this method on," he says. "Not only duckweed, which is found throughout the south, but milfoil and hyacinths as well.

"I've seen this work real well in the fall on some of the big reservoirs when the leaves die on the trees. The leaves will blow up into the coves and float on the water. That's a type of floating cover just like duckweed. You just throw it up in those leaves and retrieve it through the leaves.

"I've had great success with this up in Eufala. I was up there in November one year fishing a tournament and I got back into a spot where the leaves had blown off the trees and there were some open pockets. I took several 4- and 5-pound fish out of there."

Another place where the pattern has been successful is Toldeo Bend, the legendary reservoir on the Texas-Louisiana border. "They've got floating moss with logs and stuff around it," Rogers explains. "You can actually throw a Bang-O-Lure into the little big bass."

The ingredients in Rogers' personal junkweed gameplan consist of a 6 1/2-foot Quantum medium-action rod with a high-speed Quantum Rippin' reel. "You need a stiff rod because you never know what's under the cover, so you've got to keep them near the top," he said.

Rogers relies on 17-pound test line. "You need something that can stand some abrasion, because you never know what's under that floating cover," he says. "You never know what the fish might go down into once it hits the lure. So, it's a pretty heavy line situation. You can even use 20- or 30-pound line if you want to."

For consistent success, Rogers uses a 5-inch Bang-O-Lure. He uses a two-pronged criteria for selecting lure color for his junkweed specialty. On cloudy days, he uses a silver or gold Bang-O-Lure with a green or black back. On bright, sunny days, Rogers relies on the chrome-color, which reflects the sunlight.

The actual technique is simple.

Simply seek out any type of floating cover and either cast right into the heart of it or into little pockets of open water surrounded by this vegetation. The trick is to twitch the bait hard enough to create enough noise and movement to awaken neighboring bass, but not so fast that the fish doesn't have enough time to react to it.

"Everybody fishes topwater baits too fast," Rogers adds. "I usually twitch it two or three times. But when I twitch it, I leave slack in my line and I pop that slack out. When I do that, I don't move the bait more than 6 inches. Do that a couple of times and you should know if there's any interest in the area."

Rogers rarely bothers cleaning off the lure before it makes a return trip on his next cast.

"The only time I clean it is if stuff like real stringy moss is hanging off of it or something is fouling up the tailspinner. I like to keep the tailspinner clean because even as filthy as the thing gets, they'll hit it as long as that tailspinner is making noise. The more duckweed you get on it, the more weedless it becomes. It will only load up so much on the hooks and it's soft, so when a fish hits it, it doesn't hurt you as far as setting the hook."

Rogers theorizes why the technique is been so successful.

"The pattern doesn't surprise me," he said. "If a bass sees something he thinks might be hurt or crippled, he's going to eat it.

"It looks like anything easy to catch to a bass when it's coming overhead because it's moving slow and it's in that heavy cover. They don't investigate it nearly as closely as they would if it was sitting in clear water and there's good light penetration where they can see everything on that plug.

"And the floating vegetation like the duckweed actually helps the lure presentation. You throw up on top of that duckweed and it doesn't make a splash and it's not clear water. If you've ever watched a fish in clear water, if you throw in on top of him, any kind of splash will spook him. Then he'll come back and investigate what made the splash. This way, you're making such a silent presentation that it's over him before he knows it's there. And he just reacts."

Jimmy Rogers admits his technique is a little strange. But in this case, strange can be exhilarating.

"This technique is for the guy that loves to fish topwater and wants to fish it all day," he says. "And this is just an added technique that he can use to absolutely kill the fish. With this technique, all you see is the explosion."

Greg South plans his fishing strategy by combining a tide chart with a map of the James River.

Chapter 36

Tidal Fishing Tips

For today's accomplished bass angler — and even the experienced pro — it is the last frontier of fishing.

The modern-day bass enthusiast has mastered flipping in heavy vegetation, pitching to vertical objects, maneuvering a crankbait through treetops, doodling a tiny plastic worm at depths of 50 feet, powering a jerkbait across shallow flats, coaxing spawning fish with a small tubejig and working a jig-and-pig along a drop-off with the touch of a surgeon. And more.

PROfile

But tidal fishing still mystifies both the weekend angler and the tournament pro alike. The 1988 BASS Masters Classic on Virginia's historic James River illustrated that. Much of the tournament field didn't attempt to roll with the tide and play the tidal game, choosing instead to concentrate on a single area. Many of the most elite bass fishermen in America admitted they were lost when it came to tidewater fishing.

Virginia's Greg South is a tidal expert and two-time BASS Masters Classic qualifier.

"Tidal fishing can be a complete mystery to people who are unfamiliar with it," says tournament pro Shaw Grigsby, who grew up fishing the tidal fluctuations of Florida's Suwannee and St. Johns rivers. "It can be confusing even to the very best fishermen."

That is understandable.

Tidal fishing is a completely different world from the still-water lake and reservoir fishing that most us were educated on. Lake fishermen don't have to adjust to almost constantly changing conditions that can make a certain spot red-hot for a few minutes and then render it worthless for the rest of the day. Reservoir regulars don't have to face hours during their fishing day when their best area is high and dry.

Yet this type of fishing is well worth learning because tidal systems provide excellent habitat for bass that have been considerably less pressured than their impounded cousins. Some of the finest bass fishing in the country is located at the door step of some of America's biggest cities (Potomac, Hudson and James rivers are prime examples), but doesn't receive nearly as much fishing pressure as the more renowned reservoirs. That can largely be attributed to the perplexing nature of tidal fishing.

Tidal conditions can exist on river systems more than 100 miles from the coast, constantly changing to the beat of the moon phase. Tides on most inland rivers change once a day, featuring a high tide that inundates the marshes and a low tide that drains the shoreline.

With the exception of a few minutes of full high and dead low tide, tidal anglers face steadily changing fishing conditions.

"The key to tidal fishing is being in the right place at the right time," explains tournament veteran Woo Daves of Chester, Va., a tidewater expert. "It is a game of moving regularly from area to area to take advantage of the tide as it changes throughout the river."

"Common sense can teach you a lot about fishing the tides," Grigsby adds. "It's just like a rising water situation in a reservoir. As the tide rises and drops, the fish do the same thing — they move in and out from the shoreline. It's very similar to conditions you have in a reservoir when the water is up or down, but it takes place in a matter of minutes instead of days or weeks. It can be confusing to a lot of people because the change occurs so quickly."

Yet, tidal fishing can be the most reliable type of bass angling of all, to those who understand its intricacies.

"The tidal changes reliably dictate where the bass are likely to be holding, exactly how they are positioned and when they are going to be most active," claims Greg South, a two-time Classic qualifier and Richmond radiologist, who has fished the James River since 1972. "No other type of fishing tells you all of that."

The low tide eliminates much of the habitat that bass use (particularly along the shoreline and in the marshes), forcing them to congregate in obvious places. Those places include any object (tree, boulder or shoal) that provides a break in the current as well as the entrances to feeder creeks where baitfish are flushed out as the water drains into the main river.

With the presence of moving water, we know that bass will usually be facing the current to ambush baitfish or crawfish that are swept downstream. That is vital information for making the proper lure presentation. But it is important to remember that once the tide changes, the bass will move to the opposite side of the current break to adjust to the new direction of the flowing water. It is for that reason that bass will often be concentrated between a pair of fallen trees or large rocks.

The tide charts pinpoint the times when these river bass are most likely to be actively feeding — information that is mostly guesswork for still-water anglers.

"With a tidal system, you have a daily timetable to work with," says South, the runner-up in the 1984 Classic. "And you aren't at the mercy of some power company.

"The bass are tuned into feeding at certain points of the tide, particularly on the outgoing tide because there is less water and the baitfish get pulled out of the marshes and flooded grass areas. The baitfish are more abundant. On the incoming tide, as the water gets high, it disperses the baitfish. On the James River, I think the bass are more accustomed to resting on the incoming tide and more geared to feeding on the outgoing tide."

Most tidal veterans prefer the final 90 minutes of an outgoing tide and the first hour of incoming flow because it showcases all of the tidewater advantages — it eliminates water, positions bass in obvious places and puts them in an active mode.

And the published tide charts tell you when the fishing will be best.

"There is no substitute for experience with tidal fishing," Daves says, "but you can make up for it by studying river maps in relation to the tide charts."

The most productive approach to tidal fishing, the experts agree, is moving with the tide to duplicate the same condition (tidal stage) all along the river. With the right timing, it is possible to enjoy the most productive stage of the tide for several hours.

That is exactly how Roland Martin won a B.A.S.S. tournament on New York's Hudson River in 1984. Martin ran 60 miles south each day to get into position to fish the river's milfoil beds during the same stage of the tide. By calculating the tide tables and the speed with which the tide changed, Martin put together a stop-and-go schedule of running and fishing that put him in the position to fish the best types of structure at the right time and water level.

That strategy translated into 50 pounds of bass and a winning margin of 13 pounds.

"The secret to tidewater fishing is running the tide," Martin explains. "That is, when you find a pattern that works, you fish in a spot until the tide ceases to move, then you move upstream or downstream to a spot where the tide movement is stronger.

"With today's fast boats, you can run ahead of the tide and keep duplicating your pattern throughout the tidal system."

Woo Daves used the run-and-gun approach to tidal fishing in the 1988 Classic on the James River, but finished 6 ounces behind a man who all but ignored the tidal changes. Guido Hibdon worked a 300-yard stretch of shoreline in the Appomattox River for three days, using more battery power than gasoline, while Daves moved with the tide and fished more than 100 spots for individual bass.

Although Hibdon did not move with the tide, he could not escape its influence, which forced him to make some adjustments. The Missouri veteran had studied the Appomattox during a dead low-tide in pre-practice, noting the exact location of rocks, trees and stumps that extended from the shoreline. Once the tournament began, he simply returned to those places and used the tidal stage to dictate where he fished along each piece of structure. On a fallen tree, for example, Hibdon realized that the bass would be more toward the outside end of it as the tide lowered and closer to the shoreline end as the water climbed.

In a continuing contrast in philosophies and styles, the two subsequent Classics held on the James River were won by pros who elected to concentrate on a single area (Hank Parker in 1989 and Rick Clunn in 1990), while Daves' more traditional bump-and-run approach to tidal fishing produced fifth and fourth places, respectively.

The tidal stage that river veterans fear most is the full high tide, when the water has stopped moving, creating acres of shoreline habitat that disperses the bass. Many anglers like Greg South move with the tide to avoid having to face the fullest stage.

Catching bass during this tidal stage is, largely a matter of luck, Shaw Grigsby believes. "The best thing you can do is cover a lot of water with a bait that you have confidence in and move up inside of the shoreline or grass as far as possible," he says.

Bass will hold on a variety of cover or structure situations in a tidal system. The James River system is a prime example. In the James, the bass can be positioned on rocks, shoals, pilings or fallen trees. Yet, bass in the Chickahominy River (the main tributary of the James) are mostly likely found on boat docks, ducks blinds, lily pads and creek intersections.

Woo Daves says a common mistake made by tidal fishermen is ignoring the isolated pieces of structure found along the shoreline of the river. River bass will hold behind any object that offers some relief from the current and an ambush point.

Tidewater anglers must choose between concentrating on the main river or fishing the smaller creeks and tributaries that feed it. Each tidal river system is different. On Florida's St. Johns River, which has few tidal-influenced creeks, Grigsby works the boat docks on the main river (where the bass move when the outgoing tide pulls them from the shallow vegetation). Yet on the Suwannee River, he concentrates on the creeks.

"Creeks are my favorite because you can catch plenty of fish just working the creek mouths," Grigsby says. "As the tide comes out, the fish will always be on the creek mouths ambushing baitfish. An outgoing tide means three or four hours of fun fishing — just going from mouth to mouth and catching two or three fish off of each one."

Regardless of whether the bass are holding on main-river structure or along a creek entrance, one cardinal rule of tidal fishing holds true — present the lure in the direction of the current. A lure travelling with the current simply looks more natural to a bass waiting in ambush. For fishing current situations, Daves always positions his boat on the downstream side and casts into the flow. From that position, he can allow the current to carry him away from the structure once he hooks a fish.

Tidal fishing requires some subtle adjustments as well.

Daves keeps his worm rods rigged with two different sizes of bullet weights so that he can quickly adjust to the changing flow. When the current is strong, a 1/4- or 3/16-ounce weight may be needed to get the worm to the bottom. But as the tide eases and the water lowers, that heavy sinker will often spook fish. In that situation, Daves simply switches to a 1/8-ounce weight.

For most tidal situations, a plastic worm and small medium-running crankbait are Daves' primary weapons. Both can cover a variety of depth ranges, which is an important consideration with a constantly changing water level.

Not all of the considerations involved with tidal fishing involve catching fish. With the water fluctuating as much as 3 to 4 feet each day, tidal navigation can be difficult, at best, and treacherous, at worst.

More than half of the 42 qualifiers for the 1988 Classic discovered that either before the off-limits period began or during the official practice days. The James River's infamous mud bars collected such high-profile victims as Rick Clunn, Denny Brauer and Guido Hibdon.

"Getting stuck is easy to do," Daves says. "From a distance, you can't tell if the water is a foot deep or 50 feet deep. You pretty much have to stay in the channels and follow the channel markers until you learn a river.

"One beneficial tip that I've found to be true on this river and other tidewater rivers is to always be aware of the shoreline. If you are running up a creek and see trees on the bank, you will generally have plenty of depth. But if you see grass on both sides of the creek, don't shut the boat down because that is likely to be mud and you're likely to be in very shallow water."

The nation's tidal rivers may harbor some of the very finest bass fishing available, yet represent foreign soil to many bass enthusiasts. But a common-sense approach to tidewater will remove most of the mystery involved with fishing water that changes by the hour.

Jerry Rhyne works a Fat Gitzit along the retention wall for the cooling pond at the Sequoia Nuclear Plant on Chickamauga Lake.

Chapter 37

Seawall Savvy

Veteran bass pro Jerry Rhyne caught more than 120 bass on the final two days of the 1986 BASS Masters Classic - and he did not win.

The likeable Denver, N.C., angler finished sixth because the bass were small largemouths and few topped the 12-inch minimum length limit. But Rhyne's finish is not the important part of this story.

How many of us would like to catch 120 bass in two days? How many would like to catch 120 bass in a week?

While the fish were not enough to enable Rhyne to win the most coveted title in professional fishing, the kind of non-stop action he enjoyed would please almost any bass enthusiast. The average fisherman is happy enough many times to have his line stretched out regularly.

The significance of this story is not just that Jerry Rhyne caught a large number of bass, but where he located then. The fish were found along the most unlikely structure.

PROfile

Jerry Rhyne, a past B.A.S.S. winner, is a 10-time BASS Masters Classic qualifier.

He caught them along a seawall on Tennessee's Chickamauga Lake.

For years we have watched concrete seawalls replace natural banks along lakes in this country as waterfront property increases in value. To many, the stark, white barricade between land and water is an unsightly substitute for the natural shoreline.

But anglers like Rhyne have discovered some value to the concrete structure- it holds bass.

"Any type of concrete wall that's got some water depth along it is a good source for at least some small fish," explains Rhyne, an eight-time qualifier for the prestigious Classic. "I've found this to be true in lakes throughout the South and as far north as upstate New York.

"Yet most fishermen, including many pros, won't give a seawall a second look. That is often a mistake."

Rhyne has caught all three major species of bass next to seawalls.

"Seawalls hold bass throughout the year for one simple reason," he says. "Baitfish stay around the walls, eating algae. It may not provide the best cover for a bass, but its food source is always around."

Although he has heard reports of bass as large as 13 pounds being caught from along seawalls,, Rhyne calls these concrete structures his "limit holes." The bass aren't big, but they're plentiful.

The exception to that rule is when spotted bass move into a seawall; large spots often inhabit the walls, Rhyne says.

"Five pounds is about the biggest bass I've ever caught off a seawall. I don't fish them with the anticipation of catching a big one," Rhyne claims. "Seawalls really don't provide enough cover for a big bass. There's nothing in which it can hide."

Seawalls like Rhyne's Classic concrete compensate in quantities of fish for what they lack in big bass.

During the Classic, Rhyne concentrated on the large concrete seawall that separates the Sequoia Nuclear cooling pond from the Tennessee River. While the rest of the Classic field raced toward submerged milfoil beds and creek banks, Rhyne stayed close to the launching site and caught an amazing number of small bass by fishing a Fat Gitzit (a hollow-bodied "tube lure") on both sides of the seawall.

Using a system of fishing seawalls that was developed on the populated lakes of North Carolina and refined in places like the Thousand Islands area of New York, Rhyne didn't worry about getting strikes. The question was -- over and over-- would the next Gitzit victim measure?

That seawall had one key ingredient, Rhyne says, that made it productive throughout the year- water depth.

"You really need a depth of 10 feet or more for a seawall to be a consistent producer," he explains. "That water depth provides some overhead cover for the fish, which I think is important.

"There are a couple of exceptions, though. Even shallow seawalls will hold fish in the spring because the bass will bed around seawalls from the first of spring through early June, depending on where the lake is located. Florida lakes are different. The concrete walls there absorb heat from the sunshine, and it's

The Fat Gitzit enabled Jerry Rhyne to catch more than 120 bass during two days of the 1986 BASS Masters Classic.

the first place the bass will spawn. That's particularly true with a seawall in a canal or creek"

While the Gitzit was his ticket to more than 120 bass in two days during the Classic, Rhyne uses a variety of lures, depending on the type of wall, water clarity, time of year and the depth the baitfish appear to be holding.

In clear water, Rhyne's favorite seawall weapon is the Gitzit, which can be dropped vertically along the wall and fished at different depths. In off-colored water, he prefers a spinnerbait or crankbait, depending on how deep he guesses the baitfish to be. When bait activity can he seen near the surface, a buzzbait can be deadly, he says. The buzzbait, crankbait and spinnerbait are fished parallel to the wall.

On seawalls that have abutments or partitions that form a corner along the wall, Rhyne uses an action-tail worm like the Ditto Gator Tail; he rigs the worm on a 1/16-ounce sinker to ensure a slow fall. Believing that the bass use such corners to avoid the current, Rhyne pitches the worm directly into the corner and allows it to fall down onto the fish.

The cold water temperatures of winter dictate a slow lure presentation, so Rhyne uses a lightweight jig with a small pork trailer.

"If I had to pick one all-around bait for fishing seawalls, it would be a grub," Rhyne says. "If the water is clear, I use a clear-type grub; in dingy water, I use a white, dark green or chartreuse grub. With a grub, you can control the depth and find out the depth the baitfish are holding, which is crucial in this type of fishing. You can swim a grub at different levels, and fish of all sizes will hit it. A grub is an excellent tool for catching a quick limit of keeper fish."

Generally, seawall bass are suspended fish, so a vertical presentation is important. Only once has Rhyne found fish at the base of a concrete wall: during a tournament on the St. Lawrence River in New York. There, he caught several 4-pound-plus smallmouth bass by bouncing a jig along the bottom.

"That's the exception, though," Rhyne says.

Unusual, too, is finding large bass along seawalls. But for just the sheer fun of catching plenty of fish, these stone sanctuaries are hard to beat.

Chapter 38

Bass on the Rocks

On a dreary late February morning, Rick Clunn zips his jacket a little higher, cranks the motor and heads northward up the main channel in Alabama's Lake Guntersville. Several freezing miles later, he makes his first stop and begins casting to a small strip of riprap that wraps around a bridge foundation.

PROfile

March has just arrived as Woo Daves ventures out on the James River for his first fishing trip in several frosty Virginia weeks. His boat isn't on plane for more than three minutes before Daves spots his target and makes his first stop — a long, straight jetty.

It is mid-March now, but still cold as Roland Martin opens the rod box for the first time after making a long run across big Santee-Cooper Reservoir. Lifting out a cranking rod, he begins paralleling a line of dike riprap that stretches for as far as the eye can see.

Virginia's Woo Daves is a nine-time Classic qualifier and a winner on the B.A.S.S. circuit.

All of the above scenes were played out in the late winter/early spring period when many bass enthusiasts stay indoors, rather than brave the elements. After all, the bass are usually still in their sluggish winter mode as the water first begins its long warming climb upward. And it is still cold enough to be miserable.

But all of the above scenes produced enough fishing action to make almost any fisherman leave the fireplace. Enough fishing action to justify enduring the cold and the manmade wind-chill factor of running in a boat. Enough action to make you forget the winter doldrums.

And the common denominator in the above scenes is rocks.

Simply stated, rocks are the answer to locating the most active bass in southern lakes, reservoirs and rivers during the early spring. Whether it be a long riprap serving as a foundation or a jetty serving as a current break in a river system, these rocky structures are bass magnets. And for good reason.

"Heat," Rick Clunn says. "Riprap or any rock in the northwestern portions of a lake or reservoir will have about the warmest water available during this time of year. And the bass will seek out that warmer water and bunch up."

"The rocks retain the heat, which is a big factor during this time of year," adds Roland Martin. "The sunlight is absorbed by the rocks, which puts radiation into the water and warms it. So this is where the first active fish from the winter are found. To give you an idea just how active, this is the first place I crank each year."

Riprap and/or jetties are found in almost every reservoir and river system, except for the natural lakes of Florida. Although there are some advanced techniques that fully exploit these structures, they are simple to locate and visible objects that are usually easy to fish. Those two aspects of fishing work to the advantage of even the most inexperienced angler.

And given the extra warmth that attracts bass, these rock structures are the places to concentrate on in the early spring. Here are some techniques for taking full advantage of these man-made bass-attractors.

RIPPING RIPRAP

Although no one seems to know where the term "riprap" comes from, by definition it is a line or series of strategically placed rocks and boulders designed to protect the shoreline from erosion. It may align the foundation of bridge pilings or serve as the base for a dike or levee. Riprap can be a 100-foot section of rocks serving as a seawall in front of lakefront property or 100 miles of rocks protecting the dike around parts of a major reservoir like Santee-Cooper.

Where riprap is abundant, determining which sections of the rocks to fish can be a challenge, particularly on the big reservoirs that feature miles of this type of structure.

A cardinal rule in early spring is to concentrate on the riprap in the northwestern portions of a reservoir or the northwestern-most shore of a river system. This is the area of the lake or river that receives the strongest sunlight penetration during this time of the year.

Veteran Tennessee angler John Hunt uses two criteria for eliminating sections of riprap — depth and uniformity.

Depth is the most important consideration, claims Hunt, who avoids riprap in water deeper than 10 feet. But any portion of riprap that is adjacent to deep water (such as a line of rocks on a shallow flat near the river channel) can be especially productive.

Rock jetties have long been consistent producers for Woo Daves.

"Actually pinpointing fish on a long stretch of riprap is relatively easy, if you approach it right," Hunt explains. "I would never just randomly cast to a half-mile-long stretch of riprap, because you will waste a lot of time doing that.

"The key is concentrating on something different on the riprap. Like bass in grass lakes or even bass along a river channel ledge, bass on riprap will hold around some irregularity in that riprap. It may be where the rocks form a little point in the water. Or a big rock that is sticking out. Or a cut in the rocks that creates a little pocket.

"A straight riprap section doesn't interest me. It has to have something different on it. That irregularity will be a gathering point for bass."

Bass anglers experienced at catching riprap bass insist that the key to catching fish on this type of structure is keeping the bait in the so-called strike zone, which is usually extremely narrow and close to the rocks. The best way to accomplish that is by aligning the boat with the rocks and paralleling the riprap with the retrieve.

"There's a lot more to fishing riprap than merely casting to the rocks," Martin says. "In fact, casting to the riprap is the biggest mistake you can make.

"The way to fish it is with proper boat positioning. Get parallel with the riprap and run your trolling motor along it. I like to keep my trolling motor in 8 to 10 feet of water and cast ahead of the boat down the riprap. Keeping the bait as tight as possible to the riprap is critical."

Although some fishermen like the legendary Tom Mann have the ability to finesse a plastic worm through the rocks with great prowess, the most common riprap tool is a crankbait. A medium-diving crankbait is Martin's primary riprap weapon.

"Throwing ahead of the boat and along the riprap, I try to drop the plug in 2 to 3 feet of water and for the first 5 to 10 feet of the retrieve, the lure is coming out at an angle and really digging the bottom and bouncing off of rocks. As it bumps its way deeper, it gets down 7 or 8 feet. I'm hitting rocks and bottom during the entire retrieve. By keeping the proper angle on my cast, I have my lure hugging the bottom on the entire cast.

"One little trick I like to try with riprap fishing is the old pause trick. About halfway back to the boat, I stop the lure and let it float up a couple of feet. Then I start it again and run it a few more feet before stopping and pausing it again. This really works well at times on riprap because the water is still fairly cold and the bass are somewhat lethargic. They will usually hit the crankbait while it is stopped and it usually isn't a vicious strike, so you need to watch your line at all times."

Although a crankbait is his primary lure in the colder times, John Hunt takes a three-pronged approach to working riprap in the summer and fall of the year when the fishing can be excellent. He first works the surface with a buzzbait or stickbait in search of the most aggressive bass. Then he will crank it, using a parallel retrieve. Finally, Hunt fishes tighter and slower to the rocks with a jig-and-pig combination.

"If you work it from top to bottom like that, you'll know fairly quickly if there are any bass holding on that section of riprap," Hunt says.

Another good lure for quickly covering long stretches of riprap, according to former BASS Masters Classic champion Charlie Reed of Oklahoma, is a jerkbait — a stickbait with a shallow diving lip that can be worked quickly through an area, covering a depth range from the surface to 7 feet or so.

FISHING THE JETTIES

Jetties, sometimes called wingdams, are found on every river system, offering a series of bass-holding structures that begin paying off in the early spring and continue to be productive through late fall.

Strategically placed, jetties are positioned to maintain the direction of the flow of the river, while preventing siltation and erosion of the bank. Most jetties are located in the straight sections of a river, but many are stationed in curves and bends. By examining a quality map, you can easily pinpoint the location of a rock jetty or series of jetties.

"Jetties give the bass fisherman a very distinct advantage as long as there is current present," says Joe Hughes, an outstanding bass fisherman, who has refined the art of jetty fishing on the Arkansas River system. "Most importantly, they provide an area where two things happen: baitfish, like shad, and crawfish are attracted to jetties because they provide a break in the current. And bass use that current break as an ambush point.

"These are places where bass come to feed. And if you know where the bass come to feed in a river system — where they can feed all day long — you're ahead of the game. Jetties are one of the best places to be fishing."

The key is current.

Whether it is a swift, continuous wall of water or a subtle flow, current is what makes jetties productive. It is what positions both the baitfish and bass on these rocks. Without current, there is little reason for the baitfish to seek refuge behind these current breaks. Subsequently, there is little reason for the bass to be positioned there.

Current positions the bass at obvious places along a rock jetty. With any flow at all, the bass will be on the back side (calm side) of the jetty, particularly around the points formed by the rocks, where they lay in ambush position for food to be swept by.

Woo Daves, a veteran tournament angler from Chester, Va., stresses the importance of boat positioning for ensuring the proper casting angles to a jetty. He begins by putting the nose of his boat into the current and using the trolling motor to maintain that position. Keeping his boat even with the end of the jetty, Daves parallels both sides of the jetty with several casts. He then moves away from it and casts into the current, bringing his lure past the point of the jetty in the direction of the natural flow.

Daves emphasizes the need to examine a jetty closely to determine likely places where the bass could be positioned. He recalls a 1987 B.A.S.S. tournament on the Hudson River in New York in which he was the early leader after scoring well on a peculiar-looking jetty. The jetty was missing several rocks in the middle of it, creating a funnel effect. Using a heavy weight, Daves pitched a plastic worm into the hole and caught five bass on consecutive casts, weighing more than 15 pounds.

The best tool for working a jetty and the flowing water is a crankbait, according to Daves and Hughes, who prefer to bounce the lure off of the rocks during the retrieve. But 14-time Classic qualifier Ricky Green, another Arkansas River veteran, cites surface lures like a buzzbait or stickbait as his primary jetty weapons, particularly in the summer and fall.

The most productive jetties are shallow, but adjacent to deeper water like a river channel or creek mouth. On the James River, Daves' favorite jetties are located near large, deep gravel pits just off of the river.

"The key to fishing the jetties is making accurate casts and being mobile," Joe Hughes says. "You need to make accurate casts to take advantage of the bass in ambush position.

"And you have to fish as many jetties as possible to find the ones that are holding fish. In about six casts, you can usually tell if it is holding fish. If nothing happens after six casts, move on to the next one. And don't be afraid to return to the jetties where you caught fish."

Woo Daves calls it "patterning the jetties."

"Once you familiarize yourself with an area that has a lot of jetties, you fish them like you do bushes, logs or anything," he explains. "You just go from one to the next until you find the ones that are holding the fish. And a lot of times, you'll get a limit off of one jetty because that happens to be where the bass are schooled up."

Rock structure like riprap and jetties can provide the kind of fishing that will satisfy most any appetite. It begins when both the fish and fishermen are still lethargic from the cold of winter and continues through the fall. These rockpiles are worth checking out on every fishing trip.

Chapter 39

A Gameplan for Hydrilla

It is the scourge of skiers. It is cursed by boaters. It is despised by most fishermen.

But intelligent, experienced anglers know it can be a boon for bass.

It is hydrilla, an exotic fast-growing, stringy form of aquatic vegetation that has long dominated many lakes in Florida and has begun to make its presence felt throughout the South in places like Texas, Alabama and along the Tennessee River.

PROfile

With a growth capability of an inch per day, hydrilla, at its worst, restricts boat movement, alters the class distribution of resident fish populations and causes oxygen depletion resulting in fish kills. But that's when the vegetation has completely smothered a lake or waterway.

At its best, hydrilla can breathe new life into aging reservoirs and lakes where most of the natural brush and vegetation has disappeared over time.

David Fenton knows that as well as anyone.

Fenton, a qualifier for the prestigious BASS

Bernie Schultz, a 1989 BASS Masters Classic qualifier, is a past Red Man Florida Division champion and Golden Blend winner.

Masters Classic in 1985, guides on Texas' Lake Conroe, located near Houston. Fenton has fished Lake Conroe extensively before, during and after the emergence of hydrilla and he swears by its fish-producing ability.

"I love hydrilla," he says. "It provides the best fish cover there is. It provides everything a bass needs — food, cover, shade and ambush points. It's fantastic cover.

"It saved Lake Conroe from dying and returned good fishing to us. I believe most lakes have a cycle. From my experience, I believe most lakes reach their peak after six years or so and start to go downhill. I believe it prolonged the length of Lake Conroe's productivity. At the point when they started eradicating the hydrilla, Lake Conroe was 11 years old, yet it was still one of the top-producing lakes in Texas. But they got rid of the hydrilla, it really hurt our fishing. Now it's going through a double downhill fall because the lake is old and now, all of a sudden, there are no weeds."

While Lake Conroe regulars like Fenton, Rick Clunn, Randy Fite and Zell Rowland (all Classic qualifiers) found hydrilla to be a plus for their home water, the vegetation fell prey to real estate developers who believed a shoreline choked with hydrilla would detract from their ability to sell lots, according to Fenton.

But that's not unusual. There is a war on hydrilla in several states, particularly Florida where biologists from the Florida Game and Fresh Water Fish Commission, who have no control over herbicidal spraying of hydrilla, constantly battle with the various Water Management Districts that control the state's water supplies.

Forrest Ware, bureau chief of the commission's Division of Fisheries, is a fan of hydrilla and its ability to transform aging bodies of waters into productive fisheries.

"Hydrilla has received so much bad press over the past decade," Ware explains. "In Florida, hydrilla has been very successful in improving the quality of fishing on big lakes like Orange and Lochloosa (near Gainesville).

"But in any lake, whether it be Okeechobee or the St. Johns, you've got to have a good vegetation response to get a good crop of gamefish. It's kind of like a steak-and-potatoes relationship as far as Florida's natural lakes are concerned. Man, in his never-ending efforts to better manage Mother Nature, sometimes interferes with that process. If we can get these chemical people to change their attitude about hydrilla, we'll be better off. Rather than taking an attitude that they have to wipe out everything, if they'd let some of the plant develop and maintain a manageable level, we'd be able to produce some tremendous fishing in these lakes that we've kind of written off in past years for being degraded.

"Hydrilla can be a very useful plant if you take a management approach rather than an annihilation approach to it. But the chemical people just want to nuke every strand of it."

Ware, a fisheries biologist, would get considerable argument from hydrilla's detractors. But Doug Hannon isn't one of them.

"Hydrilla is among the very best weedy habitat because it can absorb and metabolize the high nutrient loads that we are putting in our waters," adds

Hannon, a world-renowned big-bass expert, who is also a biologist. "Not only is it good habitat for fish, but, in its way, helps keep our water a little cleaner by filtering the water coming in and puts those nutrients into a non-harmful form."

But Hannon's main affection with the stringy growth lies in its ability to hold large numbers of bass.

Fishermen who don't understand how to fish hydrilla-infested lakes regard it as an enemy. All they know is that it gets caught up in their outboard props, stops the strongest trolling motors and clings to their lures on a regular basis. To them, hydrilla, at its best, is a nuisance.

Bernie Schultz, a past Classic qualifier who lives in Gainesville, Fla., and regularly fishes Orange and Lochloosa lakes where hydrilla has a stronghold, is a hydrilla veteran. He probably understands the plant as well as most biologists and regularly puts that biological understanding to good use.

"People have the wrong attitude about hydrilla," he says. "I believe it holds a lot of forage fish.

"Some biologists have expressed the view that the balance is wrong and if it's allowed to continue to grow and overwhelm a lake, the balance of forage fish will eventually hurt the bass population. I don't agree with that. I believe it's a cyclic thing and every year the waterfowl come and remove hydrilla. And the winter freezes kill off the hydrilla. And the forage fish remain healthy and the bass remain healthy."

There is a definite art to fishing this type of vegetation. It's nothing like working a lilypad field or flipping the holes in milfoil flats.

The key to successfully fishing hydrilla is to adjust your tactics as the vegetation goes through its annual growing routine, according to Schultz. The cold temperatures of winter kill off a large percentage of hydrilla (except in southern Florida) and the plant starts its growth cycle all over again.

"There are several things to consider when fishing hydrilla and the most important one is to recognize the stage at which the plant has developed during its growing season," explains Schultz, who has refined his hydrilla-fishing system into a fine art. "The plant goes through very definite growth stages from the time it first starts to appear until it is fully grown and matted over on top of the water.

"If you pay attention to exactly what growth stage the hydrilla is at and change your tactics as it reaches each new growth stage, you'll be surprised how many different types of lures will catch fish. Most people think you can only fish hydrilla with a plastic worm, but there are times when you can use a variety of different baits and you'll be more successful than the person that just sticks with a plastic worm."

Through years of experience, Schultz has identified five distinct growth stages of hydrilla. He tailors his tactics to take advantage of the growth characteristics of the plant at each stage.

After the cold winter temperatures have killed off the hydrilla, the first stage is what Schultz prefers to as the Adolescent Stage, which usually lasts a couple of months. At this stage, the plant is between 5 and 30 inches in height and can best be found by using a flasher. Once these submergent grass beds are located, if the water depth is suitable, he actually graphs the larger beds looking for pockets, cuts and edges that could serve as ambush points for bass.

The hydrilla at this stage is little more than wispy free-standing fingers of grass. "There are certain readings you'll find with a depthfinder that will indicate this thin, sparse growth, which is perfect for crank bait fishing," Schultz says. "You can actually run a crank bait through these fingers without much problem and a bright, vibrating lure like a Rat-L-Trap or Storm's Texas Shad will really catch fish at this growth stage.

"But crank-baiting the fingers is not for everybody. It's not the most enjoyable way to fish. It's a very effective way to catch fish, but you will get hung up a lot. But I've found that's when I get a lot of impulse strikes when fishing hydrilla. When the bait gets hung on a strand of hydrilla, I rip it through these fingers and as it pulls free, I often get a strike. It's happened too many times to be an accident. I think it triggers a strike similar to the way bouncing a crank bait off of a stump or dock piling triggers a strike."

Another productive tactic during this stage is swimming a worm across the top of the underwater vegetation.

The second stage, which usually occurs through the three spring months, is the Crown Stage. In this stage, the hydrilla fingers have grown to the surface and are just beginning to curl over the top of the water. At this stage, the plant is almost fully developed and its stalks are thick — too thick to think about crank-baiting. The most effective technique during this stage is flipping the edges of the vegetation (where it meets open water) or small, open holes in the middle of the hydrilla. But spoons and minnow-type top-water lures worked quickly along the edges of this vegetation are usually effective early and late.

In the summer months, hydrilla reaches its full maturity and blankets the surface, while still remaining rooted. During this Matted Stage, Schultz concentrates on working huge openings in the grass or "contained pools of water big enough to get your boat in and still make a long cast. These big pools that are surrounded on all sides by hydrilla usually hold good concentrations of fish." Schultz casts worms, top-water lures and crankbaits throughout the day in these open-water areas.

In the late summer/early fall, hydrilla begins the downward side of its cycle. It is during this time that the plant actually smothers itself. This stage of the plant's growth is characterized by huge mats of hydrilla, which block off sunlight from its stalks, killing that portion of the plant. While hydrilla can remain alive for several months while unattached from the lake bottom, it creates huge open-water domes or caverns that provide shade from the intense summer heat and holds large numbers of bass.

The Cavern Stage is Schultz' favorite time to fish hydrilla.

"Try to visualize these huge floating mats of vegetation that have nothing but big caverns of open water underneath that are void of weed growth," he says. "These places are excellent areas for bass. They are almost like a boat dock. It offers shade and ambush points for baitfish."

To penetrate the 3- or 6-inch dense mat of surface vegetation, Schultz usually uses a 3/4- to 1-ounce pegged bullet sinker teamed with a ribbon plastic worm like a Gillraker. Once the worm breaks through this incredibly weedy barrier, you will often have an immediate strike. Texas anglers use specially-designed jigs with cone-shaped heads to penetrate the hydrilla during this stage.

The final stage of hydrilla's growth is the Dying Stage, in which the hydrilla has begun to disappear, leaving large open pockets that are usually inhabited by schooling bass that are foraging for food on the outside of the plant. A Rat-L-Trap crankbait is usually very productive during this time when the schooling fish are abundant.

When fishing hydrilla, Schultz doesn't place much emphasis on lure color. He usually sticks with silver or chrome to imitate shad or gold to copy the native golden shiners, a bass delicacy, for crankbaits, spoons and topwater lures. Dark-colored worms, along with the shad-colors have been the most productive worm colors in hydrilla.

To some, hydrilla is a nuisance. To others, it's a mystery. But by paying attention to the characteristics of the plant you will find that hydrilla is also one of the very best havens for bass known to man.

Rick Clunn enticed this 7-pound bass from the waters of the Appomattox River during the 1989 BASS Masters Classic.

Chapter 40

Overcoming Muddy Water

The early spring rains have come and for the past four days it has fallen in steady sheets. Relentless rain.

The weekend finds a slight let-up in the rainfall, but the precipitation has already done its damage. Rusty-colored muddy water is everywhere, from the back of the coves to the vegetation that lines the main river.

PROfile

The prospect of fishing amidst this reddish-brown soup is enough to dampen almost any angler's attitude. It's a typical lousy day when many fishermen would simply find something else to do.

"But muddy water isn't all bad," says tournament king Rick Clunn. "Muddy water doesn't mean that your chances of catching fish are over. Fishing muddy water just means you have to change your approach."

Texan Rick Clunn is the best clutch performer in competitive fishing.

Clunn knows well from experience. Neither his days as a Texas guide nor his tournament travels allowed him to simply skip a day or two when the lake muddied up. He has had to persevere and, as a result, has developed a system for catching fish under this adverse condition.

The first step toward catching fish is an attitude adjustment, Clunn says. You can catch bass in muddy water.

"Basically, I prefer off-colored water, whether it's muddy, murky or stained," he explains. "I much prefer it over a clear-water situation."

Thinking positively, muddy water actually offers fishermen some advantages over other types of water clarity. It positions bass at a predictable depth. The fish tend to be less spooky. And Clunn contends that bass that cannot see the lure coming into their territory are much likely to attack than fish in clearer water who have the opportunity to inspect it.

That's the good side of muddy-water fishing.

There are two bad sides — cold water and freshly muddied water — when fishing is consistently terrible.

"Muddy water isn't a problem unless it's cold water or fresh muddy water that has a lot of suspended particles in it," the Montgomery, Texas, pro says. "The worst time is when the muddy water is extremely cold — in the 40s.

"When the water gets anywhere below 50, the fishing gets tough. The metabolism of the fish is totally controlled by that cold water, so they will be extremely inactive. They don't get any sunlight penetration through the muddy water, so they simply slow down and stay that way to avoid burning any energy (calories). They just won't bite."

With fresh muddy water, the suspended particles affect the bass' food chain in the area, Clunn says, and can actually confuse a bass' senses to the point that he will simply shut down to adjust. Being very adaptable creatures, bass can usually adjust enough to begin migrating and feeding again as the particles settle.

A potentially good place to fish during days when the lake is in the process of becoming muddy is around large beds of aquatic vegetation. These grass beds will strain the floating particles somewhat, creating an environment that is more natural to the bass. As a result, it is more likely to conduct its normal behavioral patterns, like feeding.

Clunn actually enjoys fishing warm muddy water, citing the predictability it dictates.

Bass in warm muddy water will almost always be positioned shallow. And depth is the first consideration a bass fishermen concentrates on when trying to locate fish.

"I am a shallow-water fisherman," Clunn explains. "There are more fish accessible in shallow water. The muddy water keeps the fish up near the surface — so you don't have a lot of baits to worry about — and they are less spooky.

"It all boils down to light penetration. In a muddy lake, the sunlight is not going to penetrate very far below the surface. In a lake like Livingston in Texas, you don't ever have to worry about fishing below 10 feet. But in a clear lake like Lake Mead or Lake Powell, you will find fish in 80 or 90 feet. The sunlight penetrates that far down, so the bass and its food chain have no problem existing at that depth."

As a rule of thumb, Clunn looks for fish in 2 to 5 feet of water and near the bank. "Forget everything else under most conditions," he says. "If I had to pick the most important thing about fishing muddy water, it would be to stay in 1 to 2 feet of water against the bank."

Fishing in water where bass can no longer rely on vision as their dominant sense demands some adjustments as well. It will surprise many people to learn that bass in muddy water habitats develop other keen senses well enough to survive nicely, Clunn says.

It will also surprise some to hear that Clunn believes the second most dominant sense among muddy-water bass is the sense of smell. For that reason, he uses a fish attractant, like Fish Formula, on his lures.

Muddy-water bass rely heavily on their sense of hearing sound and detecting vibration. Appealing to that sense of vibration, which is detected along the bass' lateral line, is the key to scoring in muddy water, Clunn says.

Muddy water automatically eliminates some lures.

Because the fish are almost always shallow, deep-running crankbaits are eliminated. And Clunn eliminates finesse baits like small plastic worms, choosing instead to use bulkier lures that displace more water, therefore creating more vibration that can be detected from greater distances.

Clunn's muddy-water lure choices are a large bladed spinnerbait, big jig-and-pork combination, buzzbait, fat plastic worms like the Ditto Gator Trail and a large, shallow-diving crankbait. "My favorite crankbait is anything similar to the old Big O that has a fat, wide wobble, but doesn't run very deep," he says. "Remember, you are trying to appeal to their senses and which sense is the most acute in muddy water? The sense of detecting vibration."

Artificial lures should be fished slowly to allow the practically-blind bass enough time to react to the vibration it has noticed. Ideally, you should be using a bait that is bulky enough for him to detect and then give him ample time to zero in on it.

Rick Clunn's tournament success is proof positive that muddy-water fishing is not a complete wash-out. By borrowing a little of his knowledge and employing some of his tactics, even muddy-water days can be productive.

Ken Cook relies on his electronics to pinpoint thermoclines during the hottest days of the year.

Chapter 41

Summertime Bottom Tactics

The pattern of most summertime bass fishermen is predictable.

Once summer arrives, most bass anglers in lakes throughout the country continue to hammer the same shoreline structure they work throughout the year. It's the same cover where they catch fish during the fall, winter and spring, but knowledgeable fishermen will tell you that fishing for summer bass often requires a radical change in tactics.

Veteran anglers like John Hunt, Neal Parker and Bert Fischer head for deep water when the scorching days arrive and work bottom structure — a vastly overlooked type of structure — with consistent success.

"Most fishermen just don't adjust their methods when summer gets there," says Fischer, who guided on famed Santee- Cooper Reservoir in South Carolina for seven years before moving to Lake Okeechobee, where he guides out of Roland Martin's Clewiston Marina. "They continue to do the same old things.

"But the good fishermen, especially the pros, will chance their tactics for summertime, particularly when it gets real hot — the dog days. The heat of the summer has as much effect on the fish as any season. It may cause them to move more than any season. When June, July and August get here, the fish have to find relief from the sun and the heat. As a result, the vast majority of the fish

I caught at Santee during those three months were between 25 and 32 feet deep and on the bottom."

Neal Parker is an accomplished tournament pro and guide who makes his home in Lake Worth, Fla. But he grew up and guided on Kentucky and Barkley lakes, where he developed a productive system of deep-water bottom-fishing during the hottest months of the year.

"The deep-water bottom patterns are the most overlooked patterns on Kentucky and Barkley and lakes throughout the country, particularly the big southern reservoirs," says Parker, who qualified for the prestigious BASS Masters Classic in 1981. "What happens in the summertime is that 90 percent of the fishermen stay in shallow water and refuse to budge.

"But the fishermen who produce consistently in the summer have taught themselves to fish deep-water structure, which is where the heat and that intense sun forces them to move to in the summertime."

Both Parker and Fischer rarely fish the obvious deep-water structures, though. They prefer to fish more subtle bottom structure in deep water when the weather really heats up.

"Anybody who wants to do some deep-water fishing — I'm talking about the average John Doe that reads Bassmaster and reads that the fish are supposed to be on the old roadbeds and at intersections of creeks and rivers — automatically starts with those types of structures," Parker explains. "So even certain deep-water patterns are starting to get more and more pressure.

"That's why when I fish deep-water, I have a tendency toward fishing something that's a little bit different."

A not-so-obvious key to summer fishing on Kentucky, Barkley and other southern lakes, Parker says, is to fish the bottom of deep-water structure that is located near a shallow area. "What I have found in lakes all over the country is that what happens in the summertime is that most of the fish will move off to deeper water, but remain close to shallow water, where they can run up and grab a quick meal," he says. "In the summertime on Kentucky and Barkley lakes, you would find enormous schools of shad back in the bays and out on the shallow flats. And the bass would hold on the bottom of some deep-water structure, right on the edge of where it dropped off from shallow to real deep."

"Fishing the break," as Parker calls it, is a summer tactic that has produced for years. A prime example of what he is referring to is a stump row located on the (deep-water side) edge of a river channel where the water would drop from the 5-foot shallow flats to 40 feet. The fish would be holding on the bottom structure of the deep-water side, which provided shade from the relentless sun.

If the water isn't too deep, Parker uses a crankbait to quickly cover the area. For water depths that a crankbait can't penetrate, he switches to a worm, heavy spoon or jig-and-pig.

"Vertically jigging a spoon or a worm is a very productive way to catch these fish," Parker adds. "In that deep water, you can get right over the top of the structure, hold your position with your depth finder and vertically jig around that stump row or brushpile.

"That's an excellent way to catch fish when nobody seems to be catching fish during the heat of the summer."

Tennessee's John Hunt, a past Classic qualifier and winner on the now-defunct U.S. Bass circuit, believes that the common plastic grub is often unsurpassed for catching deep-structure summer bass. The attributes of the grub, he says, include a lifelike action, the ability to have its depth easily regulated, the versatility to be both cast and vertically presented and an exposed hook, which leads to successful hook-ups.

"It is hard to find a better deep-structure tool than a grub," Hunt claims. "It is particularly good in the summer."

Bert Fischer, a former tournament pro and much-publicized guide, shares Parker's enthusiasm for summertime deep-water bottom fishing. And, because of his self-taught system of fishing these types of patterns, he shares Parker's success rate.

"In the summertime, I always headed for deep-water holding areas on Santee, deep-water sanctuaries," he says. "It was automatic for me.

"After the bass had spawned out in the late spring, they would go out on creek channels and move toward deeper water. They tended to gang up, a lot of times, in a little tight school in this deeper water, some place along a creek channel. And that's where they would spend the summer. Throughout the hottest parts of summer, most of the fish would be 15 to 30 feet deep and holding on the bottom. Every summer."

But finding these deep-water holding areas takes a healthy effort on the part of fisherman, depth finder and trolling motor, Fischer cautions. The areas along these creek channels that hold the most summertime bottom bass are almost always the least-obvious to the average angler.

"Finding a deep-water sanctuary isn't something that you can just go out on a Saturday morning and just do," he says. "It's a lot of hardwork.

"I've worked one side of a 2-mile creek ledge for a week or more looking for these types of deep summer structures. I've worked creek channels for a mile or more and never pick up a fish, but all of a sudden you'll find one little spot along that creek channel that had something different about it. There would be a bend in it or a real tight stump field on the bottom of the deep side of the creek channel — something different to hold that school there. And you would find a whole big school of bass holding on this one little spot that was different from the rest of creek channel."

By spending more than 200 days a year on the water, Fischer taught himself to become very proficient with his depth finder, which is important for pinpointing the more subtle forms of structure. But when the dog days of July and August arrived, the depth finder wouldn't indicate fish on these structures.

"When I found fish in the summertime in these situations, I'd say 75 percent of the time you could never see a fish on the depth finder," Fischer explains. "They would be flat on the bottom. When they're real tight to the bottom, you won't hardly ever pick them up on the depth finder and the majority of the time when the days are real hot, they'll be flat on the bottom."

Fischer's prime summertime weapons for deep-water bottom fishing are heavy lead spoons, lead spinnerbaits like Mann's Little George, plastic worms and a jig-and-pig. Crankbaits are often eliminated because none run as deep as some of these summer structures are located.

"I've probably caught more fish on a Hopkins spoon or Little George in the summertime than I have worms, which might surprise some people," he says. "You can fish a Hopkins spoon or Little George a lot faster than you can a worm, so you can cover more water. If you find a little area of a creek channel and you catch a fish, you need to work around that area real quick. I can work 360 degrees around the boat faster with a Hopkins spoon than I can a worm."

Fischer often alternates between a plastic worm rigged Texas style and a floating worm in a Carolina rig. The Carolina rig is better, he says, for enticing bass that are holding tight to the bottom. To locate deep-water holding areas, Fischer will often troll a Texas-rigged worm along the breakline (where it falls from shallow to deep water) of a creek channel, while jigging a Hopkins spoon in front of the boat.

Fischer says that deep-water bottom fishing is not an easy technique to learn, though.

"It's hard to fish real deep efficiently," he explains. "For one thing, a lot of people don't have the patience for fishing deep and they give up on it too quickly. You're not throwing at anything you can see like a shoreline. You'll see a few stumps or brush on the depth finder and you've got to discipline yourself to work around them well. You might fish four or five places that look good with a lot of cover and there won't be a fish there. But all of a sudden, you go by a slick little stair-step on the wall of the creek channel and there will be bass all over it. You have been patient. And persistent."

Neal Parker warns that deep-water bottom-holding summertime bass often move from subtle structure to subtle structure, so it's important to search for cover in nearby areas where the fish might migrate to.

"It's an important fact to remember about fishing the bottom in the summer," he says. "They will move on you in a heartbeat.

"A lot of people believe that the fish won't move that much because of the deeper water and that weather fronts won't effect them, but that's the biggest fallacy in the world. I've found big concentrations of fish in those circumstances and went back the next day when the barometric pressure was the same, the weather was the same, the temperature was the same, the lake level was the same, but the fish were no place to be found.

"They will definitely move, so you have to be prepared for them to move. In other words, don't locate a bunch of fish deep and rely solely on them being

242

there when you return. If the fish have moved, one thing you should do is go to the closest immediate types of structure, be it deep water or shallow water. If I had a bunch of brushpiles planted in the deep water and I couldn't find any fish in them, I would probably move up shallow, thinking they moved out of the deep water in search of food. I would look to the first major point I came to or stumps or timber, anything of that nature. If I couldn't find them there, then I'd move farther out to see if they dropped off into some channels in the deeper water."

A major reason why these deep-water bass will move, particularly during the summer, can be directly attributed to the oxycline and pH breakline in the water, according to Ken Cook.

Cook, a personable Oklahoma angler who is one of the most successful professional fishermen in the country and a former fisheries biologist, says the the intense summer heat magnifies the problem of oxygen and pH stratification — layers of water that are healthy, tolerable and intolerable in lakes throughout the country.

There are times during the summer when deep-water areas are simply not tolerable to bass in terms of oxygen and pH (the amount of acidity and alkalinity in the water). While the need for oxygen is obvious, Cook emphasizes that the pH effect on bass is "tremendous. It's like blood pH on humans almost. If a human's blood pH drops a tenth of a point, it can kill you. And it effects bass almost as greatly."

The levels of oxygen and pH stratification are dictated by the amount of sunlight, which is great on summer days.

"Summer fishing is tied directly to the sun," Cook explains. "The whole thing is tied directly to the sun's effects on the water.

"Sunlight penetration controls the oxycline and pH breakline. So it usually determines where the successful fishing zone or where the most active fish are in a body of water in the summer. And it determines layers of water that are just not liveable at that time, which can be deep water in the summer."

While there are sophisticated tools for measuring the oxygen and pH levels at certain depths, Cook has a simple method that works throughout the country in the summertime and involves only a white spinnerbait.

"I've got some guidelines that the average guy can use," he explains. "You can take a sunlight penetration measurement by lowering a white spinnerbait into the water. Say you can see it down 10 feet. That means that the sunlight has to go down to the spinnerbait and come back up to your eye. So if that white object hadn't been there, the sunlight would have gone down to about 20 feet.

"That's going to give you a guideline because from the point that you cannot see a white spinnerbait any farther, that point is about 50 percent of the sunlight level. Say it's 10 feet. From 10 feet down to 20 feet would be the bottom half of the zone of sunlight penetration. A bass' eyes are set up to be the most effective in that dark zone — that 50 percent less sunlight.

"Also, it's usually in this zone that the pH and oxycline break is located. If you have no other means of determining how deep to fish, that will do it. That's a pretty good guide to start with. That's usually where a favorable oxycline and pH level exists. That's a starting point."

With a concentrated effort and a little attention to detail, summertime fishing doesn't have to be the dog days for bass fishermen. The hottest days of the year temperature-wise can also be the hottest days of the year in terms of action.

HOT OFF OF THE PRESS!

Secrets
of
America's
Best Bass Pros

Every angler knows that the key to becoming a top fisherman is spending enough time on the water to experience all that bass fishing has to offer. But even the most serious weekend angler cannot afford to spend the number of hours that the nation's tournament pros put in each year.

The Pro Advantage

With the recent publication of the new book **Secrets of America's Best Bass Pros,** you can take advantage of their years of experience. In this impressive new book, the biggest names in fishing share their innermost secrets with Bassmaster Magazine Senior Writer Tim Tucker. Every aspect of consistently locating and catching bass is explored in this fully illustrated new book.

To Order:

Send a check or money order for $10.95 (plus $2 for postage and handling) to Tim Tucker Outdoor Productions, Rt.. 2, Box 177, Micanopy, FL 32667.

Name _____

Address _____

City_____ State/Zip _____

Roland Martin

Rick Clunn

Larry Nixon

Bill Dance

Guido Hibdon

Hank Parker

Gary Klein

Shaw Grigsby

Doug Hannon

Tommy Martin

Ken Cook

Jimmy Houston

Denny Brauer

Joe Thomas

Charlie Ingram

Paul Elias

Guy Eaker

George Cochran

Charlie Reed

Jim Bitter

Rich Tauber

Woo Daves

Dave Gliebe

Greg Hines

Learn From the Pros

In the comfort of your home . . .
While driving to the lake . . .
Or sitting in traffic . . .
Or fishing your favorite bass hole!

High-quality instructional audio cassettes — a unique way to improve your skills as a bass angler!

"The Bass Sessions tapes will become among the most valuable learning tools available to bass fishermen from the novice to the most serious angler." — Shaw Grigsby

"The Bass Sessions series of instructional audio cassettes are designed to allow the country's top bass pros to share their insight into various aspects of bass fishing in a conversational forum that bass enthusiasts like myself can take advantage of at their convenience. In the Bass Sessions tapes, which are about 30 minutes in length, I go one-on-one with top bass pros with real credentials. And they willingly share their innermost secrets.

"You have my personal guarantee that the Bass Sessions series will make you a better fisherman!"

Tim Tucker

The Bass Sessions Lineup

☐ **Trophy Hunting for Bass** $8.95
Roland Martin, Doug Hannon and Guido Hibdon discuss the habits and habitats of *big* bass.

☐ **Championship Worm Tactics** $8.95
Get an insight into fishing plastic worms from the experts — Shaw Grigsby, Jim Bitter and Bernie Schultz.

☐ **Tubejig Trickery** $8.95
The three best tubejig fishermen in America — Guido Hibdon, Shaw Grigsby and Roland Martin — share their secrets of finesse fishing.

☐ **Surface Fishing Secrets** $8.95
Learn to get more out of topwater lures from veteran surface-fishing pros Jim Bitter, Steve Daniel and Larry Lazoen.

☐ **Heavy Cover Tactics** $8.95
Big bass live in some *bad* places. Shaw Grigsby, Roland Martin and Guido Hibdon reveal their most effective tactics.

☐ **River Fishing Simplified** $8.95
River fishing is a whole new ballgame from lake fishing. Experts Doug Hannon, Bernie Schultz and Pete Thliveros remove the mystery associated with fishing moving water.

☐ **Advanced Shiner Fishing Techniques** $8.95
The wild shiner is the best big-bass bait known to man and no one knows more about fishing shiners than Doug Hannon, Glen Hunter and Dan Thurmond.

Special Offer!
Order all seven tapes and receive a bonus tape *Pro Bait Modifications* absolutely free!

☐ I want to receive the tapes checked above and enclose $8.95 for each, along with $1 for each to cover postage and handling

☐ I want to receive the entire Bass Sessions Series. Enclosed is $65, which includes the cost of shipping. Send my free bonus tape.

Send check or money order to Tim Tucker Outdoor Productions, Rt. 2, Box 177, Micanopy, Fla., 32667. Visa and MasterCard orders can call 904-466-0808.

The Series Continues!

More!

Secrets of America's Best Bass Pros

Volume Two of the Bass Pro Series

If you enjoyed Secrets of America's Best Bass Pros, you won't want to miss the next volume in the fact-filled Bass Pro Series.

In **More! Secrets of America's Best Bass Pros,** the biggest names in tournament fishing share more of their intimate fishing techniques with Bassmaster Magazine senior writer Tim Tucker. This companion book to Volume One will increase your knowledge on such topics as lure techniques, bass patterns and weather conditions.

Special Bonus! **Included in Volume Two is a special bonus section detailing world champion Rick Clunn's seasonal system for locating bass. This seasonal guide takes the mystery out of finding bass in any season.**

To order your copy of **More! Secrets of America's Best Bass Pros,** send $10.95, plus $2 for postage and handling, to Tim Tucker Outdoor Productions, Route 2, Box 177, Micanopy, Fla., 32667. Money orders, checks and Visa or MasterCard accepted.